Journey Interrupted

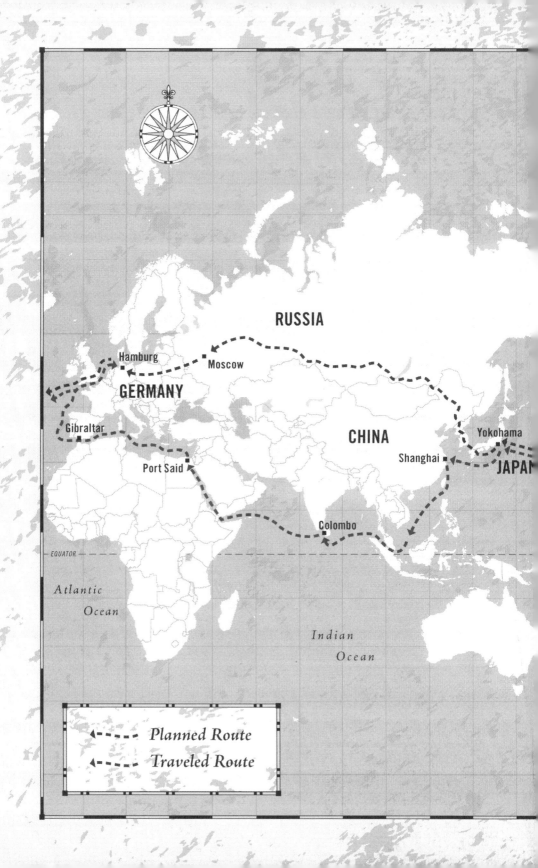

RUSSIA

Hamburg
Moscow
GERMANY
CHINA
Gibraltar
Yokohama
Shanghai
JAPAN
Port Said

EQUATOR

Colombo

Atlantic
Ocean

Indian
Ocean

Planned Route
Traveled Route

Our Interrupted Journey
1941–1950

San Francisco

UNITED STATES

New York ★

Honolulu

Atlantic
Ocean

Pacific
Ocean

EQUATOR

0 *Miles*   2,500
0 *Kilometers*   2,500
Scale at latitude of New York

© 2016 Jeffrey L. Ward

Journey Interrupted

A FAMILY WITHOUT A COUNTRY IN A WORLD AT WAR

HILDEGARDE MAHONEY

Regan Arts.

NEW YORK

Originally published in hardcover by Regan Arts in 2016.
First Regan Arts paperback edition, 2020

Library of Congress Control Number: 2015958509.
ISBN 978-1-68245-157-1

Interior design by Nancy Singer
Cover design by Richard Ljoenes
Cover and interior photographs courtesy of the author,
except where otherwise noted.
Endpaper map by Jeffrey L. Ward

10 9 8 7 6 5 4 3 2 1

To my parents, Hildegard and Enno Ercklentz,

who selflessly, courageously, and lovingly guided,

protected, and cared for my two brothers and me

throughout World War II in Japan,

and into our adulthood.

To my brother Enno,
who provided me with invaluable help,
but sadly did not live to see the completion of this book.

Freedom is never more than one generation away from extinction. We didn't pass it to our children in the bloodstream. It must be fought for, protected and handed on for them to do the same, or one day we will spend our sunset years telling our children and our children's children what it once was like in the United States where men were free.

—*Ronald Reagan*

If you're going through hell, keep on walking.

—*Winston Churchill*

CONTENTS

Part One

GOOD-BYE, USA

*M*ay 29, 1941—my father's thirty-eighth birthday—was a sunny, warm spring day in New York City. It started out just like any other during the two years since I had entered first grade at the Convent of the Sacred Heart on 91st Street, but it wasn't just an ordinary day. I knew that later that afternoon my family and I were embarking on an epic journey across the United States, across the Pacific, across Siberia, and all the way back to their native Germany. My two brothers and I had not been to Germany in four years—since I was three years old. Insofar as we could comprehend such events, we knew that the country where our parents had been born was at war with Britain.

Our German governess, Aya, who had been hired to look after my two brothers and me and had been with our family for ten years, gave us our usual breakfast. As was the routine, she walked me to school, five city blocks away from our apartment at 1192 Park Avenue. It was the last day of second grade—and my last day before we left—and on that particular morning I was feeling excited and apprehensive, as well as sad. I was excited at the thought of taking a train across the United States but apprehensive about going to visit such faraway countries as Japan and Russia. I was sad to be leaving all my friends behind, even though my parents had assured me it would only be for a short while. At my age, I was mostly unaware of wider events. I was mainly concerned with the new braces on my teeth, which an orthodontist had recently put on, as well as keeping my hair under control after having had my first permanent, which I had so desperately wanted to get before our departure.

We were at the end of our last class together when our teacher, a nun whose lovely face shone from her habit, a white and crisply starched frame resembling ribbon candy, told us to be sure to leave our desks as spotless as we had found them. That was so the next group of second-graders, who would be entering our classroom in September, would not think we were a group of sloppy, inconsiderate girls. We did what she asked, were dismissed, and went straight to chapel for Ascension Thursday Benediction, curtsying to each nun as we were always required to do. Mother Mary Ranney, my second-grade teacher, had asked me to help her decorate the chapel for the last time. I was pleased that it had turned out so beautifully.

As Benediction was coming to an end, I felt a gentle tug on the sleeve of my uniform. It was Mother Ranney, telling me my parents had arrived to pick me up. I followed her out of the chapel, and while my family and I were saying our good-byes to Reverend Mother Shea and the other nuns, the double doors from the chapel opened and out streamed the girls from the upper classes, followed by the girls from the entire lower school. I was totally unprepared for the emotional farewells that followed, as one by one each of my classmates put her arms around my neck to say good-bye. With tears streaming down our cheeks, we could barely speak.

My parents had been living in New York since they were married in 1929. My father, head of the New York office of the *Commerz und Privat Bank*, whose headquarters were in Berlin, had been recalled to the home office. With my mother anxious to see her family, as well as my father's, my father had been persuaded to return. My parents hadn't seen any of their relatives in three years, and couldn't imagine what they were all going through in a time of war. It was my mother's older brother who had suggested taking the Pacific route through Russia, because he had taken it himself from South America earlier in the year.

It was the first summer since I had started school that my family and I were leaving for Europe. For the past three summers my parents had either rented a house in Southampton or we had remained in the city. This time, however, my parents had chosen a different and exotic route to get to Germany. The upcoming trip was going to be a much longer one, across the Pacific and three-quarters of the way around the world. The idea of such a long journey made it somehow even harder to separate from all my friends, especially as I had no idea what the future held and what exactly we were going to experience on the way.

Since Great Britain and France had been at war with Germany for nearly two years, my parents had chosen to travel across America and on to Yokohama, Japan, via the Pacific. They believed the British were taking citizens of Germany and their allied nations off ships crossing the Atlantic ocean, and incarcerating them. It was also safer, they

My parents in the spring of 1941.

thought, because of the German-Soviet Nonaggression Pact agreed to by Hitler and Stalin in 1939. My father made the entire planned trip sound like such an adventure that my brothers and I were able to get into the spirit of the journey without any real concerns about our fate. Perhaps, in private, he and my mother were not quite so calm.

My parents had hired a Checker taxicab, which was waiting outside the school to take the five of us to Grand Central Station. In those days, Checkers had room for five people because—just as in London cabs to this day—they had two jump seats facing the back. We drove off, down Fifth Avenue along Central Park, which by now was in full bloom. My brother Enno was ten years old and my brother Alexander was not yet five. I was about to turn eight in less than a month. The three of us thought of the whole expedition as just a longer-than-usual trip with my parents, with the novel addition of travel by train.

My brothers, Alexander and Enno, with me in
Manhattan, spring 1941.

When we arrived at Grand Central Station, we were immediately able to board our train—the *20th Century Limited* for Chicago—as my father had checked our forty pieces of luggage onto the train earlier in the day. We were traveling with such an inordinate number of suitcases because my mother was afraid we'd run out of some of the most necessary items on our long trip and wouldn't be able to buy them anywhere, and it was unclear how long we would be staying in Germany once we got there. She had brought along plenty of soap, toilet tissue, Kleenex, peanut butter, cereals, jams, assorted canned vegetables and fruits, and a whole array of miscellaneous items necessary for the journey across several continents and cultures. She had also packed both our summer and winter clothing, in anticipation of cooler weather in Siberia.

In the taxi on the way to the station, my mood gradually changed to one of excitement again, as my brothers and I started talking about the next four or five days traveling on a Pullman sleeper train to the West Coast. It was going to be a new experience for us; we had frequently traveled by ocean liner, but never before overnight on a train. After boarding and settling into our compartments, we leaned out the windows to wave good-bye to Aya, who had come to see us off, as had several of my parents' friends. A loud whistle sounded, and we watched as the conductor called out "All aboard!" and stepped back onto the train, which proceeded to pull out of the station at a snail's pace. In the pit of my stomach I felt an anxiousness I couldn't shake off, so I went about distracting myself by unpacking for the days that lay ahead.

My brothers had gone off to explore the train with my father and soon came back to report they had discovered a beautiful dining car, and that our father had made a dinner reservation for all of us. At the appointed hour, the five of us entered the dining car and noticed that all the tables had been set with immaculately starched white linens and simple, pretty china and glassware. A centerpiece of spring flowers had been placed on each table. The aroma of food being prepared wafted through the air as the maître d' showed us to our table. Once seated, a polite and solicitous waiter—dressed in a crisp white jacket decorated with gold braiding—asked to take our drinks order.

Our parents seemed perfectly relaxed, considering the hectic preparations they had been making for our departure. My mother wanted to order right away, before the dining car became too crowded. It had already been a long and emotional day, and she thought everybody was ready to have dinner and go to bed. My parents ordered their favorite drinks—a martini for my mother and a Manhattan for my father. My brothers and I ordered ginger ale.

While waiting for our first course, our father started telling us all about the trip we had just begun and why this year we were taking a different route. Having always sailed from New York by ship in the past, he wanted to map out this new route for us, as it had been four years since the five of us had last taken a trip to Europe together.

Our father told us he had been asked by his bank to close the New York office and return all his papers to the main office in Berlin. He wasn't really keen on going back with war under way, but if he remained in New York he would have to look for other employment. He adored New York, and had always dreamed of living there. As a banker, a classical pianist, and a man utterly infatuated with the life he and my mother had created for us all in Manhattan, I knew how he and my mother had agonized about our predicament, and it looked like it might become the end of a glorious period in their lives.

My father must have reassured himself with the idea that the war could not possibly continue much longer. Hitler's rapid, brutal conquests on the European continent seemed to have been met with implacable British resolve. Surely a workable truce would be agreed upon.

My father had thought the most sensible course would be to wait for the end of the school year, then travel to the still relatively safe Germany, settle his business affairs with the central office in Berlin, and wait for the end of the war. As a born optimist, he thought we would return as soon as possible to America once the hostilities were over and the New York office was reopened.

My father went on to tell us in detail all about what an eye-popping journey he had booked; it would take six to seven weeks. After our arrival in San Francisco, the plan was to board a Japanese ship and sail via Hawaii to Yokohama, which was a port city about an hour south of Tokyo by train. He told us that unfortunately we wouldn't have a lot of time to see much of Japan, because we could only be there a week. We would leave from Japan on a ferry to Korea, board the East Asia Express, and travel through Manchuria to Manchouli (Manzhouli today), just east of the formidable Lake Baikal. There we would enter Russia and board the Trans-Siberian Railway, which would take roughly ten days to reach Moscow. We would then change trains and continue on to Berlin, where my father planned to stay a couple of days to wrap up business at the bank. The rest of us were to continue on to Hamburg to visit our grandparents.

We started preparing for our first night ever aboard a sleeper train. It had been a very long day, and I fell into my bunk dead tired, but I was unable to fall asleep right away, thinking about all that was unknown and unfamiliar that lay ahead, and missing my friends, with whom I now could not share any of my concerns. My brothers and I each had our own bunk with a curtain we could draw for privacy. I took the upper one, as I didn't want either of them sleeping above me, for fear they might accidentally kick me or step on me on the way down in the middle of the night. It was a tightly outfitted, cramped compartment for the three of us, despite our being relatively small. We had never seen a sink and toilet combined in such a novel way before. In order to use either, the others had to stay in their bunks or leave the compartment.

By morning, we had already arrived in Chicago and had to change trains to board the Atchison, Topeka and Santa Fe Railway's California-bound *Grand Canyon Limited* for the cross-country trip to San Francisco, via the Grand Canyon.

During the monotonous days of travel, it suited us all to linger as long as possible in the spacious, comfortable dining car. Our father took one of these opportunities to entertain and distract us by telling stories of his life, and of meeting our mother, as if to explain why we all found ourselves racing across the American plains. We knew little about our parents' backgrounds, and even less about the relatives we were about to see in a country we hardly remembered. We did know, however, that my father had wanted to become a concert pianist but had become a banker instead. My brothers and I prevailed upon him to tell us a lot more about his childhood and how such a radical change could come about.

My father was in a relaxed mood, as he had committed to this long journey after much deliberation. His bright blue eyes twinkled as he began, like a practiced storyteller, "I was born at the turn of the century in Breslau, Germany—in 1903, to be exact. I was the fourth of seven children, each more individual than the next." My mother smiled at this. He continued, "My father had grown up in the Rhineland, had studied medicine in Bonn—where he specialized in internal medicine—and after graduating had accepted a position as adjunct professor of internal medicine at the University of Breslau. In those days, Breslau was one of the three most important cities in Germany. It was also the second-largest city in Prussia, and it was there that my father established a rather large medical practice. What I'm trying to say, children, is that your grandfather was a very special doctor."

My father paused to light a cigarette for my mother, then one for himself. The smoke rushed out of the half-open window of the dining car.

"Several years later," he continued, "your grandfather, in addition to caring for his patients and teaching at the university, was named chief of the University Hospital and was invited by the Order of the Knights of Malta to become chief of the *Caritasheim*, to run their prestigious private hospital in the vicinity. By accepting the position, he was awarded the Commander's Cross of the Knights of Malta. Among his many patients was King Boris of Bulgaria and members of his cabinet, who came to the *Caritasheim* regularly for check-ups. The king gave my father the Offizierskreuz (Officer's Cross) and the Ritterkreuz, the Royal Bulgarian Civil Order of Merit."

One of my grandfather's colleagues was Professor Alois Alzheimer, the doctor who in the early first decade of the twentieth century had among his patients one who suffered from an illness he described as a distinct subcategory of senile dementia. In 1910, his colleagues named the illness Alzheimer's disease.

My father's mother was fifty-nine years old when she died in 1935, having suffered from heart problems for a number of years. It was a terrible loss for the entire family, as she had been such a dynamic personality. Known as Frau Professor, she was said to have been an impressive lady, who spoke a number of languages and had a natural talent for presiding as *grande dame* in her salon at home. There she entertained intellectuals, artists, aristocrats, industrialists, writers, scientists, and many poets, among them the giant of the 1920s and '30s, Gerhart Hauptmann, who was a friend, as well as her husband's patient. King Augustus of Saxony was another patient, and a frequent guest in the family home.

My father didn't wish to bore us with names we could not possibly know, but the fact is our grandmother was the center of Breslau society, and on any given evening with her one could meet Ratibors, Radziwills, Henckel von Donnersmarcks, the Ballestrems, the Schotlaenders and Schwerins (textiles), the Heimanns (banking), the Hohenzollerns, Count Yorck von Wartenburg, or Prince Reuss, all of whom were frequent guests at her salon. In addition, having had seven children, she presided over a large house and many staff. She had to oversee the children's homework and, most important, had to be sure her offspring obeyed Mademoiselle, the French nanny who had been with the family for many years.

My father proudly told us that his grandfather Dr. Tonio Bödiker had been a prominent lawyer in Berlin who, during a period of widespread social unrest in the 1880s, drafted the legislation that would create the first social security system in Germany—and the world. To pacify the working class and weaken socialism, Chancellor Otto von Bismarck had asked my great-grandfather to guide its passage through the Reichstag. The social security system he installed (health care in 1883, accident insurance in 1884, and old-age and disability insurance in 1889) was at the time the most advanced in the world and, to a degree, still exists in Germany today. My great-grandfather was later appointed by Bismarck to head the agency that administered it, known as the Imperial Insurance Agency. There is a street named after him and a monument of him in Haselünne, a town in Lower Saxony.

It was time for us to go to bed, but since we were just getting into the story, we urged my father to go on. "Not too much longer, though," he said, agreeing to continue. "I liked living with my mother, my father, my six siblings, and Ma'mselle, as we called her, in our large four-story townhouse at 26 Hansa Strasse in Breslau. I'll show it to you when we go to visit my father later this summer. Imagine it: On the first floor there was a large front hall, two salons, a library, a music room, an

My great-grandfather Dr. Tonio Bödiker.

office where my father would see patients, an office for his secretary, a kitchen with a pantry, and a dining room that could seat two dozen. The bedrooms and bathrooms were all on the second floor, with guest rooms on the third floor and staff rooms on the fourth. There were at least ten of us at lunch every day—my parents, Ma'mselle, and the seven of us—and daily my father would come home from the hospital at 1:30 p.m. sharp, having been driven there in his dark blue Mercedes by his chauffeur, Rufin, a former White Russian officer. It was usually quite a formal affair, as we were frequently joined by colleagues or patients of my father's, as well as by friends and artists. We children all had to be ready and present on the dot of 1:30 p.m. Mealtime was always very lively, because we each were expected to contribute something of interest to the conversation.

"In the summer and on occasional weekends in the spring and fall, when it was warm enough, we would spend time in the country in

Part of pre–World War II map of Silesia, where my paternal family lived until 1945.

Wolfshau by Hirschberg, at the foot of the Giant Mountains, about a three-hour drive from Breslau, through the Silesian countryside. My parents had bought a summer home there, where we had a spectacular view of the famous Schneekoppe, the highest peak in the Giant Mountain range. It was an area in which electricity had not yet been introduced—imagine that—so at night we would do our homework and our reading by candlelight before going to sleep."

Here my father paused again, somewhat dramatically, for he was about to enter a darker time.

"I was eleven years old when the Great War broke out," he said solemnly. "I remember well those four years, because they were very difficult ones for my parents, my brothers and sisters, and me. Food was often so scarce that we had to go into the fields to try and catch grasshoppers and pick thistles, for lack of anything else to eat. They were also difficult because we missed Ma'mselle, who, because she was French, had to leave Germany and return to France at the beginning of the war. She had taught us all to speak French fluently—a language we loved but were forbidden to speak once the war broke out."

My father's tone lightened again. "Ever since I was a young boy I had always loved music, and over the years I developed an even keener interest in it. I started taking piano lessons several times a week after school, and practiced daily. During my high school years, I continued taking lessons, practicing and playing, until one day it came to me that what I wanted to do in life was to become a concert pianist. However, two years after I had enrolled at the university in Breslau, I was forced to make a career change—which was a major disappointment. Music had become my passion, and I had practiced for many hours a day to improve my skills, even while studying at the university. Unfortunately, the economic crisis and financial turmoil in Germany, which was totally beyond anyone's control, made me realize I had to look differently at my future."

He explained how, in the 1920s, the German economy unraveled. It was a nightmare of hyperinflation caused by the onerous terms of the Treaty of Versailles following the First World War. Staggering reparations, the loss of overseas assets, the necessary printing of increasingly valueless currency—these factors and other results of losing the war combined to reduce the German economy to a shambles. In the chaos after the war, Kaiser Wilhelm II—emperor of Germany and king of Prussia—the Kings of Saxony and Bavaria, and all the other heads of state of the German Empire abdicated, and the Weimar Republic was established. There was fierce resentment over the terms of Germany's surrender. The future looked hopelessly grim. The incredible runaway inflation that resulted and the untold hardships that were inflicted on the people by this spiraling crisis contributed to political unrest. Employees were often paid several times a day or every few hours, so they could shop before prices would escalate, at times doubling and tripling within a very short period of time. Money had literally become worthless.

To illustrate this, my father told us this well-known allegory: "A man parked his wheelbarrow full of cash in front of his house just for a moment. He went inside to fetch something, and when he returned, he found all his money still there but his wheelbarrow gone."

With all that uncertainty and such a deteriorating economy, it is no wonder my father made the decision to go into business and to make music his much-loved avocation.

His tone of voice suddenly became animated when he said, "Ever since I was old enough, I would read volumes about America and would dream of going there one day. Now, with my new career plan, it looked like I might reach my goal sooner than I had thought. I've often told you how much I always wanted to visit and eventually move to *Das Land der unbegrenzten Moeglichkeiten* (the land of unlimited possibilities). I knew one thing for sure—I had no intention of basking in the reflected glory of my highly regarded, famous, and successful father at home—I wanted to leave and make it on my own in the 'New World.'" My father rapped the table for emphasis.

His first step toward realizing his dream came when he applied for and was given a position as an apprentice in a large family-owned import-export firm in Hamburg. The business mostly imported coffee, from the plantations the family owned in Guatemala; it was brought to the port city of Hamburg via the Atlantic Ocean and through the English Channel.

"By now it was 1924," my father continued. "The Reichsmark had been revalued, and I was suddenly on my own, a twenty-one-year-old bachelor living far away from home. I had an interesting and well-paying job, and I loved my new life. It had a lot to offer after the dismal decade of the war and postwar period. For the next two years, I made a number of trips back home to Breslau to visit my family. On the way there, I'd frequently stop off in Berlin to attend the opera and go to concerts, something I hadn't been able to do in the past. Those were very happy years."

My father paused there and glanced over at my mother for a moment before continuing to the most relevant part of his tale. "In April of my first year at the firm," he said, with some emotion, "I was invited, with my fellow apprentices, to attend the fifteenth birthday party of the boss's daughter. When I met the birthday girl, I was struck not only by her beauty, but also by her vivacious personality. It was love at first sight. The following day, I sent her fifteen red roses with a short note of thanks for a wonderful evening. I also sent one to her parents," my father added, with a sly smile. "Later, I heard from a fellow apprentice

My mother and father, a few years
after they first met.

that she had liked me too. I considered myself very fortunate indeed. At just fifteen and still in high school, she was not permitted to date, but since I had my work, my music, my studies, and my travels, I didn't have the time to go out much anyway. On the occasional weekend when we did manage to get together, we always had a grand time and enjoyed each other's company immensely. Over time we became much closer, which in turn created a real conflict when, in 1926, I was offered a job to work in America."

His new job was at the J. Henry Schroeder Banking Corporation, a British bank that had offices in New York City. "It was like a dream come true. So with a great deal of enthusiasm I took the job. It meant everything to me, finally to be able to live in the country I had longed to visit for so many years. After saying good-bye to family, friends, and my beautiful young girlfriend—whom I secretly hoped would eventually join me there—I sailed for America. It felt very liberating to have made such an important decision."

Retelling it then, with the vastness of America rolling past the train's windows, my father smiled with real pride and passion. "I was able to establish myself rather quickly in New York, a city that immediately exhilarated and intoxicated me. The tempo and the energy there seemed made for me. New York City became my lifeblood, and I quickly made many wonderful friends. I wrote to my parents that I was going to adopt America as my new country and live there forever, which must have alarmed them."

Glancing again at my mother, he said, "There was only one major problem. I had left my beloved behind—the one who would eventually become your mother."

My mother smiled back at her husband, whose story for the evening had concluded on a charming note. It was clearly time to race down the corridor to our crowded compartment, and to bed.

+ + +

With my parents and brothers at the edge of the Grand Canyon, 1941.

The train made a brief stop in Amarillo, Texas, where for the first time we heard a different, unfamiliar way of speaking. Our parents explained that the accent was called a "Texas drawl." The *Limited* proceeded on to a junction where, once again, we had to change trains. Our parents had decided earlier that we would take a side trip to the Grand Canyon, because we would have just enough time between trains to see the vast canyons carved through the rocks of the Colorado Plateau. When I went to stand near the rim, I felt terribly frightened, as if I would be sucked into the abyss. My older brother, Enno, tried to show off that he wasn't scared, and lingered at the edge, but he walked a bit unsteadily on the way back to the station.

We soon caught a train that took us to Barstow, where we boarded the *California Limited*, which would take us north up the central valley to San Francisco. Once again we heard the conductor blow his whistle and call out the now familiar "All aboard!" just before the train slowly slid out of the station. My brothers and I spent much of the remainder of the journey running back and forth through the many parlor cars. We were always on the lookout for the waiters, who usually had a little treat for us when they were not busy serving meals in the dining car.

After our arrival in San Francisco on June 3, 1941, after five days on the train, we immediately went to the Mark Hopkins Hotel with our forty pieces of luggage. The city was unlike any we had ever seen before, with its steep hills and breathtaking views. On our first evening, we dined at the Top of the Mark, a restaurant located on the top floor of the hotel and at the time a very famous and popular spot. Looking out over San Francisco Bay as dusk set in—and as the lights began to illuminate the city—made me wish we were staying there, rather than moving on again.

On our way down to breakfast the following morning we saw a stack of newspapers being delivered, bearing the headline, "Kaiser Dead." When Enno inevitably piped up and asked, "Which kaiser?" our father told us it was the exiled former Kaiser Wilhelm II, emperor of Germany, king of Prussia, who had been living in Holland.

"Is this of any significance?" Enno wanted to know.

"The end of an era, for some," said my father, dismissing a couple of generations of German history. Things were too complicated at that moment for him to explain further.

After breakfast, our parents took us on a tour of the city. Of course, my brothers wanted to get a glimpse of Alcatraz, and we all wanted to ride the famous cable cars. My mother agreed, as she wished to visit a distant cousin who had a house in the area. It was fun going up and down the hills, though we never did find that cousin's house.

The morning of June 5—the day we were scheduled to leave San Francisco—we awoke to an overcast but mild day. My parents had already arranged for transportation to take us to the MS *Tatuta Maru*, one of a fleet of passenger ships owned and operated by the Nippan Yusen Kaisha (NYK) Line, a Japanese shipping company. It was to become our floating hotel for the next two weeks—destination: Yokohama, Japan.

It was not the smooth departure my parents had hoped for. My father had asked a good friend of his—a San Francisco banker—if he would be able to facilitate getting our forty pieces of luggage expedited through customs. His friend was happy to oblige, but it turned out to be an ill-advised request, as it seemed to have had just the opposite effect on the customs officer. Instead of being able to easily board the ship, my parents were asked to open each one of the forty suitcases, which my mother—who was known in the family as the "master packer"—had packed in her usual superbly organized and tidy way. I was worried the customs people might take away my brown wooden radio, which I had asked my mother to pack, the front of which had Snow White and the Seven Dwarfs carved on it. Luckily they didn't, and after finding nothing of interest, they told my mother she could repack everything, which she proceeded to do in silence, tearing up in frustration.

The farewell parties on board, as well as the streamers and music that went along with a ship's setting out to sea, were exciting for us to experience again, and we had great fun throwing handfuls of streamers onto the dock to the crowd of people watching below. Back inside, we could still hear the band, which was alternately playing popular American songs and Japanese music, but mostly I remember a lot of John Philip Sousa marches. As the gangplanks were lowered and the *Tatuta Maru* started pulling away from the dock, the ship's horn sounded loudly several times and the music from shore became fainter.

The MS *Tatuta Maru.*

After passing under the Golden Gate Bridge, we watched it slowly disappearing into the mist of the morning as we sailed out to sea and into the Pacific.

Our voyage was to include a stop in Hawaii, during which we would be able to see some of the island of Oahu, and we would cross the international date line before our scheduled docking in Yokohama Harbor on June 19. The *Tatuta Maru* was one of the three luxurious NYK ocean liners that sailed the Pacific. The passenger areas were of high quality, many of them in the traditional European style, with highly polished wood, stained-glass skylights, fine dining rooms, lounges, a library, hair salon, comfortable cabins, and a swimming pool on deck.

Once underway, my brothers and I went looking for our cabins, anxious to see our accommodations, and as usual we wanted to negotiate any choices we might have of beds or views. The first-class accommodations my parents had booked were especially comfortable.

Our parents, obviously relieved that all forty pieces of luggage had made it on board, had had our suitcases sent to our cabin, which was right next to theirs. We noticed that all the table lamps had been glued to the tabletops so they wouldn't fall off and break during rough seas. Very quickly, with the help of our mother, we started to unpack. After a while, we told her we wanted very much to go and explore the ship. "May we go now?" we asked her. "Go right ahead," she said, cheerfully. "Let me know what you find, as I will be unpacking in the cabins for a while." It was a thrill to be allowed such independence aboard the ship.

One of the first things we observed, through innocent young eyes, was that many of the passengers on the ship looked different from the ones we were used to seeing on our transatlantic crossings, the route we had taken in the past. I mentioned this to my mother, and she explained that many of the passengers on board were from Asia—from Japan, China, Korea, or possibly the Philippines. She also explained that we would be seeing a lot more Asians once we arrived in Yokohama and told me to tell my brothers that whatever we did, we were not to stare at them. "That would be very bad manners," she explained.

The next thing we learned was our first Japanese word—*ohayō*—which means "good morning," and since it sounded like the name of a Midwestern state in America, we knew we wouldn't easily forget it. From then on we would use it proudly every morning when greeting the waiters, stewards, or any other Japanese person we would see. A few days later we were told by someone who knew the language quite well that saying ohayō alone was more like just saying "morning," but if we really wanted to be polite, we would have to say *ohayō gozaimasu*, which was like saying "good morning" in English. When I asked my mother whether she knew the word, she said that indeed she did, because her father had been in Japan and China at the turn of the century. She added that in those days he didn't even need a passport, and promised to tell us all she knew about Japan at dinner.

One reason my mother knew about Japan was that her father had traveled to the Orient on business a number of times at the turn of the century. He had brought back beautiful treasures from China and Japan, such as some famous Imari and Kutani porcelains, as well as many bronze artifacts modeled after animals and flowers. The *kiku* (chrysanthemum) was a popular design, as was the crane, because the latter signified long life. "He loved returning from his trips laden with presents for everyone," our mother told us.

We were delighted to find that a welcome dinner had been planned for the passengers, which was to be authentically Japanese. We were invited to sit Japanese-style on the floor on tatami—straw mats—and to eat Japanese food with chopsticks. We were introduced to all sorts of exotic dishes, such as sushi, sashimi, tempura, sukiyaki,

My family dining Japanese-style aboard the *Tatuta Maru*.

and miso soup, which was served with rice toward the end of the meal. As dessert we were served something akin to Jell-O, called *mitsumame*. The servings were all very small, delicate, and beautifully presented on lacquer dishes, in bamboo boxes, or on colorful Japanese porcelain. Eating with chopsticks at first presented a challenge, but we soon mastered the technique. While learning this skill, however, we ended up laughing more than we ate.

We were slowly being introduced to an entirely new culture, and observed with interest and amazement the various ways the Japanese lifestyle differed from ours. My father noticed that most of the Japanese people wore their wristwatches on their left arm with the watch face turned inward, and that they read their books from right to left, the exact opposite of the Western way. Those were the kinds of details that stood out to our curious young minds.

After almost a week at sea, there was great excitement when land was sighted in the distance and an announcement came over the loudspeaker saying we were approaching the Hawaiian Islands. As the *Tatuta Maru* sailed into Honolulu Harbor, on the island of Oahu, lovely young native girls dressed in straw skirts and what looked like bikini tops were doing the native hula to the rhythm of Hawaiian music. It was a pretty and festive sight: the girls and the band on the dock, the palm fronds swaying at water's edge in the cool breezes coming off the Pacific, behind them green lawns and stately buildings shining white in the sun.

After the "all clear" signal sounded, we were permitted to disembark. The girls at the foot of the gangplank greeted us with handmade leis, which they draped around our necks. This lovely gesture made us feel welcome and warm toward the island's inhabitants. Anxious to see a lot more of Honolulu in the short time we were allotted, my parents hired a taxi to take us to some of the local sites.

It was a beautiful, warm and sunny June day, and after a while we tired of riding around in a taxi, especially after we passed what looked like a wide, pure white, sandy beach. My parents couldn't resist letting us take a swim in the mighty Pacific, so they asked the driver to take us to the Royal Hawaiian Hotel on Waikiki Beach, just ten miles from Pearl Harbor. No sooner had we arrived than the three of us were in the deliciously cool, clear, invigorating waters of the ocean. My father had reserved a table on the terrace for lunch, under a wide, white umbrella. It was there that my younger brother, Alexander, and I committed a sin that the others would not soon let us forget. When it came time to order dessert, Enno asked for fresh Hawaiian pineapple, but Alexander and I asked for plain vanilla ice cream. My parents' reaction was instantaneous: "You can have vanilla ice cream anytime, anywhere in the world," they chided. "This is Hawaii, and fresh pineapple is right from the island itself. You should enjoy it while you have the chance."

Our family in Hawaii.

Before long, it was time to return to our floating home, but for some reason we were delayed and almost didn't make it back to the ship in time. When we arrived at the dock, we were rushed up the gangplank, which was immediately lifted, and off we sailed. At the dock, the native girls gathered once again, and again they were dancing the hula to the strains of the famous farewell song, "Aloha 'Oe." As they waved good-bye and called out "Aloha," the girls bid us farewell with dozens more of the colorful leis. "Don't forget to throw the leis back when you sail out to sea, because if they float back to us," they said, "then you'll be sure to return one day." It was with a good deal of enthusiasm that we threw our leis overboard, hoping the tradition's promise would come true.

Not quite a week was left on board the ship. During the first leg of our journey, there had frequently been a dense fog about us, but now the sun shone and the swimming became more inviting. To alleviate our general boredom, my mother decided to take her cue from our father's storytelling aboard the transcontinental train and tell us stories of her earlier life, and of the relatives we hoped soon to see in Germany.

"It is true what your father told you about our meeting," she said over lunch a couple of days after we left Hawaii. "It was at my fifteenth birthday party, which my parents held for me at our home. All the young, eligible apprentices from the firm had been invited. There was one, though, in particular who caught my eye, and that was your father."

We were seated in the rather ornate main dining room of the ship, with plenty of room to relax and listen.

"Going back, though," my mother said, "I was born in 1909, in Kiel, Germany. It is on the Baltic Sea, close to the Danish border, and was the headquarters of the Imperial German Navy. I was the middle child of three, and the only daughter—just like Hillie here," she said, gesturing toward me. "My father was a naval officer, but he came from a large merchant family in Hamburg.

"In fact, my father was born in Valparaíso, Chile. The family firm owned and operated coffee plantations in South and Central America, most of them in Guatemala. They imported coffee to Germany, but after the Great War, the plantations were seized by the local government, which had sided with the United States. The family company, which had been founded in Chile in 1856, was unable to survive these developments, and during the atrocious economic period of the 1920s and '30s, the firm was first bankrupted, then dissolved."

My mother continued, "The family returned to live in Hamburg after the end of the war. When my father's career with the navy was over, he joined the family business, having served in various parts of the world. We lived in a townhouse on the Oderfelder Strasse, a quiet, tree-lined street in a part of the city that was far enough away from the bustling business district yet close enough for my father to be able to be in his office within fifteen minutes. It was also a mere forty-five minutes from the hunting lodge my parents had bought in a little farming village, where they would spend weekends and summers when they were not traveling to South America or other parts of the world. On frequent occasions, my father would drive out with friends, taking them on shoots, often coming home with an assortment of wild boar, rabbit, pheasant, and deer. During the war, my mother had learned to conserve meat from the animals he'd shot, which provided us with food she was unable to buy elsewhere. She had also made friends with many of the farmers in the village and surrounding area and would stop in to visit them, trading some of her meat for eggs and milk from their farms."

My mother had been too young to understand the ramifications of the war, the perilous state of the German economy, or the effect these would have on her family's fortunes. She led a tranquil childhood, geared to the formalized girls' education of the times.

"When I met your father," she said, "I was still in school and had to go on to another school after that, as it was customary in my day for girls to go to a school that specialized in teaching the care and running of a household after graduating from high school. Therefore—much against my will—I was enrolled in just such a finishing school. My parents promised me a reward after completing all my courses. It was to be a trip to North and South America, which they were planning for the spring of 1928. Your father was very much on my mind, and by that time he had already left Hamburg to take a job in New York City. I considered the promised trip to be my best chance of seeing him again."

My mother sometimes spoke of being "imprisoned" at the finishing school. It was there that she reluctantly learned to clean, sew, iron, and cook, none of which she was particularly interested in or good at.

"I really didn't like it at all," she admitted to us aboard the *Tatuta Maru*. "Happily, over the years, I haven't had to do too much of that work, but as they explained to me at the finishing school, I was learning to keep house correctly so that later in life I could teach any young or inexperienced housekeeper how things were done. That's just the way things were. When school was finally out, I couldn't wait to go home to prepare and pack for our transatlantic trip to New York. I knew that, once there, I would not want to continue traveling with my parents to Latin America. I was determined to figure out a way to persuade them to let me stay in New York." With a sparkle in her eyes, she continued, "In the late spring of 1928, my parents and I set sail, and when we arrived and I saw your father again, I was convinced I wanted to stay there to be with him. I wanted to spend more time getting to know him, to see if we were meant for each other for the rest of our lives."

It was completely unheard-of in those days, especially in my mother's socioeconomic circles, for a nineteen-year-old girl to be without a chaperone. It was a sure sign of her forceful will, and perhaps of an innate power of negotiation, that she managed to convince her parents—especially my grandfather—to let her stay in New York without them. The reality was that, as his only daughter, she had her father wrapped around her little finger all her young life. She promised to see them back in Hamburg when they returned from the rest of their travels, and the fateful decision was made.

"During the time I was in New York with your father, we decided we would marry the following year, after my twentieth birthday," she said matter-of-factly. "I told my parents of this plan when I saw them again in Hamburg several months later."

What my mother left out here, because we were not yet ready to understand, was that our parents still had to overcome one major hurdle. My father was a Roman Catholic from the southeast, and my mother was a Protestant from the northwest. Quite apart from the objections the two families might have harbored from the outset, the simple fact still existed that in those days the Catholic Church did not allow marriage outside the Church. This left my mother no other choice than to convert to Catholicism. At first, her parents were dead set against their only daughter leaving their church, but once again, with a striking show of determination, my mother was able to prevail, and she immediately started taking the instructions necessary to convert.

"The following year, on Saturday, July 13, 1929," she recalled with a smile, "your dad and I were married in Hamburg, in a High Mass at the Catholic Church of St. Ansgar, a church known as *der kleine Michel* because it was across the street from the larger Protestant church, the St. Michaelis Kirche, known as *der grosse Michel*. The ceremony was followed by a large and elaborate wedding reception at my grandparents' house overlooking the Alster."

My mother's older brother, who was an ardent sailor and belonged to the Alster Piraten, the local sailing club, had arranged for an entire regatta of sailboats, colorfully decorated with flags and other insignia, to parade before them on the lake.

"In those days," my mother told us, "there was only black-and-white film, so the pictures do not do justice to the scene. It was a spectacular and colorful sight watching as a vast fleet of boats, all with their sails and flags up—the flags fluttering in the breeze on the Alster—moved slowly by. The wedding dinner was very long, festive, and drawn out— there were at least ten courses served, not including the wedding cake— and lasted for quite a while before the dancing started. The evening happily went on all night and didn't end until the early morning hours."

"I was there too," my father joked, having felt left out.

My mother laughed and continued, "The next morning, your father and I left on our honeymoon. Our first stop was Berlin. After a week there, we took the train to Paris, where we stayed another week before setting sail for New York City."

Once there, my parents rented an apartment on the Upper East Side near where my father had found his bachelor apartment. My mother set about decorating it and adjusting to her new life in the great city.

"It took a while," she said. "I had left all my friends behind, and although I had met many of your father's new friends when I was in New York the year before, I still missed the ones with whom I had grown up."

My father couldn't resist any longer. "It's true that we both missed family and friends," he said, "but things were about to get much more interesting than that. Imagine the luck: A banker and his new wife move in to their first apartment in Manhattan, and three short months later, what happens? The stock-market crash of '29, that's what happens."

"It dramatically changed life for almost everyone," my mother said. "Suddenly there were long breadlines in many parts of the city."

Both my parents had already lived through one war, had been through a series of trials and tribulations at home, and had seen bread- lines before, but that was when they were young children. Now, how- ever, they were grown-ups, and were once again facing great uncertainty. Luckily, my father was able to continue in his job at the bank, and my mother had been given some money by her parents when she left home, which she fortunately had not yet invested. My parents were able to maintain a semblance of the life they had just started building for themselves, albeit by watching their expenses carefully, not knowing if worse was to come.

"A year later, your father was offered the job to head up the New York office of the Commerz und Privat Bank," my mother said. "This was one of the three largest banks in Germany. He accepted the position, which came with a nice pay raise. No sooner had he started than he bought a brand-new Ford sedan. It was our first car ever. To celebrate, he immediately took me for a ride. The car had cost him a total of $500, which in those days was a fair sum."

My father interjected, saying, "Come on, it was my pride and joy."

Looking lovingly at Enno, Mother went on to say, "Meanwhile, in January 1931, you, Enno, were born, and we were now a family of three. That summer, with Aya—whom I'd hired by then—and the brand-new car in the hold, we sailed for Europe on one of the North German Lloyd ships, to spend our vacation in Germany. Your father was so proud of that car and was happy to show it off to anyone who asked about it. It caused quite a stir in those days, because the German economy hadn't yet recovered from the war, nor from the Great Depression in America, so not too many people owned cars then."

In the summer of 1932, my parents once again sailed to Germany with the car in tow for another month's vacation. Things there were still much like they were in America, since the recovery was yet to begin.

My mother said, "It was always good to see our family and friends there. When we returned to New York in the fall, I found I was pregnant again. This time the baby was not expected until June of the following year, so I immediately made plans to be in Hamburg to give birth to you, Hillie, with my parents by my side. At the end of May, Enno, Aya, and I sailed for Hamburg, leaving your father, who knew I would be in good hands, to follow in August—with his car, of course. It was a lovely summer, although after you were born in June, Enno showed signs that he was not too happy about your arrival. He was only two and a half, but he used to quietly go up to you while you were sleeping in your pram in the garden and pinch you, causing you to wake up and cry. By the time my mother and I investigated to see what was the matter, Enno would be off in a different part of the garden, innocently playing with his toys, not letting on what he had done. After this happened a half-dozen times, we stayed on the terrace and caught him. We realized it was quite obviously a case of sibling rivalry, which we expected would eventually pass."

"I still deny this," Enno said.

My father patted him on the knee and said, "Of course, you would."

"Two months later," my mother went on, "we were on the high seas again, sailing back to New York. You won't remember much—not even you, Enno—but part of the two summers that followed we spent visiting your grandparents, aunts, uncles, and many cousins in Hamburg and Breslau. The only year we didn't make the trip was 1936, because you"—here my mother looked down at little Alexander—"were expected in July, right in the middle of the summer. You came along perfectly on time. Then, in September, missing my parents, I booked passage on the *Europa* for you, Hillie, and for myself, leaving both of you boys behind with your father and Aya."

Partly because she came from such a large extended family, my mother never made the transition to America as completely as my father did. She always felt a stronger tug from her native Germany. More so than my father, she had one foot on either side of the Atlantic.

Addressing me directly, my mother said, "You probably don't remember anything about the return trip back to America, but it was the most worrisome and stressful one. When we docked in Southampton,

England, on our way to Germany, I was surprised to see both your grandfathers waiting for us at the bottom of the gangplank. After we greeted each other and I remarked what a pleasure it was to have them both welcome us, they told me we had to turn back immediately because your father was gravely ill with pneumonia. They said that the doctors feared for his life and that the outcome was uncertain. They said they had both come in order to be with us on the return trip. In those days, crossing the Atlantic took almost ten days, and the ship-to-shore communication was difficult at best. I immediately booked our passage back, although we were originally scheduled to continue on to Bremerhaven. Instead, we left the ship right there and spent the night in Southampton while waiting for the *Bremen*, another North German Lloyd ship, to arrive from Bremerhaven on its way to New York. The next day they joined us for the transatlantic journey. It was wonderful having them along for support, as I was obviously anxious and very concerned. Fortunately, when we arrived home, we received the best news I could have imagined. Your father had rallied and was much improved, thanks to a new sulfur drug he had been given, which helped him on his way to a full recovery.

"The last time we all traveled to Europe together was in the summer of 1937," my mother continued. "Your father once again brought along his car, this time a brand-new beautiful 1936 convertible Ford, which he had bought to celebrate Alexander's birth. I used to tease him and say I thought he loved taking the car with him—not only for the convenience of it but also to show how successful and prosperous he had become in the United States."

"I loved that car," my father said.

"I think he secretly also wanted to have everyone see what a superb automobile was being produced in his adopted country. He adored driving it all over Germany, and once again everyone had to have a spin. He loved showing it off."

Taking an art class aboard the *Tatuta Maru*.

✦ ✦ ✦

We spent the time at sea swimming in the pool and playing shuffle-board and card games with each other, and I enjoyed taking the arts-and-crafts classes they offered on board. After the novelty of being on a Japanese ship had worn off, we had ample time to read the books we had been assigned for school.

The monotony was dramatically broken one day by the steward's announcement that we were to prepare ourselves for the appearance of King Neptune—the Ruler of the Deep—as soon we would be crossing the international date line.

We had no idea what that meant, or what to expect, but wanted to know if there was going to be a ritual. After doing some exploring, we learned that this international date line was an imaginary line on the 180-degree longitude meridian of the Earth that separated two consecutive calendar days. The date in the eastern hemisphere, to the left of the line, we were told, is always one day ahead of the date in the western hemisphere to the right. Without the international date line, travelers going westward would find when they returned home that one day more had passed than they thought, despite having kept careful track of the days. Going eastward one would find that one fewer day had elapsed than one had recorded, as happened to Phileas Fogg in Jules Verne's *Around the World in Eighty Days*.

King Neptune—also known as Poseidon in Greek mythology—was an Olympian god of the sea who wielded a tall trident made for him by the Cyclops as a symbol of his station as the prime sea god. That afternoon, the captain announced the official crossing ceremony, and everyone was invited to gather in the first-class lounge the next day to join in the festivities and to meet King Neptune. We asked again what a crossing would entail and were told that the night before we were to reach the international date line, King Neptune would send a messenger informing the captain that he intended to board the ship the following day. King Neptune would then summon a group of people who were to appear before him at the ceremony, who would be prepared for an audience with the king. This preparation would involve a visit to his court, where, in accordance with ritual, they would be dunked in the swimming pool to be cleansed for the final meeting with the king. At the end, everyone would receive a certificate, which would state that one had successfully made the meridian's traversal. The following day, right on schedule, King Neptune appeared with his trident, greeted us all and, after we had been dunked in the pool, presented us with our certificates.

Several days after crossing the date line, our smooth and uneventful voyage was nearing its end. News of the war in Europe circulated among the passengers as either speculation or mere gossip, but there was no talk yet about the imminent events that would ultimately lead to the Second World War. (The fate of the *Tatuta Maru* was dire. In 1943, in use by the Japanese Navy, she was torpedoed and sunk by the US submarine the USS *Tarpon*. More than 1,400 Japanese troops died in the attack.)

The Tuesday before our scheduled arrival, my mother suggested we start packing some of our personal belongings, as she too was planning to pack the few suitcases she'd brought to her cabin (the rest of the famous forty bags had been stowed in cargo). She wanted to be sure there wouldn't be all that much to do at the very end, and she wanted us to have ample time to watch while the captain docked the ship in Yokohama Harbor. My parents must have slept soundly on that last night. It had been a seamless, enjoyable trip. Next stop, Germany—or so they thought.

Part Two

KONNICHIWA, JAPAN

*I*t was raining that Thursday morning—June 19, 1941—when the ship arrived in Yokohama. While we were finishing our last bit of packing and locking up our suitcases, we looked out our open portholes to see what we could of this new land. It was a place that had built up a certain level of mystery in our minds as being alien but enchanting. What we saw first was instantly new: There, on the dock, through the dark gray mist and rain, were Japanese men and women walking along—the women dressed in traditional kimonos, just as we'd seen in picture books. Even at that distance we could hear the *clickety-clack* of their wooden getas, and everyone was carrying unusual-looking umbrellas that seemed to be made of bamboo and oilcloth.

While still on board, our parents had heard gossip of an impending invasion of Russia by Germany. There was some question about whether or not we would be permitted to leave the ship, but this was an overreaction to what was still just a frightening rumor. In the end, the Japanese government gave us clearance to disembark, with no fuss. My siblings and I overheard our parents worriedly discussing the supposed news, and wondered what it could all mean for us.

"So much for the nonaggression pact," I heard my mother say, with uncharacteristic resignation.

"It's only conjecture," replied my father, but he was visibly concerned, though he tried to remain optimistic on the surface. "There's no guarantee the rumors are true," he said. "We will just have to wait and see."

For the week we were going to be in Yokohama, my father had booked us into the New Grand Hotel, overlooking Yamashita Park and the Yokohama Harbor beyond. After completing the disembarkation formalities, we walked down the gangplank, happy to be back on land once again. We were greeted by all we encountered with "*Konnichiwa*," which we discovered meant "hello." Shortly thereafter, my parents spotted the transport the New Grand Hotel had sent to the dock to pick up all our luggage. This was a drastically underfed horse pulling a rickety wagon. By then it had stopped raining, and once the luggage had all been loaded onto the wagon, my father hired two rickshaws we found waiting nearby, one for the three of us children and one for our parents, to take us to the hotel. It was great fun to be pulled along the streets of Yokohama.

After checking in at the front desk, we were shown to our two adjoining rooms, which overlooked the park and the harbor. The rooms

The New Grand Hotel in Yokohama, pictured in 1941.

were surprisingly small, and we noticed that hanging above the beds were gigantic mosquito nets. We would soon be grateful for these, because Yokohama, so near the water, swarmed with the insects. By then it was almost noon. My father called to us through the open doors and told us to get ready for lunch, that he would meet us in the dining room shortly. He was anxious to go to the concierge, not only to confirm all our travel arrangements for the following week but also to be sure that none of the arrangements and schedules he'd made for us had been changed. At the same time, he wanted to check out the disturbing rumors he'd heard on board. He promised to take us later to see the famous Motomachi, the five-block-long main street of shops and boutiques not far from the hotel. He wanted us to get a flavor of Yokohama.

After a quick lunch in the dining room of the hotel, we were off on the first leg of our tour. During the afternoon walking around town, seeing Chinatown and other nearby shopping avenues such as the Isezakicho and Sakuragicho, our father broke off to stop in at the Mitsui bank to see a few friends and exchange some dollars for yen. Meanwhile, I did a little window-shopping, and when I came to a shop that sold kimonos, I couldn't help but go inside to ask what the various items that were sold with kimonos were called. It seemed amazingly complicated and intricate for a Japanese woman to dress, especially when going to a tea ceremony or a formal event. Soon my mother appeared and asked what I was doing, saying she and my brothers had been looking all over for me. Before I had a chance to answer, my father came into the shop. He was still unable to confirm any of the rumors from Europe, although almost everyone admitted to having heard them too. The only thing to do, he repeated, was to maintain our wait-and-see attitude.

My mother seemed a lot more openly concerned. Like my father, she realized that if Germany really was going to war with Russia, it would be a catastrophe for the whole world. My father agreed, of course, but since there was nothing he could do about it, we would have to be patient until we knew if the rumors were indeed true. Even in times of unthinkable crisis, a family has to look at its immediate needs. Would we still be able to continue our trip? This was the dilemma. If the rumors turned out to be true, there seemed to be no chance whatsoever of our being able to make it to Germany via Russia. Everything would have to be rethought. Though noticeably on edge, my father repeated what we were so used to him saying when he wasn't prepared to give us an immediate answer: "Let's cross that bridge when we come to it." In any case, as children we were much too fascinated by everything we were seeing to be worried about something over which we had no control and whose implications we couldn't begin to understand.

We were starting to feel fatigued, which prompted our parents to hail a taxi to take us up to the Bluff, a section of town on a winding hill above downtown Yokohama where mainly foreigners lived. There were a number of homes that were in the typical Japanese style—owned by Japanese people—but most of those were gated and hidden behind thick hedges so as not to be visible from the street. We passed the Ferris Seminary, a school for Japanese girls; the hospital; the Convent of St. Maur, an international girls' school run by nuns; and St. Joseph College, a boys' school, which the driver told us was run by Marianist brothers. We merely glanced at these places like typical tourists, having no inkling what significance they would soon have in our lives.

When we had seen more than enough for our first day, our parents decided to take us to a typically Japanese restaurant to complete our Asian immersion. This time we sat on thick tatami mats covered in soft rush grass on the surface, bound on the longer sides with a cotton or brocade border. They were placed next to each other in an organized pattern, filling the entire floor of the room, except for a wide wooden or stone border at the entrance. We learned that it is the custom to remove one's shoes before entering and stepping onto the tatami, wearing nothing but socks or *tabi*, and to leave one's shoes on the stone or wooden border at the entrance. Once seated, our father asked us how we liked what we'd seen so far, and we all agreed it had been a most unusual and exciting experience. I could tell that my father was just trying to distract us from the dreaded news coming from Europe, which even Enno and I could tell was not good. Alexander was the enviably oblivious four-year-old.

The architecture in Yokohama was quite eclectic. On one avenue you would see rows of one- or two-story, houses made of wood, with sliding doors and windows—known as shoji—their wooden frames covered with rice paper. On the next avenue they might be dwarfed by taller, Western-style brick or concrete buildings, and then there was the almost totally Westernized Bluff. What stood out most to my little girl's eyes, though, were the colorful kimonos. I kept staring at passing women and girls, utterly fascinated.

My father was ordering hot sake for my mother and himself when Enno asked whether we could venture out some more the following day. Knowing we had less than a week left (assuming all went well), my father assured us we were going to make the most of our time there, and he was sure we would want to include shopping for ourselves as well as for presents for family and friends. With that, my mother suggested we order dinner so we would have time to see some of Yokohama by night.

We all decided to order something different, so we could each have a bite of what the other ordered. While waiting for the food to arrive, my mother continued our earlier conversation by saying she agreed it was very important that we go shopping, because my birthday was coming up on Sunday and there would surely be some Japanese souvenirs I'd like to open on my birthday. I knew I wasn't going to have a party, because none of my friends were around, but she assured me we'd have a family celebration that night and asked if I'd seen anything I liked. I said I most certainly had. I already knew what I wished for and responded instantly with great excitement and enthusiasm that I wanted a Japanese girl's kimono, with an obi, a pair of tabi, and a pair of zori. I wanted to see what I'd look like dressed up in the traditional Japanese fashion, and I wanted to show the photos to my friends back home when we returned. Clearly I was overstimulated by all these new experiences, and I was impressed with the kimonos I'd seen. Asking for four presents didn't seem like a lot, since I reasoned that my father could give me the kimono, my mother the obi, Alexander the tabi, and Enno the zori. Alexander then asked me how he could give me a pair of tabi when he didn't even know what tabi were, and anyway, he didn't have any money. I suggested he look at what people on the street were wearing on their feet with their getas and he would soon realize what tabi were. I said he could borrow money from our parents and pay it back when he grew up and got a job.

At that point, my father changed the subject to let us know he'd confirmed our travel reservations with the concierge, and that we could depart as planned. Apparently there had been no word of any changes, and we were due to leave as scheduled. He didn't look entirely convinced as he said this, nor did my mother when she heard this. It didn't make any sense. Any news out of Russia or Germany was likely to be propaganda. What did a hotel concierge really know?

On our way back to the hotel, we lingered here and there to see more of the city by night. It was still fairly light out when we left the restaurant, but one by one the Japanese lanterns in front of each house and shop were turned on as dusk set in. Walking down the Motomachi again, we could smell incense wafting from some of the homes, and from others we could hear the unmistakable sound of Japanese music.

We returned to the hotel and fell into our beds, exhilarated but totally exhausted.

The following day we explored Yokohama some more, and while on the Motomachi, not too far from the hotel, we passed by the store that carried the kimonos—the one where I had stopped in the day before and been transfixed by the exotic costumes. They seemed to have everything I wanted, so after my mother agreed that it looked like a very nice store, we went in to see if we could find something that fit. Meanwhile she suggested my father take the boys to Kikuya, an ice cream shop nearby, and said we'd meet them there shortly. My father and brothers liked that idea and soon were gone. My mother and I entered the shop and looked at a large variety of kimonos meant for young girls, as for every age group a different color and design are traditionally prescribed. The obi, tabi, and zori were not so difficult to find—the same type were worn by every age. I was excited when we found the perfect kimono, and I couldn't wait to go home to try them all on. Making at least some effort to rein me in, my mother said I would have to wait until my birthday party on Sunday.

On Saturday we all went to Tokyo—roughly an hour's journey by train from Yokohama—where we had lunch at the famous Imperial Hotel. It had been designed and built by Frank Lloyd Wright. He had designed it in such a way that it would theoretically withstand earthquakes of any magnitude, information that required my parents to confess that, yes, Japan was prone to extreme earthquakes. Alexander didn't like this one bit.

Frank Lloyd Wright's theory and design had been tested and spectacularly proven correct, for on the very day of the grand opening on September 1, 1923, just before noon, an earthquake of 8.3 on the Richter scale occurred near the densely populated cities of Tokyo and Yokohama. The destruction had spanned all the way across from

Hakone, in the mountains, to Yokohama Bay and north to Tokyo. It was not the largest earthquake ever to hit Japan, but it was probably the most devastating and destructive, because it had occurred at a time when thousands of homes and restaurants had already lit their charcoal hibachi grills in preparation for lunch. When the quake hit, it demolished hundreds of buildings and even more homes, destroying most of their contents. The traditional Japanese wood and paper houses ignited instantly, and firefighters were unable to keep up because broken mains made water unavailable to fight the fires. Thousands of Japanese, some on fire themselves, jumped into the river, the bay, and the canals to put out the fire or to cool off from the heat, but in the end many simply drowned. Deaths were estimated at nearly one hundred thousand, and hundreds of thousands more were left homeless. The Imperial Hotel, however, was only slightly damaged.

After lunch we took a tour of the city, walking down the famous Ginza and strolling along the moat to see the imperial palace, where Emperor Hirohito and Empress Nagako resided. It was a typical tourist outing, and my parents showed little sign of the stress they must have been under.

Sunday, June 22, was my eighth birthday. I awoke at the crack of dawn, anxious to try on my presents, but I still had to be patient. After breakfast it was straight to the Bluff to attend 11:00 mass at the Sacred Heart Cathedral. It was very crowded, and with no seats left, we were forced to stand at the back throughout the service. At one point during the Mass, I was startled to see a Japanese woman—who was standing next to me holding an infant—simply open the front of her kimono and start nursing the child. I had never seen that before but later learned that in Japan it was not unusual for mothers to breastfeed their babies in public.

When Mass was over, the rector, Father Le Bost, greeted us warmly and asked my father how long we'd been in Yokohama and whether we were planning to stay. My father replied that we had just arrived from America on Thursday and were going to be in town for a few more days before traveling on to Europe. Father Le Bost then politely told us how happy he was that we had stopped by and wished us a safe and pleasant journey, signing off with the usual "God bless" while making the sign of the cross with his right hand.

After church, my parents thought we should take a leisurely walk back to the hotel. All I could think of was my kimono and its accessories back in our rooms. My parents must have read my mind, as they began teasing me. Down the road a bit, we came upon a Unitarian church at the corner of an intersection of the Bluff and a street named the Daikan-zaka. It was a quaint and narrow street and led down the hill to the Motomachi, lined with houses and shops that all seemed as if they'd been there for centuries.

By then it was almost 1:00 p.m. and time for lunch. It was agreed that it would be fun to have a picnic in Yamashita Park, across from our hotel, with good old-fashioned peanut butter and jelly sandwiches, the ingredients for which we could find in one of the special suitcases my mother had packed. They tasted awfully good, especially because we hadn't had one in at least three weeks. After finishing our sandwiches, my father got up and said he wanted to go back to the hotel, that he had some work he needed to do before his scheduled meetings with his colleagues at several of the banks the next day. He suggested we all take a little siesta and rest for an hour, before my birthday party that evening. No one else seemed to mind—the warm afternoon sun had made everyone sleepy—so I had to continue pretending I wasn't that eager to open my birthday presents.

When we arrived back at the hotel, there was a great deal of commotion going on, and lots of people were milling around the lobby speaking in hushed tones. My father, after asking the clerk behind the desk what was going on, turned back to us, grave and downcast, and told us Germany had invaded the Soviet Union in a predawn all-out offensive. The rumors were true, after all.

A look of disbelief and shock came over my mother's face, even though the turn of events was by no means unexpected after all the rumors we had heard for the past few days. My father turned to us and said, "Come on, let's go up to our rooms. Your mother and I need to talk. We need to figure out where we go from here. Do you understand? Rest and read your books. We'll call you when it's time to go to dinner."

My birthday party at the hotel that evening turned out to be a somber celebration. With a resigned sigh, my father told us that he and our mother had to change the original plan. We would be returning home to America just as soon as he could get reservations for the five of us. We children were secretly thrilled by the news, because it meant we would be seeing our friends much sooner than we had expected and would be able to be with them for part of the summer after all. Germany wasn't home to us. All we really knew of it was distant and that it was at war with Britain.

Enno immediately wanted to know why they were making the change, displaying his inquisitive nature. Our father explained that because Hitler had invaded Russia, we could no longer take the Trans-Siberian Railway as my father carried a German passport. My mother did too, and all three of us were included on hers, despite the fact that Enno and Alexander were US citizens. Enno then asked what would have happened if the trip had been planned a week earlier, when we would have already been on the Trans-Siberian Railway. "Good question," my father replied. "We surely would have been imprisoned, and we'd have probably been lost and eventually died in Siberia," he said with complete bluntness.

He told us we probably wouldn't know the full extent of our new plan until sometime the following week, when he planned to go to a travel agency to find out how soon he could book a return passage for us. He added that since we'd come this far, before returning to America, we ought to take a short vacation in Japan and travel around the country to see some of the famous Japanese cities and their ornate temples, and also to get closer to the revered Mount Fuji, which so far we had only seen from a distance. He was trying to put the best face on our current disaster, as if it were a minor inconvenience from which we might profit in the end. We all agreed it was a wonderful idea, and my mother noted how lucky we were to have a summer vacation in so beautiful a country as Japan.

Just then the waiter came with my cake and everybody sang the usual "Happy Birthday." My beautiful presents remained unopened for the time being, as my parents were not really in the mood for further festivities. That night, failing to fall asleep, I crept out of bed and went into the bathroom where my parents had stashed my birthday presents. I couldn't resist any longer. I opened up the largest of them, the kimono, and then the package that contained the obi. I put on the kimono, and began to try to wrap the obi around my middle. I was still tangled up in this outfit when I gave up, staggered back to bed, and fell right to sleep.

The following day, we were pretty much left to our own devices as our parents went about rethinking the scheduled plans for our trip to Germany. The first thing my father did on Monday was to go to a travel agency and apply for passage back to America, making efforts to go on a neutral ship. He was told to come back in three or four weeks, as they had no space for a family of five and it could take at least that long for something to open up. When he came home, my father shrugged and said, "It looks like we may be here longer than we expected."

By now it had become clear that all the planning and rearranging would take quite a while. My parents therefore postponed our seeing Japan for a few weeks and concentrated on reorganizing their plans. They also needed not to have to be concerned about us children day-to-day, so I was enrolled in a summer program in the English-speaking section of the International Convent of the Sacred Heart in Tokyo—a sister school of the one I had left on 91st Street in New York City—for the first two weeks of July. A nanny was hired to look after my brothers. It was not a happy time for me, for I missed my family and friends. The nuns were generally much stricter than they had been at 91st Street, but both schools shared the rule that we had to curtsy every time we passed a nun. At night we slept in a dormitory with only flimsy curtains separating each bed, and once the lights were out we were forbidden to talk. We had to adhere strictly to this rule, because in each dorm there was a nun who slept in a cubicle at the entrance. If she heard even the slightest peep out of us, we would receive some form of group punishment.

Alexander's fifth birthday was coming up on July 13, for which he had also been promised a party. After rounding up as many of the children close to his age whom he'd met during our three weeks there, and some who had also been on the *Tatuta Maru* with us, it was all set. There were to be about eight girls and boys, including Enno and me. Fortunately, I was just back from my two weeks at Sacred Heart, and everyone invited could also speak English.

Our parents had hired a sword-and-fire swallower to entertain us, a Japanese man who complemented this feat with magic tricks. The afternoon of the party, the little girls and boys started arriving, and soon we were all settled in our chairs, waiting for the show to start. The entertainer was remarkable, opening his mouth and swallowing his sword, pushing it deep down into his body. He did the same with the fire, swallowing it without a whimper, and afterward everyone wanted to know how he did it. His magic tricks were equally entertaining—he

Celebrating Alexander's fifth birthday.

Alexander with two
of the hotel staff after
his birthday party.

somehow made eggs pop out of his ears—and he received a big round of applause. My mother invited him to stay for cake and ice cream, but he declined, as he had been hired for another party. While my parents worried frantically behind the scenes about getting us all back to relative safety, life went on superficially and enjoyably for us children.

Three weeks had gone by, and there was still no word regarding our return trip to America, so my father went back to the travel agency and once again was told there were few ships and even fewer clippers crossing the Pacific to the US. There were hordes of people who were migrating from different countries—either fleeing their hostile ones or looking for safe havens in different countries—so finding accommodations for five was going to be extremely difficult. We just had to be patient. My father knew the US had embargoed scrap metal shipments to Japan and had closed the Panama Canal to Japanese shipping in 1940, after the Japanese had made moves into Indochina, but he did not believe that had anything to do with passenger ships crossing the Pacific. He also knew that Japan and the US were involved in negotiations, trying to improve relations between the two countries. What he did not know was that the Japanese were continuing their aggression in China, so that on July 26, 1941 the US had frozen Japanese assets. On August 1, oil and gasoline exports to Japan were embargoed. All travel and shipping was also banned. For the moment, there was no way to return to the States. The implications of all these maneuvers worried my parents intensely but, as always, when given little choice, they remained positive and hoped for the best.

With no immediate plans for us to leave Japan, my parents booked us into the New Grand Lodge—an affiliate of the New Grand Hotel—for two weeks in August in the well-known summer resort town of Karuizawa, where the emperor and his family frequently spent their summers. It was situated in the Nagano prefecture at the foothills of

With Alexander and friends we met aboard the *Tatuta Maru*.

the Japanese Alps, in the Chubu region of the island of Honshu. We had to leave Yokohama to catch the train from Ueno Station in Tokyo. It took six hours to reach Karuizawa and on the way we saw much of the surrounding countryside of the region, with its miles and miles of rice fields, which all lay under water. There were men who worked in them seemingly around the clock. There were quaint farmhouses made of wood, with their sliding doors and windows covered only with rice paper. And, of course, the ever-present black hibachis—the small, cast-iron charcoal stoves with a grill on top for cooking—were evident everywhere around the houses. The word "hibachi" in Japanese aptly means "fire bowl."

At each and every train stop, we could hear a high, nasal voice over the loudspeaker announcing in Japanese the name of the station at

Our rustic cabin at the
New Grand Lodge.

With my brother
Alexander, fishing on
the lake in Karuizawa.

My father watching over us while we row on the lake in Karuizawa.

which we'd be arriving next. To my brothers and me it was hilarious, and we loved to imitate the announcer. Even our parents were amused, but they tried to quiet our impolite laughter.

We saw a sight totally unfamiliar to us: Japanese men walking down country roads with very long wooden poles resting on their shoulders, which they held on to by draping their outstretched arms over the poles halfway down their length. At either end of the poles hung fairly good-sized wooden tubs filled with human fertilizer they had collected from villages to take to the fields. These men were called *unkoya-san*, an indelicate literal term for the product they carried. Not a very pleasant job, we all decided, crinkling our noses.

Upon arriving in Karuizawa, a car from the New Grand Lodge met us and took us to the cabin my parents had rented. It was very rustic but comfortable enough, and we spent two carefree weeks swimming in the lake, hiking up the Hanareyama, playing tennis, and bicycling.

Enno and Alexander rowing on the lake with friends in Karuizawa.

We loved to explore the area while our parents visited the local antiques shops looking for treasures. On one of those days, while walking near the railroad tracks, we saw a highly polished burgundy train with black trim rolling by with all its dark curtains drawn. We noticed that the Japanese people, who also had been walking near the tracks, had stopped to face the train. Bowing down deeply from the waist, they remained that way until the train was completely out of sight. When we inquired about what we had just witnessed, we were told that it was Emperor Hirohito's imperial private train, which was taking him to a villa in Karuizawa. Apparently, it was customary for all Japanese subjects to bow down and not look at the train when it passed, despite the fact that the emperor and his empress sat behind drawn curtains. He was, in the eyes of the Japanese, a deity—a god who was to be treated with the utmost of respect, to the point of worship—and therefore not to be gazed upon directly.

Before our two weeks in Karuizawa were over, my father began to get nervous and was anxious to return to Yokohama. He wanted to see if anything had opened up for us in the way of space on a ship bound for America, but we begged him to stay for the full two weeks. He acquiesced, but we could tell he was on edge.

At this point it was mid-August. On one of our last days in Karuizawa, while walking in the countryside, we came across several Japanese children who were out picking flowers on the plains. One of them spoke English, so we struck up a conversation. It turned out they were picking flowers to put on the graves of fallen soldiers. Thinking this was a really nice thing to do, we asked if they would like us to join them and help. A short while later, a photographer appeared, and when he asked if he could take our picture while picking flowers, we innocently said yes, seeing no harm in being photographed with our newfound friends. Two days later, the concierge at the hotel showed us that our picture had appeared in the local paper.

The photo that appeared in the Karuizawa newspaper, *Asahi-Shin Bun*, in August 1941.

墓前へ 村 車 高、心 の 花 束

靖國第四年の盂蘭盆を迎へた輕井澤町旧輕井澤青少年團幼年部では"お國のため戰死した兵隊さんや遺族の方に感謝と慰靈をいたしま せう"と野山に咲き競ふ秋草の探取をはじめ十四、五の兩日、一同は、この貢心籠めたを采を戰士勇士の墓前や遺族を訪れて捧ぐる豫定であるが、且下同町に滯在中のドイツ幼年諸君も、これを聽いて"僕等も仲良しの國、日本・兵隊さんの英靈を慰めませう"と純情溢ふる〻可憐な枢軸共同戰線を張り麗しくも愛らしい枢軸友好強化風景を展開してゐる【寫眞は日本の兒童と共に仲よく、英靈に供ふる草花探取中の獨逸ヒルデ・ガード孃やイリーキン君、同町野澤ケ

We couldn't possibly read the newspaper article because it was all in katana, hiragana, and kanji. Translated into English, it read:

A CHERISHED BOUQUET FROM THE PURE HEARTS OF CHILDREN

Four years after the Manchurian incident began, at the time of Urabon [a Buddhist event to honor the spirits of the deceased], in the town of Karuizawa, the old Karuizawa youth group—a division of young children—decided to collect autumn flowers that were blooming in a nearby plain and deliver them to the graves of fallen soldiers and their families to show their gratitude. They were to collect them for two days on August 14th and 15th. Young German children who were vacationing in town heard about this plan and decided they would like to join them for this event, to also honor the soldier's spirits. These innocent children of pure heart worked together to strengthen their bond, in the beautiful unfolding scenery.

Upon our return to Yokohama, my father immediately went back to the travel agency and to the neutral shipping lines to see if anything new had developed while we were gone, but again he was told that with the ban on Japanese ships going to the US, it would be quite some time before they could find passage for a family of five on a neutral ship. Again he heard, "Come back in three or four weeks, and we will see what we can do. Right now there is just nothing available. Perhaps we will have something for you then."

Meanwhile, at the hotel, the atmosphere had changed radically. New rumors had it that the place was teeming with spies, and every encounter was met with suspicion. Scare stories were flying all around Yokohama and Tokyo, and many prominent people were being taken to the security police for questioning.

Finally my father, discouraged by the fact that it could take a long time to secure passage back to America, decided he could no longer keep the three of us out of school. He applied to the two English-language schools we had passed on the Bluff when we first arrived in Yokohama—St. Joseph College for my brothers and the Convent of St. Maur for me—both of which accepted us, albeit on a temporary basis, until we could return home to America.

St. Joseph College, located at 43 Yamate-cho (the main street on the Bluff) was a Catholic boys' school founded by Brother Louis Stoltz and five other Marianists in 1901. It was attended by about seventy students. The Convent of St. Maur was established in 1872 by the missionary Sisters of the Infant Jesus to provide children drawn from the international community of all nationalities and religious denominations with a quality English-language education based on an understanding and appreciation of people's differences. Despite the fact that its buildings were devastated by a typhoon in 1884, demolished by an earthquake in 1894, then left in ruins again in 1923 during the Great Kanto Earthquake—which caused the deaths of many of the pupils, staff, and sisters—the institution nevertheless survived and was thriving when I entered the elementary school in the fall of 1941.

By then my parents had moved us from the New Grand Hotel to a furnished house on the Bluff at 66b Yamate-cho, which my father had rented on a temporary basis from the Unitarian church next door. It was near the corner of the intersection of the Daikan-zaka and the Bluff, a section of Yokohama where most foreigners lived. It was also very convenient, because it was an easy walk to school for the three of us.

School was actually quite fun. The nuns at St. Maur were not nearly as strict as those at the Sacred Heart in Tokyo, and it was nice that we no longer had to curtsy each time we passed them. My daily hour-long Japanese lesson was the most challenging course but at the same time was a blessing, because as I became more proficient, I could start conversing with the Japanese people I encountered who didn't speak English.

My mother went about arranging the house and unpacking most of the forty suitcases, leaving the household goods and the canned foods in their suitcases in a separate storage room. There we would

Our rented house
at 66b Yamate-cho.

The living room at
66b Yamate-cho.

The Japanese amahs.

go to pick out whatever was not available in the stores. She started by hiring two Japanese housekeepers, known as amahs—one to do the cooking and the other to do the cleaning, laundry, and pressing.

She also spent a considerable amount of time trying to get to know the area better in order to do the shopping. She was pleased that at the bottom of the hill there was the Motomachi—which we had seen on our first day in Yokohama—where she could buy just about everything. She also found a wonderful chocolate shop that was run by a Russian woman called Frau Gusev and her store became a favorite of our family. On the way back up the hill there was a stylish flower shop named Miyazaki, run by the owner, Miyazaki-san, and that too became a must-stop for my mother because of the beautiful selection of plants, fresh flowers, and floral arrangements.

The Miyazaki flower shop in 2005, seemingly unchanged from the 1940s.

My father, on the other hand, went about the business of communicating with everyone he thought could help us out of our predicament. These included his friends not only at the US banks but also at the Japanese and German banks. He even tried the consulates, but all to no avail. Fortunately for him, there was an upright piano in our rented house. To calm himself during the many frustrations he encountered, he would sit at the piano for hours playing all his favorites—Beethoven, Brahms, Chopin, and Wagner. I remember his agonizing over Beethoven's *Moonlight Sonata*, as his fingers did not always move as quickly as some of the movements demanded, mainly because he hadn't practiced for some time. When it came to playing Wagner's "Magic Fire Music," though, he threw himself into it with such gusto that he could heartily enjoy the dynamic sounds he was still able to produce and we, who were almost always listening from some part of the house, loved to hear him play it.

He was also able to join a tennis club, where he and my mother played a couple of sets a day. At the club, they met quite a number of people from the Yokohama foreign community, from several different countries, who had been living in Japan for many years. From them, my parents received much local and political knowledge about Japan. My father always liked to be up on everything, and he made sure to keep himself and the rest of us informed. His new friends told him about special Japanese inns (*ryokans*), where he would arrange for our family to stay on the occasional weekend. There we would sleep on tatami floors with futons under and over us for cover at night. When it came time for a meal, the futons, pillows, and sheets would be rolled up and stored in a closet, and we would be served food at a square table set up for the occasion.

Baron Mitsui from the Mitsui bank was an acquaintance of my father's from his banking days, and when they would meet, Mitsui

My father's upright piano.

was always extremely cordial—as were the majority of Japanese in those days. They would mostly talk about finance and politics and were pleased and hopeful when Admiral Kichisaburo Nomura, long regarded as pro-American, was appointed ambassador to the United States. They both knew Nomura was a capable and knowledgeable diplomat who was well versed in foreign affairs, and they hoped he would be successful in his mission of avoiding war.

While we waited to hear from the travel agents, life went on in Yokohama—but not without worry and stress. It didn't help matters when, that fall, after school was in full swing, as I was playing with a few new friends I had invited to my house for tea, I was suddenly bowed over in pain. I could no longer stand up. I threw myself onto my bed and curled up in the fetal position. My friends, alarmed at seeing me in that condition, went looking for my mother, who—after seeing me lying there rolled up and in tears—called the doctor and asked him to come to the house. He arrived shortly thereafter, and after he had finished examining me, he and my parents stood at the foot of my bed talking in almost inaudible whispers. At one point, though, I thought I heard the doctor—a Dr. Wirtz, who, we later found out, didn't have a medical license—say, "She has acute appendicitis." After he left, I asked my mother what he had said and what was so cute about my appendix. She replied, "He said you had an acute appendicitis attack and will have to go to the hospital immediately to have your appendix surgically removed. Your appendix has become infected." She went on to explain that people didn't really need an appendix, that it was a spare organ.

I asked whether the operation would be painful, and she said not really, as the doctor would put me to sleep. That way, I wouldn't feel a thing. She did say, though, that perhaps after the anesthesia had worn off, I might have some discomfort, but in a few days I would be feeling well again and would be able to do everything I'd always done. I asked when I'd have to go, and she said "Right now," adding that she and my father would take me to the same hospital I saw every day on my way to and from school. Because I couldn't walk, my father carried me downstairs into a waiting taxi, and we went to the hospital. There I was put on a gurney, and soon my agony was over. My mother was right: The first few days after my operation were rather awful, but once home, in my own bed and with the bandages removed, I slowly began feeling a lot better and eventually was even anxious to go back to school. Such small dramas are the norm, of course, but I'm sure my parents were relieved that all had gone so smoothly in a completely foreign land.

Monday morning, December 8, 1941, dawned in Yokohama and began just as every other Monday morning had during those past three months. We still had no news about open berths for our passage back to America. As soon as one of the amahs had given us our breakfast, we were off to school. We didn't see our parents that morning, as they hadn't yet come downstairs before we left. The day at school was also not a particularly memorable one, but it would become indelibly etched in all our minds the moment we returned home from school. There, in the living room, we found our parents sitting with a friend, speaking in low voices, so we could not make out what they were saying. The moment they saw us, my father, whose face was almost ghost-like, spoke up in the firmest tone he could muster and said, "Come here and sit down with us. Something terrible occurred earlier today. It is unbelievable, but it happens to be true. This morning the Japanese attacked Pearl Harbor in Hawaii. We saw the area when we were there, remember?" We nodded. "Incredible," said my father, still letting the news sink in even as he tried to explain. "A total surprise attack on Sunday morning there. Apparently they have destroyed most of the American fleet."

Among the children, only Enno could begin to understand. "Warships? And sailors too?"

"We only have the earliest reports. No one knows how bad the casualties are." My father looked at the floor and shook his head. There was no use trying to explain. It was a catastrophe beyond belief.

With that, Enno asked how we were going to get back to America now.

"That still remains to be seen. A lot will depend on what happens next, but I think we can be certain the US will declare war on Japan after this. That could mean we'll be stranded here at least until the war is over. But we'll see." "We'll see" had become our father's mantra.

My immediate thought was that I was not going to see my friends for a lot longer now. At eight years old, I could not comprehend the magnitude of what had just occurred and how it was likely to affect the whole world. There was no way I could absorb the implications: I was living in a country at war with the country I considered to be my home, and at the same time America would surely be drawn into war against Japan's allies, including the country of my birth. In my little universe, all I cared about were my friends back home, from whom I received letters filling me in on their lives in New York.

Alexander saw me looking sad—sensitive as he was—and said that maybe I'd see my friends sooner than I thought, that our father would be able to get us back before Christmas. Our father told us there was not much we could do except, once again, to wait, hope, and pray. "It's all in the hands of God," he said, with an air of resignation. "But I'm sure we'll get back home safely. It's just a matter of time," he added, as if verbalizing the thought would make it happen. Little did he know then how much time it would take, and what it would take to get there.

And sure enough, as he had surmised, December 10 brought the US into the war, and with a determination to fight to the finish. Britain too declared war on Japan. The following day, Germany and Italy declared war on the US. In a personal microcosm of the world's general conflagration, our family's immediate fate was sealed.

+ + +

Up until December 8, 1941, the Japanese had been extremely polite, always friendly and helpful to us. From that historic date forward, however, things changed quite dramatically. On the Bluff, at every corner of almost every intersection, including ours at the Daikan-zaka, there had always been police booths with officers stationed in them. Now, despite the fact that we were German nationals, our amahs said they had been told they would have to report all our comings and goings, all our activities, and get the names of everyone who came to our house. They were told to list the names of all our guests and submit the list to the policemen on duty, on a daily basis. From that point on, unfortunately, we had very little social contact with the Japanese. In truth, they had been told to despise and look down on white foreigners.

The community's mood had completely changed. Soon, my father was called in for a meeting with SS Colonel Josef Albert Meisinger, head of the Gestapo in Japan. Meisinger, wearing that brutal uniform and a disapproving scowl, asked my father why he had enrolled his children in English-language schools and not in the local German school. My father replied that we weren't at all proficient in German, and because we'd always attended English-language schools in New York, it was therefore the natural place for us to be. Colonel Meisinger insisted on the point, saying that now that war had been declared, my father should change us over to the German school. Meisinger actually told him, "Your kids are speaking English? That's a lost cause. After the war, no one will be speaking English anymore." My father told him point blank that he had no intention of taking us out of our current schools, that we were already enrolled in the best Catholic schools in Yokohama, and that we were going to remain right where we were. He let Meisinger know in no uncertain terms that he was not going to make us transfer to other schools.

Colonel Meisinger then suggested that my father join the Nazi party. This too, my father refused to do, and the result was that, from that day forward, we were under constant and close surveillance. Apparently, my father was now considered "politically unreliable" by the Nazis and the German authorities. Colonel Meisinger gave my father the creeps, and no wonder. He would later be remembered as the Butcher of Warsaw for his sickening actions in Poland before he was stationed in Asia. After the war, Meisinger was arrested in Japan and sent to Poland to face charges of war crimes. He was forty-seven years old when he was tried and executed.

Still unable to travel in either direction, we had no other choice but to remain in Japan for however long it would take to secure passage back home. It quickly became quite clear that we would probably have to adjust to an entirely new way of life in an unfamiliar culture, which was at war with the US and allied with Germany. Soon after that, my father went back to our schools and enrolled us permanently, with the proviso that when the time came and we were able to return to America, he would take us out.

It was then that we started learning, in much more detail, about Japanese culture. We started studying their language, with their two alphabets, katakana and hiragana, and the Chinese characters, known as kanji, the most difficult of them all. First we were taught katakana, the easiest. When we had mastered katakana, we were taught the more complicated hiragana. Both were phonetic, which enabled us to spell foreign names and places quite easily.

The most challenging of all was not an alphabet but kanji, which consisted of thousands of characters, much like Chinese ideograms. Only Enno was old enough to be taught how to write kanji. He was told that one would have to know at least 3,000 of those characters to read a newspaper.

It was mandatory that I take an hour of Japanese each day. As I became more proficient in speaking and understanding Japanese, it was

あ a	い i	う u	え e	お o
か ka	き ki	く ku	け ke	こ ko
さ sa	し shi	す su	せ se	そ so
た ta	ち chi	つ tsu	て te	と to
な na	に ni	ぬ nu	ね ne	の no
は ha	ひ hi	ふ fu	へ he	ほ ho
ま ma	み mi	む mu	め me	も mo
や ya		ゆ yu		よ yo
ら ra	り ri	る ru	れ re	ろ ro
わ wa				を wo
ん n				

ア a	イ i	ウ u	エ e	オ o
カ ka	キ ki	ク ku	ケ ke	コ ko
サ sa	シ shi	ス su	セ se	ソ so
タ ta	チ chi	ツ tsu	テ te	ト to
ナ na	ニ ni	ヌ nu	ネ ne	ノ no
ハ ha	ヒ hi	フ fu	ヘ he	ホ ho
マ ma	ミ mi	ム mu	メ me	モ mo
ヤ ya		ユ yu		ヨ yo
ラ ra	リ ri	ル ru	レ re	ロ ro
ワ wa				ヲ wo
ン n				

Left: hiragana, Right: katakana

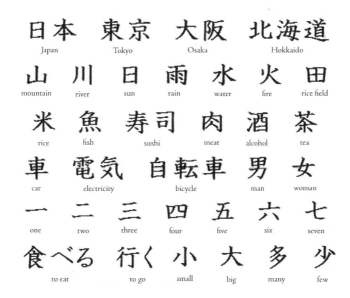

日本 Japan   東京 Tokyo   大阪 Osaka   北海道 Hokkaido

山 mountain   川 river   日 sun   雨 rain   水 water   火 fire   田 rice field

米 rice   魚 fish   寿司 sushi   肉 meat   酒 alcohol   茶 tea

車 car   電気 electricity   自転車 bicycle   男 man   女 woman

一 one   二 two   三 three   四 four   五 five   六 six   七 seven

食べる to eat   行く to go   小 small   大 big   多 many   少 few

Kanji

much easier to understand their culture. Both Enno and Alexander took judo lessons, and I took lessons in ikebana, the Japanese art of flower arranging. I was also taught how miniature bonsai trees are grown and how they are treated to retard their growth. The nuns and brothers who were our teachers came from many different countries, and though each spoke several languages, all were fluent in English. It was truly an international school, and we blended in very comfortably. They introduced us to the two major religions—Shintoism and Buddhism—on excursions to various shrines and temples.

During the Christmas holidays, our parents took us to the Japanese theater in Tokyo, where Kabuki plays were performed. Kabuki was usually about historical events, moral conflicts in love relationships, or both, and the actors used old-fashioned language that we couldn't begin to understand, not yet having mastered contemporary Japanese. Even though they spoke in monotonous voices and were accompanied by several traditional Japanese instruments, we were nevertheless entertained and definitely amused.

My father missed having music at home, so he decided one day to assemble a Victrola he proudly brought home in pieces, together with a collection of classical records he'd found on the Motomachi. Not being able to work, he took advantage of the upright piano and basically went back to his first love and what he originally had wanted to be—a concert pianist. It was great therapy for him while he did not and could not find work or any type of occupation.

Our first Christmas in Yokohama brought with it many happy surprises. For instance, we were delighted to find we could buy a real Christmas tree and many Western decorations. We even found Christmas records to play on the Victrola. Coming from Europe, we always celebrated the birth of Christ on Christmas Eve. After dusk, when it had turned dark, we lit the real wax candles our father had carefully mounted on the tree. At that point, he turned on the Victrola

In my kimono by the Christmas tree with my cat, Mooshi,
and my brother Alexander.

and played Christmas carols. After exchanging presents, we had dinner, and later that night we all attended midnight Mass. What was
particularly special was that, thanks to Frau Gusev's chocolate shop on
the Motomachi, we had many of the traditional chocolates and candies
we were accustomed to having at previous Christmases in America.
I wore the kimono with the tabi and zori I had been given for my
birthday, and I felt very festive in my Japanese dress. Instead of toys,
our parents gave us beautiful Japanese Hiroshige prints to hang on the
bare walls of our rooms. The boys were also given a dog, a black-and-
white mongrel they named Flora, and I was given a sweet little black-
and-white cat, also a mixed breed, which I named Mooshi. We siblings
gave each other typical Japanese geisha and samurai dolls. We also gave
each other origami kits, with which we could practice the technique
we had learned of folding paper into cranes, flowers, goldfish, or swans
without using any glue or scissors. We also added funny little touristy
trinkets we had found on the Motomachi.

✦ ✦ ✦

Oshogatsu, as New Year's is called in Japan, is the most important holiday celebrated in the country. Businesses are closed from the first of January until the third, as that is a sacred time for families to gather and visit with each other. Since January 1 is considered such an auspicious day, it is said that it is best to start the day by viewing the New Year's first sunrise, known as *Hatsuhinode*. Traditionally it is thought to foretell the entire year to come, and must be free from stress and anger. It is to be full of joy. Every year is considered completely separate, with each New Year providing a fresh start. Before the end of the year, therefore, all clothes and houses are thoroughly cleaned; entrances are decorated with ornaments of pine, bamboo, and plum trees; and all work is completed, so as to leave the old year's miseries and troubles far behind, in order that parties and celebrations can be enjoyed to the fullest. A traditional Japanese New Year's dish is *omochi*, a rectangular cake made of rice and water. When it is toasted, it turns golden brown and puffs up like a little cushion, and when dipped into soy sauce it becomes quite tasty.

As the New Year dawned, there was still no word from anyone my father knew in Japan, including his friend Baron Mitsui. We remained in what my parents hoped was just a holding pattern, and a very temporary predicament. Meanwhile we had to continue on with life, although we were definitely much more guarded in all our words and actions.

In January, Enno celebrated his eleventh birthday with a few of his friends from school, including one who had celebrated his birthday three weeks earlier and with whom Enno had formed a close friendship. His name was Isaac Shapiro—Ike, for short—and he was one of five brothers whose parents had originally come from Russia but who at this point were stateless. Ike already spoke Japanese fluently because he was born in Tokyo on January 5, 1931, the same year as Enno.[*]

Reading the *Japan Times* was the only way our parents could get any news in English, but they suspected much of it was propaganda. My father had also brought with him a short-wave radio—an Emerson—but he used it only secretly and on rare occasions, as we were being surveilled. On infrequent attempts he was sometimes able to pick up the *Voice of America* broadcast from San Francisco. My parents told us only the news they thought we could understand. It was on one of those days that they called us in for a serious meeting to impress upon us once again that as long as there was war, we would have to watch our actions and learn to keep our thoughts to ourselves and our mouths shut unless we were among family. They made us aware that we had to refrain from discussing anything with anybody that could even remotely be interpreted as being anti-Japanese or anti-German, as the consequences could be dire. All in all, I got the impression my father was more wary of the Germans—Meisinger, in particular—than he was of the Japanese authorities. There was further tension between my parents and some in the German community in general, because they disapproved of our being taught in English, from American textbooks.

Later that winter we were introduced to another Japanese tradition, a festival called *Hina Matsuri*, also known as the Doll Festival or Girls' Day, which is celebrated every year on the third of March. It is

---

[*] Six years after the war ended, in September 1951, while standing in line to register for the fall semester at Columbia University in New York City, Enno recognized his friend and classmate from Yokohama, who was about to enter Columbia Law School. They had a very warm and happy reunion. Now, 65 years later, Isaac Shapiro is not only a well-known and respected attorney with the law firm Skadden, Arps, Slate, Meagher & Flom but has also written a book about his and his family's experiences in Japan during World War II, titled *Edokko*, which in Japanese means "Son of Tokyo."

a day on which families who have daughters wish them a happy and successful life. The families display their doll collections, which represent the emperor, empress and the Imperial court, together with peach blossoms, in their home. They display the dolls so that all bad fortune can be transferred to them, before the dolls are taken to a nearby river and set afloat.

Toward the end of March it was cherry blossom time in the Tokyo and Yokohama area, a spectacular sight none of us had ever seen before. We were excited that spring was coming at last, and went out for long walks to admire the beautiful *sakura* (cherry) trees. On one of our walks on the Bluff, we met a French couple and their two daughters with whom my parents had become acquainted at the tennis club. They told us they'd been all over the Bluff and in town by Yamashita Park looking for blooming cherry blossom trees, all of which they had photographed. My parents said nothing at the time, but they later made sure to warn us to not even think of taking our cameras out of the house to photograph anything, as that could be misconstrued and might spell trouble.

Other events contributed to my parents' unease. Soon after we arrived, they had met and befriended a stunning Eurasian woman named Marieli. In her late twenties, she had a Swiss father and a Japanese mother, and she frequently came to visit us. She spoke Japanese, English, and German, which was very helpful to my parents, who had not yet learned Japanese. One day she disappeared. When my father heard she had been imprisoned, he went to bring her some food and tried to find out the reason why. She had no idea, nor did anyone else. People assumed she was suspected of being a spy.

On May 5, there was yet another festival, and by the time we were dismissed from school in the afternoon, it was going on in full force. This time it was the annual Boys' Festival, *Tango no Sekku*, and much like on the Girls' Day in March, families prayed for the health and future success of their sons. It was a festive celebration at which color-ful paper kites in the shape of carp were hung all over, and lots of sa-murai dolls were displayed—symbols of strength, power, and success in life.

On Saturday April 18, 1942, with school closed for the weekend, my brothers and I were sitting at lunch with our parents shortly after noon when we heard the wailing of air-raid sirens. We were used to this because of previous practice drills, and at first we thought it was just another false alarm. But then we heard the unmistakable sound of low-flying planes in the distance, and we realized it was the real thing. Alarmed, we went outside to see what was happening. Far away, we could see antiaircraft shells exploding over the city of Yokohama and in the northern sky. In the direction of Tokyo I spotted a plane that had been shot down dropping to the earth with black smoke trailing it. From my vantage point it looked as though it was going to crash into the bay. It was far enough away that we didn't have to worry about it hitting us. It started zigzagging and dropping so rapidly that we knew it had been badly damaged. Alexander covered his eyes, not being able to watch the plane careening downward, worrying that it might ex-plode at any moment. It was much too far away for us to be able to see it hit the ground, crash, or explode, and for all we knew it might have fallen into the bay. Both Alexander and I were still shaken and scared but were assured by Enno that we had nothing to worry about if we just stayed inside the house until we heard the all-clear signal. Shortly thereafter the signal sounded, and to our relief, nothing had happened to us or to anyone in the neighborhood.

What we had just witnessed, we soon learned, was the audacious air attacks later known as the Doolittle Raid. Our parents read in the paper that American B-25B planes led by Lt. Col. James Doolit-tle had flown over Tokyo and dropped bombs over military targets.

Sixteen bombers destroyed an oil tank farm, a steel mill, and several power plants. Targets to the south, in Yokohama and Yokosuka, had also been hit, including a few schools and supposedly an army hospital. Japanese propaganda ridiculed the raid, calling it the Do-Nothing Raid, and boasted that several B-25Bs had been shot down. In fact, none of the bombers were shot down in Japan. All sixteen planes cleared Japanese airspace and, low on fuel, crashed in China and the East China Sea, except for one, which made it to Vladivostok in Russia. The Japanese captured eight crewmembers who had hidden in a coastal Chinese village and executed three; one died during his internment and the other four survived the war as POWs. The plan for the raid was not so much destruction as it was to unsettle the Japanese people and make them lose faith in their leadership. I have no way of knowing what the plane was that we saw dropping out of the sky. It was just a surreal moment in our lives—war from a distance—and we had seen a corner of a great morale-boosting and terrifically inspiring American success.

Notwithstanding the war's raging on, life for us, at least temporarily, went on with a semblance of normalcy. Considering the violence and chaos in so many parts of the world, and living in a country that was going to fight its war to the bitter end, things were still pretty good for us. We drew our blackout curtains every evening and slept fairly well.

More than a month had gone by when at breakfast one morning Mother asked whether we had seen the French friends we'd met on the Bluff with their two daughters the day we were out walking during cherry blossom time. My father replied that he hadn't really wanted to tell us the disturbing news, but he'd heard all four of the French family had been imprisoned on charges of espionage not too long after we'd seen them. He guessed that the Kempeitai (the military police of the Imperial Japanese Army in World War II) thought our friends were taking pictures of Yokohama to give to the enemy so they could see whether there were some areas of interest to target. He wasn't sure whether they were Vichy French or Free French, so it might also have been politically motivated. He said he would inquire at the tennis club the next day. The thought of being sent to prison just for taking pictures of cherry blossoms in bloom seemed strange to me. But this was what the war was like among civilians.

This was also the reason he kept on telling us to be very careful and to be constantly aware of our actions and how they could be interpreted or misinterpreted by others. With virtually everyone under suspicion, so much could easily be misunderstood. The last thing any of us wanted was to be arrested because of some silly or innocent move on our part. After that incident, we became increasingly cautious and more than ever did our best to be observant and aware of all our actions. We also watched closely what was going on around us and immediately reported to our parents if we saw anything suspicious. He would always be concerned that something like what had happened to the French family could happen to us if we weren't vigilant.

One Sunday, while walking back from church, my father spotted a charming Japanese gazebo made in a pattern similar to American latticework. The difference was that rather than flat pieces of wood, bamboo poles were used, tied together at each crisscross by black rope. When we arrived back home, my father asked us whether we liked the gazebo we had seen, because he thought it would be fun to have one in our garden too. He added that he would need our help to put one together. It would be a family project. The three of us enthusiastically agreed to help, so the first thing Monday morning my father went out early to pick up all the materials needed to get started. I wondered whether we had the skill and the know-how to erect the gazebo, after we had so enthusiastically agreed to help build it.

Enno standing in the completed gazebo before
wisteria was planted.

When he returned, my father motioned to us to come on out, as he couldn't wait to begin the project. He also asked our gardener—a Mr. Hara, or Hara-san, as we called him, who came with the house—to help. My father chose the corner of our garden to the right of the front entrance to the house, announcing that it was the perfect spot.

That same summer, Alexander and I were left at home alone one day with only the amahs and no particular activity. Enno had gone off somewhere with Ike Shapiro, and our parents had gone to play tennis at the club with friends. We decided to take the opportunity to investigate what was so great about the cigarettes our parents seemed to enjoy so much. We took one of their packs from the house, lighting the first one in the house with matches from the kitchen, and then proceeded to go, each with cigarette in hand, to a grassy hill above the Daikan-zaka on the other side of the street from our house. There we sat, lighting one cigarette after another from the original cigarettes, smoking away, until we started feeling sick. Suddenly, from our perch up on the hill, we saw our parents walking home from the club. We quickly put out our cigarettes in the grass, cleaned the dirt off ourselves, and hurriedly made our way back home. As we entered the house, our parents, who were in the living room, called to us to come and say hello, but we shouted back, saying we just wanted to go upstairs and wash up and would be right back down.

After furiously brushing our teeth and scrubbing our hands, we came down to the living room where they were sitting, listening to music, and gave them each a kiss. They asked us what we had done while they were gone, and we told them we had just played around in the garden and across the street with Flora and Mooshi, and we had read some books too. Then they asked what else we did, whereupon Alexander said we hadn't done much of anything else. My father couldn't understand why, if we'd done nothing much else, we had to brush our teeth, so we told him we had eaten some berries and wanted to clean our mouths. Then came the bombshell. He started quizzing us, asking why a whole pack of their cigarettes was missing, and proceeded to tell us that the amahs, Hatzue-san and Shizuko-san, had told him we had both lit a cigarette before we left to go out.

Knowing a lie was considered even more of a serious violation than the actual offense, I said we wanted to try out what was so good about the cigarettes they seemed to enjoy so much. My father told Alexander to go to the kitchen and bring him a wooden cooking spoon, as this called for a spanking for each of us. He felt this would be a firm reminder never to smoke again. Alexander dutifully brought in the spoon, and with that my father made us lie facedown over his knees, one after the other, with me going first. He gave us each three good whacks, which hurt, but not really as much as it hurt our pride and humiliated us in front of our mother and Enno, who had since come home. We were too proud to cry and bit our tongues. With that, our father gave us each a kiss and asked us to promise him never to try doing that again. We both promised him and ran right out of the room licking our wounds. We were furious at Hatzue-san and Shizuko-san for ratting on us and vowed to get revenge.

We got our chance a few weeks later one weekend afternoon when, for some reason, Alexander and I were in the kitchen while the amahs were taking their afternoon rest. Their coats were hanging on hooks by the kitchen door, and I noticed that one of them had rather a big, bulging pocket. I peeked in to see what was inside, and there, to my amazement, I saw two new bars of soap, still wrapped in their original wrappers, that were just like the soaps my mother had brought over from America. I quickly ran to my father, who came to take a look. Sure enough, he confirmed the soaps were ours. My father knew the amahs would lose face and would feel compelled to leave immediately if he confronted them. Since good amahs were hard to come by, he didn't want that to happen, so he simply removed the soap from her pocket and put it right back where it had come from, in the storage room. Had the amah asked for a bar of soap, he would have gladly given her one, but having stolen it, she had to be taught that she could not get away with that in our household. Alexander and I chuckled to ourselves at the thought of the amah whose coat it was finding the soap missing and realizing she had been found out.

Since my mother had packed every conceivable item she could think of before leaving, we now had almost everything we needed that we couldn't find in Yokohama. There was soap, Kleenex, toilet tissue, canned foods, oils, peanut butter, cocoa, and all sorts of delicious snacks we may have wanted or needed. We had, after all, planned on a long trip before it was cut short and we ended up being stranded. This was a great help, because when food started to be rationed, we still had food that was no longer available, which my mother—with uncanny forethought—had brought with us.

At one point, my parents decided to hire a Chinese cook who could speak Japanese and help us with the shopping, the rations, and the chickens we had since acquired. His name was Li Tai-Liu. Hara-san had been so helpful with the building of the gazebo that my father asked him to help build the chicken coop. From then on, Li tended the coop at the back of the house near the kitchen entrance.

In the beginning, Li was a creative and good cook who introduced us to many different types of Asian dishes, but as time went by and meat became scarce, he would frequently come to my mother and ask, in halting English, if it was all right if he made hamburgers, whereupon he would make a circular motion with his right hand, which my mother understood to mean he was suggesting putting the meat through the grinder. At first she would say that was fine, but after a while she and my father began to wonder why he so frequently wanted to make hamburger, and they became suspicious. Then it dawned on them that he was probably substituting the cow or lamb meat in our rations for horse, dog, or cat meat, keeping our meat to sell on the black market. After doing a bit of sleuthing to see if their hunch was correct, they discovered to their disappointment that he had indeed been doing just that, and Li was dismissed.

During the summers of 1942 and 1943, we were still able to take day trips around Yokohama. With school out, it was the perfect time to see some of the surrounding area and go to a beach nearby. There was a beautiful one at Enoshima, which is a small island at the mouth of the Katase-gawa River that flows into Sagami Bay. The island is approximately two miles across and about an hour's drive south of Yokohama on the Pacific shore of the main island of Honshu.

I was distraught when I lost my wristwatch in the sand one day, knowing it would be too expensive to replace. When we returned the following day to try and find it, Alexander, having seen me so upset the day before, started digging in the sand to see if he could by some miracle find it. I had long given up hope of ever seeing it again, when from behind I felt a gentle tap on my shoulder. It was Alexander, who was dangling my wristwatch under my nose. He asked me whether that was the one I was looking for. I shrieked with delight and thought it really was a miracle that he was able to find a watch that had been buried in the sand overnight on that vast beach.

On another one of our excursions, my parents took us to Kamakura where we were told we simply had to see the famous *Daibutsu*, the Great Buddha. It was just a forty-five-minute trip from Yokohama, and there we discovered the giant statue of the Amida Buddha, which was crafted entirely out of bronze. It stood almost fifty feet high and was said to be the second-largest Buddha statue in Japan. Many people went inside and walked all the way up into his head, where there were two windows from which one could look out. Although he was impressive, we were content to remain on the outside.

Once, on a long weekend, my parents took us to Hakone and Miyanoshita, where they had booked us into the Fujiya Hotel. It was a charming, Western-style Japanese hotel. (After the war, General MacArthur and his high command made their summer headquarters there.) Upon our arrival, we were enchanted by the multitude of koi swimming in a pond near the main entrance. We were permitted to feed them with a special food we could buy at the front desk, and the koi would crowd each other out snapping up the food. There was also a large swimming pool, in which Alexander might have drowned had it not been for Enno's quick reaction after noticing our younger brother had disappeared under the water.

We went for a drive to Lake Yamanaka to have a picnic and to get closer to and admire Mount Fuji, probably the most recognizable mountain in the world. It is still considered an active volcano, although it has been dormant since 1707, and most of the year it is covered in a blanket of snow on the top third of its peak. Fuji-san, as it is affectionately referred to in Japan, has long been regarded as sacred by some Japanese sects. It is always a majestic sight, as it stands alone in the wide countryside, surrounded by lakes. For Christmas, my parents had given me a woodblock print by Hokusai depicting Mount Fuji at cherry blossom time, and to this day it is still one of my favorites.

Although the official season for climbing Mount Fuji is in July and August, we were told that the climb up was mainly on black volcanic sand and rock and that because the summit was much colder than the base, we would be better off viewing it from a distance. Our parents agreed and took us on a boat ride on Lake Yamanaka instead, after which we had a picnic lunch on its shore. From there we could admire Fuji-san in all its glory. The nearby Hakone-Yumoto *onsen* (Japanese for "hot springs") was our next stop. After a long day of sightseeing we were happy to immerse ourselves in one of the many hot springs, while admiring more of the spectacular mountain views.

One of my dearest friends in Yokohama was a young Japanese girl my age who lived in the house next door to us. Like my father in his youth, she was studying to become a concert pianist. Her name was Yoshi Shiono. Although I could not see her too often because she needed to practice for hours after school, we nevertheless got along very well right from the start and spent as much time together as we could. It was she who showed me how to correctly put on a kimono, and she taught me many other Japanese traditions, including the writing

With Yoshi Shiono in Yokohama.

of kanji with a paintbrush. She showed me the symbol for "tree" and then proceeded to show me that three of the characters together— one on top with two underneath—made the symbol for "forest." She also showed me the symbol for "woman" and smiled when she put one character on top and two characters underneath, a combination that formed the symbol for "noise." We had a good chuckle over that.

I was excited the day she actually had the time to show me how to dress in a kimono, as up until then I would just slip on my flowered silk kimono and tie a sash randomly around my waist. I had never been shown how to wrap the long obi around me, and since it was not too comfortable anyway, I usually just left the obi on the shelf. When she invited me to her house, she showed me her immaculately neat closet in which there were kimonos of all types, fabrics, and colors neatly folded on shelves. She had beautiful brocade and silk obis and braided silk cords, also in a variety of colors.

Japanese tradition dictated that the colors, patterns, and types to be worn—of which there were a large number for almost every occasion—depended on the age of the one wearing them and on the season. Girls, as in Yoshi's case, could wear pinks, yellows, reds, and colorful floral patterns in the spring and the traditional *yukata*, an informal, unlined kimono made of cotton and worn with a narrow sash, in the summer. Most often these were worn to the bathhouses or on warm summer evenings, as they were simple in both style and construction. In the fall and winter, reflecting the seasons, darker shades were worn, on which bamboo and various Japanese good-luck symbols were popular. Young single women would wear long-sleeved *furisode* kimonos—a sign they were available for marriage—and once married, they would wear *houmongi* kimonos for weddings and tea ceremonies. Frequently, the more formal ones had the family crest embroidered, stamped, or painted on them.

Yoshi showed me how she put on the various layers, starting with a knee-length *hadajuban*. She then slipped on a second undergarment called the *nagajuban*, which she said was worn to add collar definition to the kimono but was not worn with the casual summer yukata. Over these layers, she added a beautiful furisode silk kimono with long sleeves and, finally, the obi, a wide brocade sash about twelve feet long and twelve inches wide. She wrapped the obi around her waist and up a little higher, so that it covered her ribs, and then folded it vertically at the back and looped it around in such a way that it looked like a little pillow on her back. She then tucked the remaining fabric under and, using one of the silk cords, tied the obi in place, bringing the cord to the front, where she made a knot, tucking the ends in the cord on either side. Then she put on her white tabi, which had one socket for the big toe, and fastened them at the back of the foot. She then slipped on her zori. She also showed me her bulky overcoat with sleeves that were designed to hold the lighter sleeves of the kimono and all the undergarments underneath, which she wore in the winter. It seemed to take forever to get dressed like that, but the result was truly beautiful.

When August came to an end and school was ready to start again, things were looking pretty bleak. Fortunately, the bank was still paying my father's salary, but at a much-reduced rate; it was paid out to him at one of the banks in Yokohama. Before and even later during the war, German banks maintained yen deposits with correspondent Japanese banks, while at the same time Japanese banks maintained mark balances with correspondent German banks, so with this reciprocal agreement, our father was able to get paid in yen by transfer from a Japanese bank. Although life was not as costly there as it had been in New York, it required our parents to start adjusting the budget accordingly.

One day my mother and I were at home, just puttering about, when my father told us he was leaving to take the boys for a haircut. After about an hour, they returned, calling to us from downstairs, saying they were back. Mother replied, saying we were upstairs, and asked if they were coming up. My father called up to say they'd be right there, and suddenly all three of them appeared in the doorway grinning from ear to ear. My mother and I just stood there looking at them, aghast. They'd come home with what the Japanese referred to as a *bozu* cut. Their heads had been completely shorn, and not a hair was left, making them look totally bald. It was the funniest sight we had seen in a long while, and we roared with laughter. My father reminded us that we had to start cutting back on expenses, and this was certainly a good place to start, because they wouldn't need another cut for at least two or three months. He added that the Japanese frequently had their hair cut this way anyway, for reasons of hygiene.

With the winter upon us, and the war in full force, there was still little hope that we would be able to leave Japan. We continued going to school and tried to see as much as possible of the country on weekends. Enno went around town on a bicycle my father had bought for him and would gladly do errands for our mother just to have a reason to get around and see the sights. Often I would tag along, sitting in what the Japanese referred to as a *reeah cah*—from the English "rear car"— because it was a two-wheeled wagon with a wooden floor attached to the back of the bike. Enno would ride us all over downtown Yokohama, where we window-shopped on the major avenues, such as the famous Motomachi, Bentendori, and Isezaki-cho. Coming up the Daikan-zaka to return home was the only hurdle, as we had to walk up the steep hill to our house, pushing the bicycle with the rear car attached.

Having been a passionate roller skater back in America, I often thought what fun it would be to have my skates in Yokohama, as I could go to school with them and skate all around the Bluff and the city below with great ease. I would also not have been dependent on Enno and his bicycle with the rear car.

One cold and bleak November day the heating system malfunctioned, and the house was freezing cold. While waiting for it to be repaired, my father said he would take us into town to warm us up. As we were walking along the road, he turned to my mother and said, "All right, here's where we part. We are going into this *ofuro* (bath). It's divided into two sections, one for women and one for men. Shall we meet back here in about forty-five minutes?" Turning to my brothers, he said, "Come with me, boys; here's where we're going in."

My mother and I went in the opposite direction to the other side of the building. There we walked through two big wooden doors into an immaculate public bathhouse, and on into an area much like an office reception room. An attendant handed us towels, washcloths, and a brush and led us to a room where we could change. There was a locker of sorts, in which we could leave our clothes. The attendant told us the rules; they were strictly enforced—one reason why everything was so sparkling clean.

We proceeded to undress and go to the bath hall, which was in a large, white-tiled room the size of a banquet hall. There we had to look for an available faucet, at which it was the custom to wash oneself from head to toe. When my mother and I located a faucet, we started washing with the brush that had been provided and then thoroughly rinsed off all the soap with a large wooden ladle that was hanging by each faucet. We helped each other rinse off our backs, and when the last remaining suds were gone, we were ushered into the vast Olympic-size communal tub. I had been so busy following all the rules that I hadn't noticed the various shapes, sizes, and ages of the many women in the bath hall until I was sitting in the large pool where the water was very hot—it must have been at least 105 degrees. It was a curious sight to see, mainly because I'd never seen any naked people before, other than my mother and a few friends when we changed into bathing suits or into pajamas at slumber parties. There I saw girls of all ages, most of them wearing the same hairstyle appropriate to their straight black hair. It was a simple do, worn straight on each side of the face and with bangs also straight down over the forehead and just touching their eyebrows over their almond-shaped eyes. I saw teenagers, young women with babies, and some old women with very wrinkled bodies. When we had soaked enough and were ready to get dressed, we stepped out of the pool and saw that we had turned as red as boiled lobsters. By now it was time to meet my father and brothers, so we hurriedly slipped on our clothes and went outside. We were still so hot that when we left the bathhouse and went out into the freezing cold, the inner warmth stayed with us for quite some time before we reached home.

At the end of 1942, our second Christmas and New Year's Day in Japan came and went with still no hope in sight of returning home to

New York, and even worse, there still was no communication whatsoever from anyone outside Japan. We remained on food rations, and it seemed we were given ever-tightening restrictions, which by now included not being able to go to Kyoto, Osaka, or Nara to see the famous temples. The events taking place on faraway islands at the beginning of the war were now coming closer to home. We received relatively little good news and were fed much propaganda. At the tennis club, there were so many rumors flying about that it had become increasingly difficult to distinguish between stories that held truth and those that were simply unfounded hearsay.

Sometime in the fall of 1943, while we were all at home, we heard loud explosions coming from downtown Yokohama. As we ran from our house to the top of the Bluff to see what was going on, we saw

The hospital on the Bluff—Yokohama, 1941.

huge clouds of thick, black smoke billowing up from the harbor, where three German battleships had docked a few days earlier. A few hours later, those of us living on the Bluff were asked to take in wounded survivors. The officers and crew of all three ships had been forced to jump from the ship; many of them had drowned, others were seriously injured and had been taken to the hospital on the Bluff.

Those who had not been hurt badly enough to need emergency medical care, but who needed either a place to sleep or to recover from their minor injuries or both, were put up at homes on the Bluff. Our parents, seeing how young and scared and in pain some of the German sailors were, took in a corporal and a lieutenant, both of whom my mother nursed until they were well enough to return with their fellow shipmates and continue on to an unknown destination. While they were at our house, they told us they had no idea what had happened, because neither had been topside when the explosions occurred. They knew, however, that they had not been bombed from above. They told us the explosions had come from within the battleships. They thought perhaps deliveries had been made to the three ships, all of which contained explosives, with exploding devices timed to go off at just about the same time. Sabotage was the only explanation they had at the time.

Because there was an unobstructed view of the Yokohama Harbor and further out into Tokyo Bay from the Bluff, the explosions triggered more suspicions among the Kempeitai. Soon we heard there was to be a mass evacuation of foreigners living on the Bluff; we were to be sent out of Yokohama and into the countryside, mainly because we would be unable to observe all that was going on in Tokyo Bay. It was also easier to keep control over all the occidentals from different countries if we were isolated in one or two villages rather than being spread out over many large cities. We were later told authorities suspected spies had been living on the high ridge all along, which they had not been aware of, despite all the policing on the Bluff.

Stories of espionage were not mere paranoia. When we arrived in Japan back in the summer of 1941, living in our expat midst was a character named Richard Sorge, who represented himself as a German journalist. His history was well-known: a war hero from the 1914–1918 conflict and winner of the Iron Cross for valor; a member of the Nazi Party; a bon vivant, womanizer, and a drinker. In October of that year, the community was scandalized by his arrest on charges of spying for the Soviet Union. The story that emerged was as thrilling as it was frightening. Richard Sorge, who was so trusted by the Germans that he worked right out of the German embassy when he wanted to, had been a lifelong communist, devoted to the cause and to the Soviet Union. He had previously organized a spy ring in China, and the ring he oversaw in Japan was spectacularly successful. He had initially warned Stalin that the intelligence he had gathered in Japan pointed to a German invasion of Russia. Russia ignored this tip, to its extreme detriment. Sorge's next coup was to advise Stalin that the Japanese strategy was going to be directed toward the Pacific, not Eastern Russia. This time Stalin and his commanders listened to Sorge, to the point of committing all their resources against Germany. This made an incalculable difference in the outcome of the war, causing many to consider Richard Sorge the most successful spy in history.

My parents might have gone on seeing Sorge at the tennis club or at cocktail parties on the Bluff, considering him a hard-living journalist behaving hedonistically through treacherous times, had his spy ring not been uncovered in October 1941. In prison, he lived in the hope that the Russians would make some sort of trade for his freedom. They did not, and disavowed any knowledge of their most useful operative. The Japanese hanged Sorge in Tokyo on November 7, 1944. Decades later, he would be lauded as a national hero of the Soviet Union, but in his time of greatest need, he was betrayed.

The general atmosphere in Japan had become tenser than ever, and all the signs pointed toward the evacuation of foreigners from the cities. At the end of the summer, the buildings and grounds of St. Joseph College had been taken over by the Japanese army. The remaining Marianists and other foreigners were forced to leave and move to Gora, and a small school was set up in the halls of the Park Hotel there, where classes were conducted. St. Maur had also closed its doors, and the nuns, who had not been sent back to their countries in 1942, were sent to different parts of Japan.

In January 1944, my brother's best friend, Ike Shapiro, and his family moved to Tokyo. As Ike wrote in his book, this was during the time he and Enno had begun concentrating their energies on girls and generally living their adventurous adolescent lives . . . and now they would be separated. By the spring, my parents were also told they would have to look for a house to rent in either Hakone or Karuizawa, and they would have to move very soon. When our parents returned from Hakone, which then was roughly a three-hour trip by train from Yokohama, they thought they'd found a perfect house for us with a beautiful atrium in the center. However, while we were packing up our house in Yokohama, word came that the owners of the house in Hakone had decided to take it off the market, and so it was no longer available. With that, the search began again, though by then there were no more houses available in Hakone. That left our parents no other choice but to rent, sight unseen, a house in Karuizawa, the mountain resort we'd visited in the summer of 1941. It was the last and only house that was still for rent.

When we were all packed, we were told trucks would come to pick up our furniture and our remaining pieces of luggage. We might have had less luggage had we eaten more of the food my mother had brought along, but owing to her thrifty ways, we still had quite a bit left despite the three years we'd already lived in Yokohama. She had wisely rationed our private supply, not knowing how long it would have to last.

Mooshi and Flora were going to be part of the hand luggage, in which we were planning to hide them because of the rule against transporting animals on trains. We decided to take the chance, though, because we couldn't bear the thought of leaving our precious pets behind.

It was early in the morning when the trucks came, but we could already feel that it was going to be another very hot summer day. After everything was loaded onto the trucks, they took off, and we in turn prepared for the train ride, made a bit more complicated because of the two animals. The vet had given us tranquilizers for Mooshi and Flora, which my mother had fed them earlier, and while we waited for them to get sleepy or at least drowsy, we punched holes in their makeshift cardboard boxes so they would have plenty of air. Once we had accomplished that, my father called a taxi and we headed for the train station in Yokohama.

We had no problem with the animals on the line from there to Tokyo, but when we changed trains in Tokyo for the six-hour ride to Karuizawa, it was another matter. We were worried and scared that something awful might happen on the way up to the mountains, as the conductor on our section was a stern and angry-looking man. We took turns going to the snack/bar car, because we weren't about to leave the animals unattended. Several times during the ride, Mooshi let out a weak meow and I was mortified, but when I looked around the car to see if anyone had noticed, several people were sleeping and a few of those who weren't gave me a knowing but understanding smile—or so I hoped. I prayed it would not happen when the conductor came around to collect our tickets. By then I was also praying Flora wouldn't be discovered, as she had begun panting loudly in the heat of the day. I began to perspire not so much from the heat as from nervousness, and suggested to Enno that he get some water for Flora so she would stop her panting. It was a relief to find that it worked, and soon I became drowsy myself, dozing off for a while.

At Takasaki Station I was awakened by the announcer—the same one, it seemed, whose nasal voice had made us laugh so hard on our first trip there three years earlier. Thankfully, all was still quiet, and I felt relaxed enough to take out a book and read. At Yokokawa, four electric locomotives were added to our train to provide additional pushing power for the ascent to our final destination—Karuizawa.

Upon our arrival, we immediately freed the suddenly much more peppy and happy animals and started walking toward the main road, the *machi*. This time we were not being met by a car or taxi because we were not staying at the Mampei Hotel and there was now a shortage of gas. That meant we not only had to walk up to the machi with our suitcases, but farther on up to the Atago-yama, where we would find our house. Flora was thrilled to be out of her box and ran around in circles with excitement, but Mooshi was still too groggy and couldn't be left to walk alone on a street that was strange to her. I picked her up and carried her, which was much easier, because it had cooled down quite a few degrees from the heat in Yokohama. Still, with each step I wondered how much longer it would take to reach our house.

Just before the right turn that led to the Mampei Hotel, we turned left onto a road that led us over a little creek to the Atago-yama, where we'd been told we would find our house. It was late afternoon by the time we came to the road and by then it had cooled down even more. The sun had set behind the mountains, creating a beautiful backdrop for our little village. Walking up the long hill on an unpaved road, to a totally strange house on the Atago-yama, left us tired and out of breath. There, before us, we found a two-story wooden clapboard house with a porch that wrapped all the way around from the front of the house to the end of the left side. There were two wooden sliding doors that opened up to a large living room. Too tired to go in, however, the three of us first threw ourselves down on the front steps leading up to the porch, happy that we'd finally reached our latest home away from home.

Our house on the Atago-yama, still there in a photo my brother
Enno took on a 2005 visit.

It had been a long, hot, anxious, not-very-interesting train ride, and
now at our new home on the Atago-yama in Karuizawa, there was
much to be done. It occurred to me as we unpacked that in my eleven
years we had already moved three times—first from Larchmont, New
York, to our Park Avenue apartment in New York City; from there via
the New Grand Hotel to our house at 66b Yamate-cho, Yokohama;
and now to this house in the mountains. I wondered how many more
moves we would have to make before we finally reached home again.

My thoughts were interrupted when I heard my mother calling,
"Children, come pick out your bags and bring them upstairs to your
rooms. Your father is hungry and wants to take us out to dinner very
soon, so take a quick look around the house and decide which room
you each want. You can unpack when we return."

Enno, Alexander, and I all gave a deep sigh, as we too were hungry.
We walked up the steps onto the porch and from there entered the
large, square, rustic, wood-paneled living room in which the movers

had left our furniture and all our suitcases. We started rummaging through everything, looking for our belongings. When we found our bags, we carried them upstairs and arrived at a square hall, which was more like a large landing off of which there were five doors. These led to three bedrooms, one bathroom, and a small hallway. At the top of the stairs, looking to the left, there were two rooms. Each had a view out over the front garden of the house. My parents had chosen the room on the left, and Enno and Alexander wanted the one on the right, which was fine by me, because I was thrilled to have the one room that had tatami mats. It was at the back of the house and looked out onto the hill going further up the Atago-yama. The door to the bathroom was straight ahead from the top of the stairs, and the door to the left of the stairs opened up to a small hall leading to the staff quarters, the room where our amah would be living.

We heard our father call to us, saying we should come down and help bring up all the wooden pieces that made up our beds. He said we would assemble them quickly once we had identified them, because that wouldn't be too difficult. My mother said she would help us make our beds, with her famous hospital corners. I called back saying I didn't think I'd need a bed because I could very easily sleep Japanese-style on the tatami mats. I said all I'd need would be a futon or two, with a top and bottom sheet. With that, we all swung into action. When we finished putting the beds together, the rooms started taking shape. We left the bureaus, desks, and chairs until the next day when we could round up some extra manpower.

The next morning when I woke up, I couldn't understand why I was itching all over, as all my windows had screens on them. I looked around my room to see if I could find any signs of mosquitoes or the like but found nothing. I knew something had bitten me during the course of the night. There was no evidence of it until I sat down on the tatami mat to fold up my sheets. There on the tatami, I noticed a tiny black dot—smaller than a pinhead—near where I was sitting. When I bent down to look at it more closely, it suddenly jumped up high and came back down again just as rapidly. I tried to swat it with my hand, but it was much too fast and elusive for me to even lay a finger on it. I went downstairs to ask my mother for help, because I knew I couldn't sleep there another night.

"*Ohayō-gozaimasu, Oka-san, Oto-san* [Good morning, honorable mother and honorable father]," I said, in what I thought was my politest Japanese, bowing deeply as I entered the kitchen. They turned to me and replied, "*Ohayō-gozaimasu, Hirri-san* [Good morning, Hillie]," not bowing quite so deeply.

"Look at me," I said, showing them all the bumps and welts on my body. "I'm being eaten alive, and I don't know by what. All I know is that I itch all over and can't stand it any longer. Do you have anything for me that will take away this maddening itch?"

My mother suggested we first determine what it was that bit me, so I told her that all I knew was that I found nothing but a tiny black speck on the tatami and that when I went to look closer, the speck jumped up and down, but I couldn't swat it or catch it. That's when she told me she suspected—from the way I described it—that I could very well have fleas living in the tatami mats, adding that she'd go up to investigate right after she finished preparing breakfast.

I asked her why the amah she had hired wasn't making breakfast. She told me she had been in earlier that day and said the moment she'd arrived that she had a very sick mother in Hiroshima and therefore had to leave immediately to take care of her. There was nothing my mother could do but to let her go. I asked what we were going to do now, and she nonchalantly replied, "We'll just all have to pitch in until I can find a replacement for her." With that she motioned to me to come upstairs so she could have a look at my bugs.

The boys had just awakened and were coming down the stairs for breakfast as we were going up. We went to my room, kneeled down on the tatami and, to our amazement, saw many little dots jumping up and down, which confirmed my mother's earlier suspicion that they were fleas. She told me we were going to the village later that morning and she would inquire at a specialty store to see if there was anything they had that would get rid of fleas. She suggested that meanwhile I should keep the door to my room closed so we could try to contain them there. She also said she'd see if she had something to relieve my itch. If she didn't, she thought we'd surely find something in the village.

My father came along with us, as he had to register us in the local community. My brothers joined us as well. The walk back down to the village was on the same narrow road we had taken the day before. It was bordered on each side by a three-foot wall made entirely of lava rocks from the nearby Mount Asama, an active volcano. No cars were permitted on the unpaved road, but there weren't many cars, and hardly any gas, anyway.

When we arrived on the machi, my father took the boys and went about the business of registering us, while my mother and I went looking for both flea repellent and something to relieve the itch, because what my mother had found in her medicine case wasn't working.

Once these chores were accomplished and we were settled in, we started venturing out to familiarize ourselves with the parts of Karuizawa we hadn't seen in 1941. It was mainly a summer resort and the cold made it difficult to stay there in the winter, as most of the houses and cottages did not have central heat. The architectural style of the houses varied. Many of them were rustic, and not always pretty, as the settlers of the town were not just from Japan but included Westerners who came from many different countries as well as many different cultures.

One day, not too long after we'd arrived in Karuizawa, Flora, Mooshi, and the chickens suddenly all started acting up in a most peculiar way. Flora was constantly barking, and Mooshi was meowing and hissing with her back hunched way up. The chickens were fluttering around, making funny clucking noises. Shortly thereafter the ground underneath us started shaking and rumbling. It happened that I was standing at the front of the house at the time. I had heard horror stories about how if the earth opened up underneath you in an earthquake, you could fall in and be squashed to death. With that in mind, I kept jumping up and down with my legs far apart, watching anxiously to see that the earth wasn't opening beneath me. Fortunately, it didn't, and a few minutes later—it seemed like an eternity—the earthquake subsided and the animals went back to acting normally again. Later I thought to myself that they must have sensed something out of the ordinary was about to happen. It was my first unsettling, scary, and eerie earthquake experience.

In the old days, Karuizawa had remained fairly undeveloped as a town, because the volcanic soil from Mount Asama, together with the high altitude and misty climate, made it almost impossible to grow crops. It had originally been a rest stop in the old Edo period (1603–1868) as it was on a trade route on which the journey was usually made on foot. In Oiwake–Karuizawa, just north of Naka-Karuizawa, several old ryokans could still be seen along the way.

Not too far from the Naka-Karuizawa Station, at the foot of Mount Asama, there was an area called *Oni oshi dashi*, which translated means "what the devil spewed forth." These were massive lava beds that had formed several hundred years ago, after Mount Asama had its most devastating eruption in 1783. An entire town had been buried, along with many of its inhabitants. One could see just where the lava had overflowed in large black streams, and where a village on the side of the volcano had been totally destroyed and buried. Years later, a shrine was

Author's photo from 2005 of the shrine that was built on the hardened lava beds.

built on top of the lava beds, on the original site of the village, in honor of the hundreds of people who lost their lives in the eruption.

Wandering through the lava fields one day, we came upon a most spectacular view of Mount Asama, which we wished we could photograph but were afraid to, again because of how it might be interpreted or misinterpreted. (There was a possibility of retribution of some sort, if our taking of photographs was viewed suspiciously.) Occasionally, we could see sulfur smoke steaming out from the top of the crater.

Karuizawa had originally been discovered by Westerners in the late nineteenth century, when many missionaries from the Tokyo area became aware of the cooler climate there and developed it as a summer resort. The nearby Shiraito Falls, which translated means "white thread," were named for the water that cascades out of the rocks in slender, frothy strands. It was a beautiful sight.

Frequently, we'd go hiking on the Hanare-yama, the smaller mountain lying closer to Karuizawa in front of Mount Asama. The top of this smaller mountain had a perfect view of Mount Asama and Karuizawa, but once again we were too afraid to take any photographs. From time to time we'd spot a bear and, if lucky, a Japanese goat-antelope (kamoshika). Although it was illegal to climb to the top of Mount Asama, many people did. It was not that difficult a climb, although it was quite steep in certain places. We only went as far as Oni-oshi-dashi, however, and never did climb to the top. My parents told us we had to stay below, because they didn't want us to take any chances that could land us in trouble.

Another day, we rented bicycles and rode past endless rice fields to a nearby village, where we had been invited to the home of a farmer my parents had met while out exploring. It was an unforgettable fall day with a chill in the air. The ride was invigorating. The farmer and his wife, who were extremely polite and hospitable, invited us into their home for lunch. We took off our shoes and walked through two half-opened sliding shoji doors made of rice paper and up stone steps into a tatami room, where we saw a square table in the middle of the floor. The farmer and his wife invited us to sit down at the table on the tatami mats and told us that if we crossed our legs in front of us and brought them toward our body—yoga style—we would be able to feel the warmth of the charcoal embers that had been placed in the pit below the table. The farmer's wife then placed a futon over the table and our crossed legs and placed a square wooden board the size of the table over the futon.

She brought out chopsticks with several bowls containing soy sauce, ginger, wasabi, and the delicacies she'd prepared for lunch. A little fish, eel, and shrimp, a beef delicacy, and finally the lunch was completed with miso soup and a bowl of rice. It was a delightfully authentic Japanese meal. Our parents enjoyed it, but we three children ate rather reluctantly, not sure what exactly we were being served. Happily relaxed and warmed by the red charcoal embers, after lunch, we could have easily leaned back on the tatami mats with the futon covering us and taken a nap. That was exactly how the farmer and his wife slept at night when the weather turned cold. They told us all they did was just lie back and cover themselves with another futon while the smoldering charcoal kept their feet warm. On our way home, my thoughts wandered to my friends in New York and how different our lives had become since we left on that spring day in 1941. It felt as if I were living in some kind of surreal dream.

Another one of the many wonderful things we discovered about the town of Karuizawa was the *onsens*. Once one entered an onsen, it was much like the *ofuro* in Yokohama, as it was also separated into two parts—one side for the men and the other for the women—and in each side there was an anteroom in which there were lockers where one could change and store one's clothes before entering into a larger tiled room. In the middle of the room was a large indoor-outdoor natural hot spring, and on the walls surrounding it were faucets, basins, brushes, and small wooden ladles with which one was required to wash and rinse oneself thoroughly before being permitted to soak in the hot springs. It felt so good to just sit and soak, particularly when the weather started turning colder in the fall. Despite all our explorations, we still had to be careful and aware of the dangers that might surprise us. Even though it wasn't overt, we had to keep assuming that we were being observed at all times and had to keep vigilant.

My parents were a very popular couple—people seemed to gravitate toward them—and their outgoing personalities were engaging. They were well-known wherever they went, not only from the Yokohama days but by now also in the Karuizawa foreign community.

They made friends with the Danish minister and head of the legation and his wife, the Tillitses, who they discovered were actually distant relatives of my mother's, and were now neighbors on the

My mother and friends in Karuizawa.

Atago-yama. Many people from different countries had been evacuated to Karuizawa, which by then had become a veritable League of Nations. There were a number of French, Portuguese, Spanish, Italian, Russian, Swedish, and German people all living in and around the town, several of whom my parents had known in Europe, before the war. In the end, Karuizawa became an occupied village, in which the Japanese government had chosen to contain foreigners. They had shepherded us all into one town in order to keep an eye on our movements and to note those with whom we socialized. Ever since the incident in Yokohama Harbor, when the three German battleships exploded, they feared there might still be spies among us. They couldn't be sure, but then neither could we.

In the late summer of 1944—despite the fact that my mother and I had found a flea repellent and an anti-itch cream that first day in the machi—my tatami mats still remained home to a number of surviving fleas. For the approaching winter, each home was to be given a single stove to heat a part of the house. Our house, however, having been constructed of wood almost fifty years earlier, was just not safe enough to have a stove installed in any room. Fortunately, a house two doors down had just become available and we were given permission to move there. I was so relieved and happy to be able to leave the room where the fleas had made my life so miserable.

There was a lawn on each side of the driveway to the new house, and the driveway curved to the left and then again to the right. It ended directly in front of the center of the house, and there were steps going up to the veranda that wrapped around the three sides of the building. Upon entering there was a large room that was apparently meant to be used as a dining room. It was not my parents' preference, but there was no other room in the house suitable for dining. Because it was the closest to the kitchen, that's where we ended up having our meals. Straight ahead through the dining room was a door that led to a hall and to the kitchen. On the right of the dining room was the living room, in which my father put a baby grand piano he found in the village in a second-hand store; it still sounded quite good after he had it tuned. The hall behind the dining room led to a staircase and to the one bathroom in the house as well as to a library/bedroom, which my father used as his office. At the top of the stairs the door to my parents' bedroom, which was over the living room, was straight ahead and the door to my brothers' bedroom, which was over the dining room, was to the right. I had to go through their room to reach mine. The one stove we'd been allotted was installed in my room, as it had the easiest and simplest access to ventilation. To the left of the stairs over the kitchen was a storage room. That was it. The one bathroom downstairs was typically Japanese and had a window that looked out onto our garden in the back. There, in front of the window, was a wonderful long, deep, oval wooden hot tub, in front of which were wooden planks on the floor, and upon which were several wooden buckets. To the right was a type of sink, at which the soap and scrub brushes hung in full view as a reminder to everyone to scrub themselves before entering the hot tub. The buckets were there to rinse off the soap after washing before entering the tub and soaking in the clean, hot water. To the left of the hot tub, in a little separated unit, was the toilet.

Although there was no electric hot water or gas heater, we did have electricity, but it did not power the stoves in the kitchen nor was there any in my room. The stoves were fueled with wood. In the fall and spring, when it was warmer, we cooked in the kitchen, but the moment it turned cold, in the late fall and winter, we cooked in my room and ate there as well. It was also where all of us would congregate when the deep winter came and the weather was unbearably cold. My dressing table was used as a desk, at which we would all take turns doing our homework. Even our pets had by now become acclimated to their new surroundings and stayed in my room with us. Mooshi would even sleep in bed with me and help keep me warm in the well-below-freezing temperatures.

We had moved the chicken coop we'd brought from Yokohama to the back of the new house and had replanted the vegetables we had dug up from the garden of the old house, not knowing how long we would have to remain in Karuizawa. Our chickens were still producing eggs on an almost daily basis and our parents had been able to buy a few large sacks of potatoes, which they stored on the porch. By now my mother had also interviewed and hired a very lovely Korean girl to help in the household, but with no more room in the house, she could not live in. She came as a day worker instead.

We were slowly settling into our new home, and everyone was given their daily routines. Enno was elected to do most of the errands with his bicycle. I was to take care of Mooshi, a new cat we named Tiger that one day had just come to stay, and Flora, our mongrel. I was also in charge of setting the table for meals, which my mother insisted had to be done properly so there'd be some semblance of order and style in our lives. First, I had to set place mats on the dining room table, and then she would tell me to take the silverware—which my parents had bought quite inexpensively in Yokohama—and place it and the napkins on the place mats in the correct way. I was sure she was making me go through this routine to teach me how to be a homemaker, for which she'd been forced to go to school and had hated every minute. Alexander, who by now was eight, was responsible for the chickens and the chicken coop. His job was to feed the chickens, clean out the coop, and collect the eggs the hens had laid that day, as they were a small source of protein for us.

By the end of 1944, everyone in Karuizawa had been put under village arrest and we were no longer permitted to bicycle to the neighboring villages. We were basically confined to our village, where there wasn't much to do other than walk to the machi for our food rations, go to the doctor if and when necessary, and, of course, venture to the pharmacy for medicine if needed. Fraternization with the Japanese, and vice versa, was strictly forbidden. There was no communication with the outside world except for the little Emerson shortwave radio our father had secretly brought with him, plus my little carved wooden Snow White radio, which transmitted very little, and all in Japanese, rendering it useless to us. By now, we were totally isolated up in the mountains, where we remained under surveillance until the end of the war.

My mother loved working in the garden and had started preparing it for the winter when one day the owner's gardener came along with the same intent. He told us, in effect, that we were not allowed to speak to him but that he wanted us to know he would continue to take care of the grass, trees, shrubs, and bushes as long as he was not caught talking to us, nor we to him. We assured him that because he was obviously doing his job very well, there was no need for communication and that we would never even acknowledge him. However, my mother told him if he needed to communicate with us for any reason, he could do so through our part-time Korean housekeeper.

Right after we made our move, my mother enrolled us in a make-shift school off the machi, within walking distance of our house. We attended only three days a week because there was not enough fuel to heat the school for five days. Classes were taught mostly in German, which presented a problem because our German was not very fluent, having only learned to speak it at home with Aya, and only rarely with our parents. The classes started late enough in the morning so that we didn't have to leave the house and walk to school in the dark, as there were no street lamps. On Sundays, we went to St. Paul's Church. One day, after Mass was over, my father discreetly pointed out a man from the Gestapo whose name was Alarich Mosaner. He would come to the church at the end of Mass and observe which Germans in the community had shown up, because the Nazis frowned upon church attendance. He would then make a report as to who had been seen at the Roman Catholic church. That was a bit worrisome, because Herr Mosaner was head of the Hitler Youth in Japan. He was the right-hand man to Josef Meisinger, the SS colonel and chief of the local Gestapo—the same man who had met so ominously with my father in Yokohama.

In late autumn—the leaves had already fallen—my parents invited the Danish minister and his wife for dinner. Their house was just down the hill from ours at the fork in the road, and they had only to walk up the hill to our house on the Atago-yama. They had become very good friends during the war, since having discovered a distant relationship with my mother, so my parents saw them frequently. During dinner, my father thought he heard a rustling sound outside and asked me to see if there was someone about. Sure enough, as I opened the door and walked out on the porch, I saw a dark figure disappear around the corner of the house. It was then that we realized—just like in Yokohama at the top of the Bluff—that we were still under surveillance and actively being spied on. At that point, though, it was not clear whether we were being watched by the Gestapo, the Kempeitai, or both. It appeared that they still wanted to know with whom we were associating and what we were doing.

By November, the weather had turned a lot colder, and with it, our food rations became even scarcer. They consisted of a handful of rice per person per day, soybean paste—with which our parents had learned to make miso soup—a loaf of bread per week for our family of five, and a pound of butter per person per month. My father had learned to cut a loaf of bread into thirty-five prosciutto-thin slices, so we would each have one slice per day. We would compliment him that he actually managed to get such evenly cut slices out of each loaf.

Because we were each given our own pound of butter and told we could use it as we wished, it was amusing to watch how everyone consumed it differently. My mother would make her pound of butter last all month by scraping a tiny bit on her slice of bread every day and using it sparingly on vegetables, but some of us wanted instant gratification and devoured the whole pound in a week by spreading it on thickly, saying, "We're going to eat, taste, and enjoy our butter until we run out, and then we'll just do without for a while." We figured that we could always spread some of the soybean paste on the bread in the interim. It became a standing joke, and we used to laugh about it, but my mother would wisely hide her butter safely somewhere, so no one could snatch any of hers. We still had a few of our own vegetables from the garden, and, luckily, the hens were still laying eggs, which helped augment our meager diet. Meat and fish were nowhere to be found. The mere act of survival began taking up more and more of our time, as we had to find food for ourselves and the chickens, search the area for more potatoes, and find someone to sell us wood for our stove. It also became exceedingly cold to set the table. The silverware was like ice and stuck to my fingers, but when I complained, my mother insisted I put mind over matter, put on a pair of gloves, and proceed with my job.

Once, when we had run out of wood, my brothers and I had to go up the hill into the woods to try and cut down a few small trees. We had just finished felling the first little one, which we had chopped up into smaller, more manageable pieces, when we were approached by someone who identified himself as the owner of the property. He told us we had to hand over the wood to him, otherwise he would report us to the authorities. Not for a moment did we hesitate, remembering our parents' warnings over the years. When we arrived home empty-handed and told our parents what had happened, rather than being upset with us, they praised us for having done exactly the right thing. That evening we had a cold supper.

When my father went to town, I would frequently accompany him to pick up the ration coupons we needed to give to the shopkeepers in exchange for food. There really wasn't much else to buy, except maybe some of the Imari or Kutani china our parents had started collecting. As we had done so many times to get to the village from the Atago-yama, we'd walk out of our driveway, turn right, and go all the way down the hill until the fork in the road met another one on the right. We didn't know many people who lived on that road, but there were many houses all the way up the mountain into the hills. We would continue on our street all the way down across the small bridge over the little stream that gave off a charming gurgling sound. On the machi there were rows and rows of typical Japanese village houses and stores on each side, and at night it was never totally dark because in each house the lights were kept on to scare away the bad spirits, just like on the Motomachi in Yokohama.

The foreigners in the Karuizawa community during that year and a half were, on the whole, very kind to one another, mainly because we were all occidentals in an Asian country, but also because we had no support from anyone and needed to help and support each other. We were essentially living in a type of cocoon where it was imperative that everyone hang together for survival. If someone heard something bad had happened or was about to, it would spread through the community like wildfire. Everyone tried to warn everyone else if and when they happened to hear of an impending problem. There were no more than a thousand foreigners in the community, but most everyone in the village watched out for everyone else. We never knew whether, among that large group, there were some who were Nazi sympathizers, so it was best to keep completely neutral in casual conversation. Most of the time it seemed everyone pitched in and helped, until we'd hear an isolated story about espionage or betrayal.

Everyone went through the same deprivation when it came to food—everyone except for the diplomats at the embassies, who had quite an abundant supply of provisions. They had a huge warehouse full of supplies that had been seized from Allied ships captured by the German Navy and ended up in Japan. They in turn had the food shipped to Karuizawa, but access to that food was limited to diplomats. The German naval attaché's sons were friends of my brother Enno, so occasionally we would be invited to their house, where they would share some of their food with us, although not too frequently, because they had their own families.

One day, a man came to our house and asked to see my father who, when he saw what the man was selling showed an interest and started negotiating. What he ended up buying was half an animal—which my father took to be half a cow—and decided he'd share some with our neighbors, the Tillitses. That night, my father who, unlike my mother, loved to cook, made us the most delicious meal, giving us each a nice large piece of meat—something we hadn't tasted in months. We enjoyed every bite. The following day, my father offered a piece to the Tillitses, as well as to another neighbor, and they were all delighted at the prospect of tasting meat again. When the Tillitses sent their Italian chef, Luigi, to pick up the meat, he took one look at it and with his eyes wide open just said "*Cavallo, cavallo.*" The half an animal my father had bought the day before turned out to be half a horse. It had been so long since we'd tasted meat that we had no idea we'd eaten horse meat. It was so delicious that none of us could tell the difference, nor could we have cared less.

Deep into winter now, we could really understand why Karuizawa up until then had only been a summer resort. It was brutally cold and it snowed incessantly. One morning after waking up to a fresh white blanket of powdered snow, we were sitting at breakfast admiring the beautiful scenery when we heard a rumbling noise we'd never heard before. Puzzled, all of us ran to a different window, wondering if we could see where the noise was coming from. All of a sudden, it started raining little black, dust-like particles, which changed the pristine white countryside into a depressing gray terrain. Later in the day, we heard that Mount Asama had erupted that morning, but fortunately it was only a minor eruption.

Alexander, the youngest at eight years old, had only the chickens to take care of by day, so Enno and I decided to make him the chief bed-warmer by night. We agreed to pay him one Japanese sen (a fraction of a US penny) per night to climb into our beds and warm them up for us with his own body heat. Alexander, for some reason, didn't seem to feel the cold as much as we did, nor did he seem to mind it, because he willingly did his new job. We would crawl in with every piece of clothing on that we owned. Just our noses and our mouths would be exposed, as most nights the temperature ranged between −25° C (−13° F) to −10° C (14° F). The only heat we had in the house during the day came from the stove, but at night it was so unbearably cold that we literally had to sleep with all our clothes on, as well as our gloves, scarves, and woollen caps.

With the extreme cold came several other problems. For one, all our water pipes in the house had frozen, which meant we had no water with which to cook, bathe, or flush the toilets. The only way we could get any water was for the three of us to go farther up the Atago-yama, where there was a well. With two pails in hand for each of us, we'd hike up the hill being careful not to slip on the icy road. After pumping the water and filling all six pails, we would start our trek down the hill again. With the road covered in a sheet of ice, it was impossible not to slip, so in order to bring the pails back down relatively full, we had no choice other than to sit on the ice and slide down to our house. We inevitably spilled some of the water on the way. After bringing the water home, we first had to boil it so we could defrost the toilet. Then we'd boil some more, wash ourselves, and fill the tub with what was left, so we could each have a good soak. Sometimes we'd have to repeat the procedure if there wasn't enough left with which to cook.

We did a lot of walking on those cold days, and with our very limited, meager diet, there was not a bit of fat on any of our bones. I suffered terribly from long periods of exposure to the cold and freezing weather. Ultimately this led to my getting frostbite, which my mother knew could cause severe tissue damage. I had already had terrible chilblains—a condition that is frequently confused with frostbite but which manifests as ulcers that affect the extremities and cause damage to the capillary beds in the skin and is caused by exposure to extremely cold temperatures. The chilblains caused redness, itching, and inflammation, mostly to my toes and fingers, and was very uncomfortable. These red and itchy regions of the body had the potential of developing into painful blisters, but fortunately I was spared that discomfort. I was also fortunate that the death of the tissues didn't lead to more serious complications, such as gangrene. The only thing I noticed was that my skin had an increased sensitivity to cold or heat after it had been exposed for the first time.

We had another unpleasant surprise when we found out that the sacks of potatoes my father had bought on the black market were totally frozen and would not thaw out until spring when everything else started to thaw out as well. At that point, they no longer tasted like potatoes, but since we were hungry, we ate them despite their sweet, not-very-appetizing flavor. My parents had a real knack in that they always seemed to be able to make the best out of a bad situation. They instilled in us the determination never to give up, to keep on going, keep on doing, and keep on dealing with whatever happened. It was a matter of survival, and they told us that if we followed what they tried to teach us, we would have a better chance of seeing our ordeal through to its end.

Alexander made the saddest discovery of that winter when one morning he went to get eggs from our chickens and found our rooster stuck to his perch, frozen stiff. As Alexander looked around the chicken coop, he noticed that the hens too had succumbed to the freezing weather and were lying motionless in a corner. He realized that our meager supply of protein had come to an end, and with it his chore. We did not know then that we were experiencing one of the coldest winters on record, ever, in the history of the Japanese Alps.

During the winter months, my father, not having been able to work, had more time to play the piano. He would sit for hours playing his beloved Chopin, Wagner, and Liszt. He was still trying to perfect the *Moonlight Sonata* and would work on one particularly difficult movement for hours, which turned into days. It was also a way of keeping his hands warm throughout the day. When he wasn't at the piano, he played records on the old Victrola he had single-handedly rebuilt in Yokohama, which he had brought and reassembled again in Karuizawa.

For more practical distraction, my father had his secret shortwave radio, which he thought would keep him in touch with the outside world, but soon he wondered whether most of what he could tune in to was propaganda emanating from the Japanese radio stations. He still couldn't ask anyone, because nobody dared admit to having a radio, for fear of retribution. Even though it was a cooperative community, we nevertheless still had to be on our guard. We never could be quite sure that anyone we confided in might have been dispatched by either the Kempeitai or the Gestapo to watch and listen for any suspected spying or other often, erroneously perceived, wrongdoing. My father sent one or all of us children outside to act as lookouts. It would have been disastrous if someone were to have found out and reported him to the authorities for having listened to the radio, so we never said a word about it. In fact, he only listened to the radio as long as there was no one other than family in the house. He'd heard on the radio that there had been an attempt by a number of German aristocrats on Hitler's life that past summer.

Events seemed to be happening so fast, and on such a broad canvas, that it was impossible to keep up. Just the first months we spent in Karuizawa saw a mind-boggling tumult of action—every corner of Europe and Asia seemed to be a front. It was difficult to gauge the overall progress of the war, so vast was its scope. Even so momentous a development as D-Day itself had come and gone without our hearing about it for some time. My parents had long since given up any talk of a truce or of some sort of winding-down of the conflict. This was war to the bitter end both in Europe and in the Pacific. The only question was how soon a turning point would be reached before the Allies would get the upper hand and win the war. From various reports over time, my father did begin to get a sense that the war in Germany, which had been raging for more than five long years, was reaching a violent but inevitable conclusion in favor of the Allies.

After surviving one of the coldest winters we'd ever experienced, we were relieved to feel that spring was finally in the air. In April, it became a lot warmer, and toward the end of the month, wild cherry blossoms appeared and the trees began to sprout leaves. In May, we spotted wild birds in an array of different colors just about the time the cherry blossom season was coming to an end.

With spring also came the news that on April 30, 1945, Adolf Hitler had committed suicide. A week later, on May 8, 1945, it was announced to the whole foreign community in Karuizawa that Germany had surrendered unconditionally. That was the first official news anyone had about the events that had transpired in Europe, and it was met with great jubilation. People were hugging and kissing each other, and tears were streaming down many of their faces. Relieved as they were, our parents were nevertheless exceedingly distressed, not knowing whether their families in Silesia, Bavaria, and Hamburg had survived the war. All they'd heard was that Berlin lay in ruins and that Hamburg was a ghost city. Apparently, only the outer walls of Hamburg's thousands of buildings remained standing.

The months that followed Germany's surrender—the period between May and August—became even more tense and worrisome as time went on. We were no longer under international legal protection. Instead of feeling relieved and hopeful that we'd soon be able to return to a normal life, we now experienced a heightened concern for our safety. People were essentially stateless, and the war was still raging on in the Pacific with no end in sight. There was no food, because US forces had sunk all the ships that used to supply Japan, with the result that we had an ever more severe food crisis on our hands. Toward the end of July, a rumor circulated that the Japanese armies were mobilizing and preparing to mount a major offensive, determined to conquer their enemies. During this period, we observed many more soldiers patrolling the area where the *gaijin* (foreigners) lived. Despite the fact that Germans were allies of the Japanese, from the time Germany had surrendered, there had been an increased fear that we all might be imprisoned. This awareness gave us a feeling of tremendous unease, which made us even more vigilant about not "stepping out of line" in the eyes of the Japanese. It was impossible for us to know for what reason they might decide to incarcerate us at any given moment, so it was imperative that we watch our every step.

It had happened to the French family with the two daughters in Yokohama. And it happened to Herr Engel, a German businessman friend of my mother's back in Hamburg since before the war. He had gone to live in Japan for his job in the late 1920s, and, as he had gone very native, we affectionately called him Engel-san. He was already living in Karuizawa by the time we arrived, but by that fall he had disappeared. No one knew what had happened to him and, unable to find him anywhere, we lost touch. Later, we heard what we had already suspected, that he had been taken prisoner. Nobody knew why, and there was no information about what Engel-san had been accused of, but soon the news spread throughout the community that he had been incarcerated and apparently tortured. It was surmised that the Japanese suspected him of being a double agent or a spy. For whom, no one knew—probably not even Engel-san himself.

Many months later, sometime toward the end of May, we were thrilled to hear that Engel-san had been freed. He came to visit our parents almost immediately after being released from prison. I remember the day vividly. Coming home from school that afternoon I jumped up the front steps, landing on the porch with a loud *thump*. Instantly, my mother appeared and told me not to make so much noise, that Engel-san was inside and had jumped when he heard the bang of my abrupt arrival home. She told me he had just come from prison and was visibly shaken and emotionally and physically extremely fragile. Nevertheless, she did want me to come in and say hello. What I saw was a man who looked like a shadow of his former self. He was ashen, drawn, and stick-thin, with eyes like deep, dark, hollow pools sunken in his face. He was definitely not the man we had known and remembered. He told my parents what had happened to him while he was away, how he had been tortured and beaten, and how ever since he had been released he'd become terribly fearful and nervous—fearful that the police would come back and haul him off to prison once again. It was hard to know how we could help him, other than to lend him all the support we could, but my parents didn't feel as if it would be enough. They thought he needed a doctor who could help him rehabilitate and recover from the extreme stress and the nervousness and mental exhaustion from which he was suffering. They felt that if he had professional help, he could readjust to the world outside sooner and could begin going forward with his life again.

At school a few days later, a classmate of mine told me that on her way to school that morning, she had seen a terrible sight. She was still in shock, shaking as she recounted having seen a man hanging lifeless from a tree by the roadside. I inwardly wondered whether that could have been Engel-san. By the time I arrived home from school that afternoon and told my parents what my friend had seen, they had already heard the sad news, and it indeed was Engel-san who had hanged himself. He was desperate, a totally broken man who could no longer live with the memory of the nightmare he had endured. His suicide was a traumatic experience for my parents and for us children. He had been such a good friend, and it was heartbreaking to have seen him so totally distraught and destroyed.

Engel-san and my parents had mutual friends named Wobker and

Schleeps, two gay men who had been together for a very long while and who were a barrel of fun. We used to love to go to their house, which they had decorated with great taste. Music would always be playing when we came to visit, and they allowed us to play with their pet monkey and would tell us funny jokes. They too were in shock over the loss of their friend, and it once again brought home to us how much danger we were in and that we had to remain exceedingly vigilant. The threat that we could be taken away at any moment was very real. My parents—thankful that up until then we had been left alone, had not been taken prisoner or tortured, had not been subjected to any of the horrendous inhuman treatments about which we kept hearing—never let down their guard.

It was an even greater hardship now for my parents, as they not only had to continue dealing with all the uncertainties—such as food for the family and clothing for the three of us, who were continuing to grow— but also because they were living with the constant fear and concern for their and our safety, as well as for our future. From time to time, with the knowledge that he was unable to do anything about our current predicament, my father would go into a deep funk out of total frustration and feeling of powerlessness. He would stop playing the piano and would just sit in his chair, listless, pensive, and gravely worried.

My mother was always there to help during those times and would try to perk him up and encourage him. She reminded him of what he had so often told her, that they couldn't afford to be downcast and had to remain hopeful, that our survival was at stake, and that he had to keep being informed and stay on top of what was going on, for we all depended on him. Most of the time she was able to help him regain his positive outlook, and he would start playing the piano again. At other times my mother would be the one to become discouraged and depressed about our predicament, especially when she saw we were still hungry after she had put all the food there was to eat on the lunch or dinner table or when it was so cold outside that it made going out of the house impossible.

It was at those times that my father would look for ways to encourage my mother and help her work her way out of her sense of hopelessness. Most of the time they were successful in getting each other back to where they were able to regain a certain degree of equanimity and to continue being able to face the daily challenges and struggle to survive in a war that had caught them so off-guard in such a different and unfamiliar country.

Our greatest worry as children was what would happen to us if one or the other or even both our parents became ill or were suddenly taken away from us like Engel-san. Imagining us up in the mountains, alone with no relatives and very few friends, was more than I could bear. I'd often cry myself to sleep at night just thinking about what might become of us. As for our parents, they were desperately worried about what might already have happened to their families, most of whom were living in the eastern and western parts of Germany close to both fronts. There had been no communication for years, and now there was even less hope of hearing anything, as we were much more closely guarded by the Japanese than we had been before Germany's surrender. It was a time of heightened stress.

Up until Germany's surrender, my father had been receiving a salary from the Commerz Bank because he had been recalled to the home office by the bank. Now, having been stranded, he was, in effect, still working for them. We were able to live on his income, mainly because there was not much to buy except for the food we could find. On occasion, though, my parents would go antiquing for treasures and would pick up a beautiful piece of Imari or Kutani or a piece of furniture, such as a *tansu* (a chest of drawers) or a dining table, all of which were relatively inexpensive at the time. Because of its low height, my parents used the dining table as a coffee table. They loved collecting. After coming home, they would be excited when they had found something exceptionally beautiful, rare, or special.

Then in May, the money transfers were no longer forthcoming, and my father was unable to receive his salary. Fortunately, though, having been an astute banker, he had put us on a budget and had handled our finances wisely, so we weren't immediately destitute.

We welcomed summer like a long-lost friend, and it felt especially good to be able to sit in the warm sun and let it permeate my body. I still had remnants of chilblains, but they too seemed to be improving. We had survived the harsh winter and in the process had not only learned from it but had also learned to appreciate our close, supportive, and loving family. What we had experienced that winter was a valuable lesson in what the human spirit can endure, and it seemed that our emotional development came from that period more than from any other. At best, the three of us children were spectators of the maneuvering our parents had to do, to keep us all well and together as a family. At times, the reality of what had happened and was happening to us became very personal, and we became focused and involved in the process.

Tiger, the cat I'd been given after our move to 867 Atago-yama, did not survive—but not because of the cold. One day, Tiger simply went missing. He looked just like a tiny tiger, and it was terribly upsetting not knowing where we could find him again. I cried for days, and I remember sitting on my father's lap, inconsolable about my cat's disappearance, when he said to me, "Don't worry, we'll find Tiger; he'll come back. You were very good to him." Then one day, Tiger did come back, but it appeared as if he'd been tortured, because he seemed to have gone completely mad. He was not the same cat I had known.

He hissed and clawed at us when we tried to get near him, which led us to believe he'd gone through some traumatic experience. Because his behavior had become unrecognizable, and dangerously so, we were forced to put him down a few days later. With no vet in the area, we had to quickly drown him in a deep barrel of water. My father had said I could not keep him under any circumstances, as he'd become another problem we didn't need. Had Tiger not changed so drastically, I might have been sorrier, but it was nonetheless heartbreaking to see him and the way he acted when he returned.

Flora, our black-and-white mutt, survived the winter but had become very thin. Mooshi, my sweet little black-and-white cat, succumbed not only to the freezing-cold winter but also to old age and malnutrition. Both Mooshi and Tiger had been my cats, whereas Flora had belonged to my brothers, but now she belonged to everyone in the family. For the first time, I was without any pets of my own, and it made me sad. I asked my father if we could replace at least one of my cats, but he felt he couldn't let me have another cat—not because he didn't want me to have a pet of my own, but because it would be unfair to the new pet as we ourselves barely had enough to eat. He explained that he hoped we'd be on our way to America very soon, and would mean we'd have to leave the cat behind. In thinking about it, as disappointed as I was, it made sense. It would have meant another separation.

Toward the end of July 1945, the war in the Pacific still showed no signs of coming to an end. In fact, it began to look like it was coming closer to our little enclave in Karuizawa, for occasionally we'd see a fiery, bright orange-yellow sky on the horizon in the distant southwest. We knew the city of Takasaki was located around that area, because there was a train station there at which we had stopped twice before on our way to Karuizawa. Takasaki Station was at the foot of the mountains, where there was a junction and where steam engines were exchanged for four electrical engines. That way, the trains would be able to make the steep climb up to Karuizawa from Tokyo's Ueno Station. Also coming from that general direction, we could faintly hear the wail of air-raid sirens, and we assumed Takasaki was being bombed. That made it clear to us that what we had seen on the horizon was actually a city burning. We could almost make out what we were sure were flames shooting up into the air. It was the most ominous and frightening sight, and we couldn't understand why the bombing was coming so close to our relatively obscure little resort village. Later, we learned that because at Takasaki there was such an important railroad junction, it was of great interest to the Allies. We hoped that where we were would be of little interest to anyone and that our summer resort town, which had been turned into a holding camp for foreigners, would be spared. The bombings in Takasaki continued for at least another week, and occasionally we would see the sky light up again in the distance. There was also a report that Osaka had been subjected to a major air attack that had left the city badly damaged.

On the morning of Wednesday, August 15, 1945, we were awakened to the news that fighting had ceased, that the war was over, and that His Imperial Majesty, Emperor Hirohito would—for the first time in history—be speaking to his people on the radio, scheduled to be broadcast at noon.

I remember being elated by the news and running out onto our driveway with my parents and brothers. We were jumping up and down for joy, shouting, "The war is over! The war is over!" We hugged each other so tightly that it took our breath away. We were jubilant at the thought that our stay in Karuizawa would soon come to a happy end and that we were finally going to be released from our village arrest and from a long period of isolation from the rest of the world. Having been forbidden to leave Karuizawa for most of the last year of the war, we hadn't been permitted to travel even to the next town. We couldn't wait to return to Yokohama and, at long last, America.

After we had all calmed down, my father and I went down to the machi to see the reaction of the people in the village. As we neared, we could hear the radios on in almost every shop and we could see that everyone was listening with rapt attention to someone making an announcement. We assumed it was the announcer saying that his Imperial Majesty would be speaking to his subjects at noon. I remember arriving at the store of one of the shopkeepers we knew and standing in the entrance listening to the radio with a lot of villagers. It was impossible for us to understand what the emperor was saying, especially because he was speaking in a different-sounding Japanese dialect, one that even the average Japanese person did not seem to understand. So, we just watched the people's faces to see what their reaction was. They showed remarkably little emotion. They didn't cry, they didn't laugh; there simply was a kind of dark cloud over their heads. It was amazing to us that when the emperor had finished speaking, many of the people began to smile and nod their approval. Only later did we hear that not only had the emperor spoken in the imperial dialect of Japanese, which was difficult for native Japanese to understand, but he had also very carefully chosen his words, stating that he had accepted the terms of the Potsdam Declaration, never once using the word "surrender." He focused almost entirely on the fact that the enemy had discovered such a cruel and inhumane weapon that he felt he could not subject his people to any further devastating events such as had taken place at Hiroshima and Nagasaki. By sending his message in this manner, he was able to prevent many Japanese men and women from losing face and therefore possibly committing widespread hara-kiri.

We walked back up the Atago-yama to our house, where we found some friends who had congregated just to talk about what we thought might happen to us now. That evening, we sat around the dinner table, which I was once again asked to set, happily tired from the emotional day we'd just spent. We were having the usual miso soup and whatever could be scraped together, when we started making plans to return to Yokohama and America and discussing how we were going to implement all those plans. Falling asleep that night was not hard—it had been a thrilling day, and we were all totally spent.

When we had arrived in Karuizawa in the early summer of 1944, my father had hoped we would be able to depart before the start of the school year at the beginning of September, but now it was the middle of August 1945—more than a year later—which made him quite anxious to return to Yokohama. He wanted us to be able to at least start the new school year there before leaving for America again. With no information on when we could leave, my father re-enrolled us for a few months in the makeshift school we'd been attending. They told us they would take us out the moment we received the okay to return to Yokohama. They encouraged us to stay positive and said things such as, "Look, it wasn't exactly pleasant to have to spend the war in this freezing mountain resort, but it did keep us out of harm's way when Yokohama was being bombed," or, "Who knows what we'll find in Yokohama now, after all the bombing that took place only a few months ago, so please be patient?" That was the hardest thing to be, because we had already been patient for so long.

We shuddered when we learned, much later, that toward the end of the war in the Pacific the Japanese government had a plan to kill all Westerners if a hostile invasion by American troops were to take place. The concern of the Japanese was that the occidentals would constitute a fifth column behind their lines. Fortunately, the Kempeitai was ordered to abandon that plan after the battle of Okinawa in July and the dropping of the atomic bombs on Hiroshima and Nagasaki in August. With the broadcast of the emperor's speech, the war was essentially over. Thanks to the American occupation of Japan, our lives were spared.

A few days later, we received a transcript of the emperor's speech, which my father read to us:

> In conformity with the precepts handed down by our Imperial ancestors we have always striven for the welfare of our subjects and for the happiness and welfare of all nations. This is precisely why we declared war against Great Britain and the United States. It was not our intention to infringe on the sovereignty of other nations or to carry out acts of aggression against their soil. Despite the valor of our land and naval forces, despite the valor of our heroic dead and despite the continued efforts the situation has not taken a turn for the better and neither has the aspect of the world situation taken a more favorable turn. Moreover, the enemy has employed its outrageous bomb and slaughtered untold numbers of innocent people. Accordingly, to continue the war under these circumstances would ultimately mean the extinction of our people and the utter destruction of human civilization. Under these circumstances how were we to save the millions of our subjects or justify ourselves to save the spirits of our Imperial ancestors? We must express our regrets to our allies who have fought alongside us for the emancipation of East Asia. Let us therefore face the long road, each of us, as one united nation in firm fidelity to the Throne and in full confidence in the indestructibility of our Divine Land, and let us resolve to bend all our energies to future reconstruction. Let us be strong in our moral principles and firm in our ideals.

Not long after that gloriously happy day when the war was finally over, the first wave of American armed forces and MPs arrived in Karuizawa in their Jeeps—four-wheeled vehicles with open sides that we'd never seen before—loaded down with cameras as if they were tourists. It was a thrill to see them, and it seemed they too were pleased to see us, because we were able to speak English fluently, without an accent. For them it was as refreshing to be able to communicate with us as it was for us to be able to communicate with them. They would give us rides around the village in their Jeeps. They gave us candy—which we hadn't seen in years—and some of their K rations, which they hated, but which we devoured with gusto. In turn, we showed them around and helped them find whatever they needed. After their arrival, the Japanese soldiers who had been monitoring our every move simply disappeared, much to our relief. No longer being constantly policed allowed us to be rid of the tension we'd been living with. The American forces had come to free us from our village arrest, and we were told we could leave Karuizawa anytime we wished. We were even free to return to Yokohama.

No sooner did we get the clearance than my father sent Enno, who by now spoke Japanese quite well, to Yokohama on the train to see whether we could rent our former house on the Bluff. That night, he stayed at the New Grand Hotel. When he returned the next day, he told us we would not recognize parts of Yokohama. Most of the city had been leveled and was like a wasteland, but many of the houses on the Bluff seemed to have fared better. Because they had been built either out of brick, stone, or stucco, in the European style, they had withstood the firebombing better than the Japanese houses, which were built of wood and rice paper. Enno found he wasn't able to rent our original house because it had been the rectory of the Unitarian church next door and would be needed as such again. He did succeed in finding another house down the road at 46b Yamate-cho, across from the Ferris Seminary, the missionary school for girls.

46b Yamate-cho, Yokohama, in 1945.

He went on to tell us that the seminary had been turned into the headquarters of the 209th MP station in the latter part of August. While at the hotel, Enno had had a chance to talk to some of the army and navy officers who were also living there, and he raved about the friendliness they all had shown him. In the course of their conversations, they told Enno about the historic ceremony they were honored to have witnessed the morning of September 2, on board the USS *Missouri*. The ship had arrived in Tokyo Bay under the command of Fleet Admiral William F. Halsey Jr. at the end of August and had been chosen to be the venue for the most significant event officially ending World War II. General Douglas MacArthur, the Supreme Commander of the Allied Powers, had accepted the Japanese surrender, led by Mamoru Shigemitsu, the Japanese minister of foreign affairs for imperial Japan, and General Yoshijiro Umezu, the chief of the Imperial Japanese Army, who had come aboard to sign the Instrument of Surrender. In effect, from that day forward, General Douglas MacArthur became the interim ruler of Japan until 1949, when the US State Department became more involved and MacArthur lost control. The Japanese later gave him the nickname of "Gaijin Shogun" ("foreign military ruler").

Alexander and I, meanwhile, had returned to our makeshift school while waiting to return to Yokohama. One morning a few weeks into the fall term, there was a considerable commotion when we arrived, because the mother of one of our classmates, a White Russian girl, had come to school to inform our teacher that her daughter would no longer be attending school there. Apparently, late in the afternoon the day before, on her way home from school, a young American soldier had befriended her and had asked if he could give her a lift home. She accepted his invitation and happily jumped into his Jeep without a moment's hesitation. Instead of taking her home, though, he had driven her deep into the woods, where he had brutally raped her.

When I came home that afternoon and recounted the story to my mother, she took me into my room and started telling me about what she referred to as "the birds and the bees." I had just turned twelve three months earlier. In those days, no one spoke about sexuality at my age, so it was a subject about which I knew nothing. A while back, I had asked my mother, when I saw that Flora was in heat, whether women too went into heat, and she had just answered me curtly with, "Yes, but only when they're older." Just then we were interrupted by my brothers coming home, and she changed the subject, telling me, "I'll talk to you about it some other time."

This, it seemed to me, was that "other time." My mother broached the subject gently and quietly, not wanting to be overheard. After going into much detail about what I was to expect would be happening soon, she impressed upon me that under no circumstance was I to go anywhere by myself or with any man, be it a soldier, an MP, or even a

Japanese man. She said, "You have two brothers with whom you can go anywhere, but just don't ever go anywhere alone." She explained that most of the soldiers had been on ships for a long time and hadn't seen a woman or a girl for months. Now on shore, they were free to relieve their pent-up sexual urges and would look to find someone who'd willingly have sex with them. But then there were others who, if they couldn't find a willing partner, would just go after a girl and force her to have sex. If the girl resisted, the man would overpower and rape her. I realized then that my mother was being even more protective of me than ever. Both my parents put the fear of God in me and explained that I was to heed their warnings and take them seriously. No matter what I was offered, whether candy or food, I was to politely always say "No, thank you," and go on home.

Because of my classmate's traumatic experience, their admonishments sank in. I was now faced with a new set of fears and started hanging around with my brothers a lot more. I was envious of them that they didn't have those restrictions and could pal around with the GIs, who often gave them candy, chocolate, and tins of their despised Spam and K rations. They did, however, bring some of them home to share with the rest of us. At that point, the soldiers were receiving "real" food and were glad to pass the rations on to us.

After Enno returned from his initial trip to Yokohama and told my parents it was safe enough to go there, he and my father went back down together a week later to make the final arrangements. In the meantime, we started to get everything ready for our move before the cold winter months were to set in again. A few days later, my father and Enno returned home and shared with us the many interesting experiences they'd had. For one, they told us that on the train to Tokyo there had been a German man whom neither he nor Enno had ever seen before. Curious, they engaged him in conversation and found that he had been living in hiding all the past year, because he'd been the radio operator for Richard Sorge, the notorious German spy for the Soviets. He had gone into hiding because he was afraid of being arrested. A little while later, they heard that the last anyone had seen or heard of him was on that train. Apparently, after arriving in Tokyo, he had gone directly to the Soviet mission, put on a Soviet uniform, and been sent quietly to Russia.

When we told Father and Enno that we were more interested in whether we'd have a place to live that fall than in some radio operator we didn't know, our father told us that he'd rented the house Enno found for us and that we were all set to move in the following month or, at the latest, in early November—just as soon as we could pack up and hire movers to help us with our furniture. The house was located not far from our original one, and although some windows were still boarded up because they

In Karuizawa before leaving for Yokohama, in the fall of 1945.

were missing windowpanes, the house was actually very nice—perhaps nicer than the one at 66b Yamate-cho. My father told us we would see that on the Bluff there were still plenty of signs of the bombings.

Everyone was so busy trying to put their lives back together that we couldn't get things done quite as quickly as we would have liked. My father told us he had seen many American ships in the harbor, a lot of Jeeps and trucks on the roads, and that the streets were teeming with soldiers and sailors. "It's quite a change from the old Yokohama, but it will certainly be an improvement over our year in Karuizawa," he said.

Anxious to get settled before Christmas, we started packing up our belongings once again. It was beginning to get chilly, making us swing into action faster. Our parents used this opportunity to teach us teamwork. We called the moving company to tell them we were ready, but they informed us that one of their trucks had broken down and there would be a delay sending some of our things down until the truck was fixed or they could find a new one. Not wanting to wait any longer, we asked the owner to at least send our beds, the kitchen boxes, and the Victrola, which he promised to do. With that, we locked up the house, gave the key and the inventory to the movers, and—loaded with packages and suitcases—were on our way to the train station. Nothing had changed much at Karuizawa Station since our arrival there sixteen months earlier, but we were not prepared for what we saw on the ride down to Ueno Station, especially from Takasaki on down. So much had been destroyed that we would not have recognized the towns had it not been for the signs.

It was the end of October, and despite our being terribly sad and depressed at seeing Yokohama—the city that we had once known as a bustling metropolis was now mostly in ashes—we nevertheless were happy to be out of Karuizawa before another cold winter set in.

Yokohama in ruins, 1945.

Because our newly rented house was directly across the street from the entrance to the 209th MP station, we saw a lot of MPs coming in and going out of the original Ferris Seminary, which had been turned into their headquarters. In a very brief time—because we were able to converse with them in English—we got to know most of the MPs there and were quickly adopted by them as their mascots. They invited us to have meals with them in their mess hall, where we joined them in their chow line. After lunch or dinner, they told us to clean off our trays, just like they did. With our eyes popping out, we watched as they summarily chucked leftover food in the trash. We were so shocked at what we saw that Alexander asked for permission to dig out the hot dogs and sausages, which, when boiled in hot water, might still be edible. Not only did they grant him permission, they also sent him home with GI-issue food they were so tired of but that to us was a treat. We knew our parents would be only too happy to boil up the hot dogs and sausages, to have something other than the soybean paste we'd been living on for so long.

Frequently, when they held movie screenings in the auditorium of the former girls' school, we were invited to watch the latest ones from Hollywood. We particularly enjoyed the double features, because we hadn't seen movies in close to five years. I still had the same restrictions as I'd had in Karuizawa, and I was only permitted to go across the street with at least one brother.

General MacArthur's first priority had been to arrange that Emperor Hirohito was neither tried as a war criminal, for which some Allied political and military leaders were pushing, nor asked to abdicate, as was suggested by Prince Mikasa and Prince Higashikuni of the imperial family and Tatsuji Miyoshi, one of a number of intellectuals who held this view. MacArthur, in his sensitivity, farsightedness, and infinite wisdom, rejected both recommendations, knowing that either

General Douglas MacArthur meeting with Emperor Hirohito on
September 27, 1945.

action would be enormously unpopular with the Japanese people who revered their emperor as if he were a god. MacArthur's decision to keep him on the throne and work with him proved to be the best solution for everyone. In hindsight, it boggles the mind how nuanced his understanding of the Japanese people was, especially at a moment that might otherwise have elicited vengeful instincts of retribution.

At roughly the same time—toward the end of 1945—the Marionist brothers from St. Joseph College returned to Yokohama and with the aid of both the Japanese and the occupation forces started restoring the school, which had been damaged by bombs. Toward the end of the war, all the buildings of the Convent of St. Maur had been leveled by the Allied bombings (the school wasn't rebuilt and reopened until 1948), with the result that I was unable to return to classes there. Meanwhile, my parents were informed that St. Joseph College would reopen the following September, but this time as a coeducational school, assuring me a place to go. While waiting for St. Joseph to reopen, we spent most of our time across the street with our newfound friends, who would frequently take us into downtown Yokohama in their Jeeps.

By now we had moved into the house we had rented at 46b Yamate-cho. Upon entering the house, a narrow hall led to two facing doors, one to the kitchen and the other to the living room, at the base of the stairs. In the far end of the living room on the opposite wall of the door to the dining room was a fireplace, and to the left of it, there was a giant hole in the ceiling where an unexploded bomb had fallen in. The bomb had been removed by the time we arrived, but the hole was still there, waiting to be closed up, along with two more windows that had also been blown out and were still boarded up. In the far corner of my upstairs bedroom was a giant hole, through which I could look down into the living room. Because the bomb had come through the roof, I also had a hole in my ceiling, which went right through the roof to the open sky. There was nobody available until after the New Year who could come and repair the roof and the ceiling, as there was a great deal more extensive work that had to be done elsewhere on the Bluff so the houses could be inhabited.

Back out in the hall, there was a bathroom to the left of the stairs, over part of the kitchen, and my brothers' room was on the right over the library. To the left of the bathroom was another room, which was also over the kitchen. That's where my parents had stored the little bit of food that was left—mostly orange marmalade, jams and jellies, and the cans of K rations that had been given to us by the American soldiers. Over time, and very mysteriously, jars of orange marmalade began disappearing. Only when my mother went out into the front garden one day did she notice a lot of the empty jars on the grass under the storage room window. She immediately called my siblings and me together and confronted us with her discovery. When neither Alexander nor I said we knew anything about it, my brother Enno confessed. He said that sometimes at night he got so hungry that, when he saw us all sleeping, he would quietly go and consume whatever he could find, after which he'd throw the evidence out the window.

By Christmas, the rest of our furniture still hadn't arrived, and there was nothing we could do but improvise. We made do with wooden crates, on which we sat in the library on Christmas Eve and played Christmas carols on the Victrola. Once again, my father had managed to come up with a live Christmas tree, and once again, he placed real wax candles on it before hanging up the meager decorations my parents had saved from our first Christmas in 1941. There were no presents, as there still was nothing to buy, but there was a lot of Christmas spirit as we sat around the tree singing to the Christmas music being played on the trusty Victrola. Happy to be back out of the cold weather in the mountains, we were all in the best of spirits and ever so grateful to be safe. It was by no means warm, but it was a lot warmer than the Christmas the year before. On our way to the dining room, where my mother had set up our usual fare of miso soup, rice, and the few vegetables she had found at the market, we noticed that it had started snowing outside—as well as through the giant hole in the roof into my bedroom and straight down into our living room.

Later that evening, we walked farther up the Bluff in the snow, to the same Catholic church we had attended many times before leaving Yokohama. This time it was to attend midnight Mass. Now that peace had been restored, we had much to be thankful for and we prayed that the Lord would guide us and give us the hope and strength we needed to face what lay ahead, thanking Him also for having brought us safely to this point. At home after Mass, we hugged, kissed, and wished one another a merry Christmas before happily falling into bed. That very first postwar Christmas would be indelibly etched in all of our collective memories.

Shortly after the New Year and Oshogatsu celebrations were behind us, the balance of our furniture finally arrived. Our parents went about arranging it all and found a spot for the ebony baby grand piano my father had bought in Karuizawa. It desperately needed tuning, although it first had to be reassembled, as it had been much too big to transport with its legs attached. By then, the hole through the ceiling of the living room and my room had been repaired, and the panes in the windows of the living and dining rooms had been replaced. Finally, we could see outside and even let some sunshine in.

Early in the New Year, we began meeting the "dependents," as they were called, of the officers to whom houses had been assigned on the Bluff, and life started to normalize again. There were a number of teenagers we met while playing on the Bluff, and each one of us had a favorite. Enno met a young boy about his age named Jean Schanze, the son of a

Colonel Schanze. He was part of the Eighth Army under the command of Lieutenant General Robert L. Eichelberger, who had come to Yokohama in August 1945 as part of the occupation. Enno also had a girlfriend by the name of Gail Smith. My special friend was Evelyn Melberg, who was originally from California. She was the daughter of a US Army colonel and a French mother named Germaine. She had two sisters—Maxine and Marilyn—but both were much older. They had been among the first group of dependents to arrive in Yokohama on a ship named the USNS *Fred C. Ainsworth* and were assigned a house on the Bluff fairly close to ours. Evelyn would often bring along some chocolates, knowing we didn't have any and couldn't buy them on the market yet.

With Evelyn Melberg in Yokohama.

Anxious for us to return to America as soon as possible, my father started inquiring about where he needed to go and what he needed to do to reactivate his, my mother's, and my reentry permits, which had expired after six months and therefore—more than five years later—were no longer valid; Enno and Alexander, born in the US, were American citizens and did not need such documents. The American consulate in Yokohama had been closed during the war years and had not yet reopened. There was no Department of Immigration that he knew of. He was led to believe that there was an American embassy in Tokyo, because someone had told him they had seen the American Flag flying over the embassy building on September 5, just after the signing on the USS *Missouri*. Upon hearing the news, he decided to take the train to the capital and take all of us with him so he could show us postwar Tokyo.

When we arrived at the Tokyo Station on the Marunouchi side, the wide street facing the Imperial Palace was still there but a large part of the station had been destroyed during the firebombings of 1945. It was quickly rebuilt and was operational by the late summer. Instead of three stories, it now only had two and had lost its impressive dome that had been a replica of Amsterdam's Central Station. We walked toward the palace and turned left onto the main street on our way to visit the Imperial Hotel, where we had stayed before the war. The same Frank Lloyd Wright hotel that had so brilliantly survived earthquakes had been badly damaged by the bombings during World War II.

We continued on with our father to the American embassy and waited while he spoke to someone in the administration office. Not too long afterward, he came out of the office with a very discouraged look on his face. What he heard distressed him greatly. He was told that part of what MacArthur was currently dealing with was what to do with all the foreigners, particularly the Germans, who had been living in Japan either voluntarily or, as in our case, involuntarily. He told us there were rumors that all German nationals would be returned to their country of origin, but so far there was nothing to back up that rumor. At least there was some good news, because Enno and Alexander were going to be given Certificates of Citizenship by the Allies.

At that point we were ready to return to Yokohama, as we had seen enough of the many buildings in ruins, a bleak and depressing reminder of the war that was finally over. On our way back to the station we happened to pass the Dai-Ichi Building just before 5:00 p.m. This was General MacArthur's headquarters, and we saw that his limousine and his motorcade were waiting for him. We decided to stay and see if we could catch a glimpse of the hero, and sure enough, at the dot of 5:00, two rows of MPs flanking the steps coming down from the building were commanded to stand at attention and present arms with their rifles. General MacArthur came out of the building with his signature corncob pipe in his mouth and bounded down the steps and into his waiting limousine. A huge crowd had gathered to watch. The limousine, led by half a dozen motorcycles and flanked by several more on each side, sped off. It was an impressive sight and great showmanship, sure to be psychologically intimidating. The six-foot-plus-tall and fit MPs had been handpicked by the general and towered over the much shorter Japanese. Later, we heard that every weekday this performance was repeated when the general arrived at 9:00 a.m. sharp and again when he departed at precisely 5:00 p.m.

That spring and summer, we had lots of time to do many different things with our new American friends, often going to the beach or to visit Kamakura to show them the giant Buddha. We even took them to Karuizawa one weekend to show them where we'd gone our first summer, walked them along the Kumoba Pond and took them to the Atago-yama to show them where we lived during the last year of the war. From time to time, we also saw the friends we'd made in Yokohama before the war, those who hadn't been evacuated to Karuizawa with us, but who were evacuated to Gora or Hakone that same summer. Of course, we also continued spending time across the street, and frequently our MP friends there let us bring our civilian friends over to watch movies.

Enno took a job with the harbor master as a translator and could not always join in our escapades, but he came back to tell us of interesting things he had seen and amusing stories he had heard. He mentioned having seen a number of DUKWs (pronounced "ducks"),

The three of us happily back in Yokohama in front of 46b Yamate-cho in the fall of 1945.

Lt. Chuck with Alexander and me, across the street from our house in the spring of 1946.

which were amphibious vehicles that had been developed for use in the war. At times, Enno would be asked to drive army nurses to Enoshima and Kamakura on their days off and to act as their translator and tour guide. At only fifteen, Enno handled the three-quarter-ton army truck remarkably well. Another time, he was asked to drive a Captain Kesselring, who suggested to Enno that he bring his family with him.

Enno with his Jeep in Yokohama.

With my mother, Captain Kesselring, and Alexander.

Over time, we started to acquire an extensive and sometimes colorful army vocabulary. It was all so much fun, despite the fact that the times were still pretty uncertain and worrisome for our parents. As kids, though, we easily and happily adjusted to our new life, confident that we were eventually going to return safely to America. Our parents, too, were actually starting to have a much better time, as they began meeting more of the army and navy officers and their wives, many of whom were being housed on the Bluff. There was a General Charles A. Willoughby, a major general in the US Army, who was serving as General MacArthur's chief of intelligence. He was born in Heidelberg, Germany, just before the turn of the century and came to America in 1910 at the age of eighteen, after attending Heidelberg University. Then there was a General Charles S. Ferrin, known as "Chick," who was a brigadier general in the field artillery. Our parents met him through a friend of theirs from Austria named Carlie, who had been married to a man she later divorced because he had taken a young Japanese male lover. Our parents took their friend Carlie, now a single mother, under their wing and became her confidants. She had become desperately unhappy after having a devastating love affair with General Ferrin. He had promised to send for her when he returned to America, but she never heard from him again. Only much later she learned what he had neglected to tell her: He had a wife and children back home.

Then there were the Schanzes and the Melbergs, who became good friends and on occasion invited us all to their homes for dinner. There was also a navy captain (later a rear admiral) by the name of Beverly Mosby Coleman, who at the time was port director in Yokohama. Sometime after, he was transferred to Tokyo as chief defense counsel for the Tokyo Tribunals opening the IMTFE (International Military Tribunal for the Far East) on April 29, 1946, but he resigned six weeks later on June 18, objecting to some of the trial procedures, which he thought were not in accordance with US practices. That same month, he returned to Washington, DC, for duty in the Bureau of Ships.

Captain Beverly Coleman during a break in proceedings at the
1946 war crimes trials in Tokyo.

At one point my mother, concerned about her family in Hamburg, asked the Tillitses whether they could possibly help find out news about her and my father's families in Germany. She had a cousin, Karen von Neergard, who lived in Stockholm, Sweden, and thought perhaps through the Tillitses' Danish relatives they could make contact and eventually find her family through the Red Cross in Germany. To my mother's surprise, a few weeks later, the news came back that her parents, brothers, and many cousins had all survived. Most of my father's family, who were from the east, had been forced to flee to Bavaria from the Russian invasion in February 1945. During the flight, my father's youngest sister had been killed. He was also told that his youngest brother, who had been working in his Frankfurt office, was killed when his building was bombed in an air raid. No other details were available. It was terrible news. My parents were both deeply saddened and also frustrated that they were unable to communicate with the rest of my father's family.

On September 15, 1946, with Brother Soden as director, the newly repaired and rebuilt St. Joseph College finally reopened as a coeducational school with twenty-five students attending. The three of us were among those first twenty-five, but a week later the school had grown to a student body of three hundred. My friend Evelyn also was among the first twenty-five but subsequently transferred when an American School opened up.

That same fall, I was confirmed at the Church of the Sacred Heart on the Bluff, with a fair number of occidental as well as Asian children and adults. It was a festive occasion, although due to continuing shortages no reception was planned.

A few months into our first term, my parents discovered that Alexander was in the habit of playing hooky a great deal of the time, going off to socialize with soldiers and sailors. He didn't speak Japanese that well, but being the outgoing type, he loved going down to

My parents, Enno, Alexander, and I (black arrows) at
Confirmation Day in Yokohama, 1946.

the city. He didn't really want to go to school but preferred spending time with many of the sailors in the harbor, with whom he could speak English. He was frequently invited on board the ships docked by Yamashita Park.

Every now and then one of the brothers at St. Joseph College would inquire whether Alexander was sick. My parents had no idea where he could be and asked Enno to search for him. He found that most of the time Alex was spending the days at the military barracks in Yamashita Park, directly across from the New Grand Hotel. I was unaware of all of this because, by now thirteen, I had made many American friends who were also teenagers, such as Evelyn, Gail Smith, and Sharon O'Hanlon. I was frequently invited to go with them on fun trips in their cars, which was a special treat, because my own family had no means of transportation.

Several wonderful events stand out in my memory. The first was the evening we all, including Evelyn and her parents, drove to Tokyo to hear my Japanese friend Yoshi Shiono give a piano recital in a huge concert hall. We were so impressed, because at sixteen she already was a world-class artist. Of course, she had worked hard all the years I'd known her, and it had paid off. Another time, our parents took us to the local concert hall to hear the renowned Wilhelm Furtwängler conduct Beethoven's *Ninth Symphony*. We had heard it many times on our Victrola, but hearing it performed live with a full orchestra and chorus was our most exciting experience in a very long time. We were also invited one day to go to the opening of a new movie that had been released in America in mid-March. It was being shown in a downtown theater that had been built with bricks and mortar and had therefore largely withstood the bombings. What little repair was needed had already been done. The movie was *Gilda* and starred Rita Hayworth and Glenn Ford. It was by far one of the all-time great movies of the 1940s, and the dance Rita Hayworth performed while singing "Put the Blame on Mame" was nothing short of sensational. Having seen the movie, I was determined to learn to sing and dance and to go into the movies.

The second postwar Christmas was upon us. There still wasn't much to buy, but at least we were no longer on a starvation diet. Not that there was an abundance of food available, but between our neighbors across the street and our American friends, all of whom generously shared some of their stores of food, we were no longer starving.

Shortly after Christmas, my father was quietly alerted by some of his friends in the armed forces to the fact that we were very likely going to be repatriated to Germany and that he should try to make the necessary arrangements to have his belongings shipped there as soon as possible. This should preferably be done through neutral friends,

With my brothers and Flora in the fall of 1946, six
months prior to our departure from Japan.

because everything would otherwise be sold after our departure from Japan. This, of course, came as a terrible blow to my father, as he had been working tirelessly through many of those same friends to return to America. Apparently, it was to no avail, because the order had come from General MacArthur himself. He supposedly had already informed the Japanese government that all German nationals were to be deported to Germany.

Several weeks into the New Year, my father received the news he so dreaded to hear, that we should prepare ourselves to be repatriated back to Germany by the end of February. He was told we did not need to pack anything and were to leave all our belongings behind. There would not be enough room on the troop transport ship for anything but two pieces of luggage each. What he had been warned about at the end of the year in Tokyo was now going to be implemented. MacArthur was definitely going through with his decision to send all German nationals home and had arranged for them to leave Japan in a relatively short time.

Again, my father went to Tokyo to speak with someone at the consulate to inquire whether we might be qualified for an exemption because he, my mother, and I had been issued reentry permits in the spring of 1941, and particularly because both my brothers were US citizens. He was told that an inquiry would be made, but ultimately the orders came back from the high command that *all* German nationals would have to leave and that it would be impossible for us to return to the United States directly, despite the fact that several of my father's friends in the army and navy had tried to intervene. He was reminded that our reentry permits, which had originally been valid for six months, had expired in November 1941, and the office of immigration and naturalization had not yet started issuing entry permits. All efforts were unsuccessful, and no one at headquarters could go against orders. It had been an exercise in futility.

Visibly upset by the news and the realization that, once again, it looked as if we were going to lose all our possessions, my parents met with our friends the Tillitses—the Danish diplomats—and Carlie who, as an Austrian citizen, was not being repatriated. Because my father had been unable to send or wire payments to the US, when we did not return in the fall of 1941, all the contents of our New York apartment had been auctioned off and were a total loss to us. He did not want to have that happen again, especially because he and my mother had collected some beautiful things while in Japan.

When the Tillitses and Carlie heard the story, all three were as appalled at the news as my parents were. Over a cup of tea, they started talking about several options we might have, but none seemed to be viable. Having to leave behind all the Imari and Kutani china my parents had collected, as well as some of the tansus, side tables, lamps, and the coffee table they'd bought was unacceptable, and all agreed they would try to find a way to salvage everything.

The next day, the Tillitses came to the house and offered to take some of our furnishings with them, as they were scheduled to go back to Denmark in March and were packing up anyway. After their arrival in Denmark, they would ship everything to my mother's parents' house in Hamburg. Because Germany had surrendered, my father was no longer receiving a salary from the bank, so he had to start selling some of the jewelry he had given my mother over the years. There were still a few sentimental pieces left, which they also gave to the Tillitses in a small suitcase, making the assumption it would be safe in the hands of a diplomat.

Later in the day, Carlie came over and said she would be happy to include whatever we wanted to have sent with her shipment to Austria, as she was planning to return home as well. She also said she would ship them on to us in Hamburg as soon as they arrived and the circumstances permitted. That included all the Japanese antiques, the silver and china, the beautiful bronzes, the bibelots, and the objects my parents had collected over the close to five and a half years we were in Japan. She said she didn't believe there would be any problem bringing our belongings over as part of her household shipment. My parents appreciated very much their friends' kind offer and started packing up, sorting out what items we'd be taking with us and what would go with the Tillitses and Carlie.

The day before our scheduled departure, my brothers and I were busy helping our parents take all the smaller items over to the Tillitses and Carlie, while the larger items, which had already been packed up, were being picked up by a truck and delivered to them. All that was left in the house that evening were the two pieces of hand luggage per person that we were permitted to take with us, and our beds, which my parents had not planned to ship to Europe.

The next morning, February 15, carrying only our permitted hand luggage, we left our house on the Bluff and climbed into a waiting school bus. It proceeded to take us to the town of Uraga, a seaport south of Yokohama at the entrance of Tokyo Bay. It was approximately a two-hour drive. Still a bit sleepy, having gone to bed late the night before, most of us slept all the way. By the time we arrived at the docks, we were wide-awake again. To our great surprise, Colonel Schanze was waiting to greet us. He had come to say good-bye and to see that everything was going smoothly. There, in front of us, loomed the SS *Marine Jumper*, a US Navy troop-transport ship that had been loaned to the Japanese by the US Navy for the purpose of deporting the "enemy aliens" back to Germany, as the Japanese Navy had been totally destroyed. This was a new ship, just two years old, capable of carrying nearly four thousand troops.

The SS *Marine Jumper*.

After a while additional buses started arriving, carrying more German nationals from various parts of the country. It was an extremely well-orchestrated boarding procedure, with no time being wasted. Everyone was immediately herded over to what looked like a Quonset hut, at the entrance of which passports were being checked. We were then asked to proceed through the hut to the ship. As we were about to exit the hut, we were made to remove our outer clothing and shoes and were sprayed with DDT. Despite our very vocal and strong objections, they went right ahead and sprayed us, saying those were their orders, that it was a precautionary procedure purely for our protection. We hated the feeling but were powerless to resist. At the same time, my father was told that it would not be necessary for him to make arrangements for us to be picked up at Bremerhaven. Everyone would first be taken to a camp in Ludwigsburg, near Stuttgart, in order to be "de-Nazified." Every effort was being made to root out Nazi war criminals.

Shortly thereafter, we boarded the ship. My father and Enno were taken separately way down into the bowels of the ship, into a large room for men only, where they were assigned two bunks, one over the other, in a stack of four and among rows and rows of bunks. My mother, Alexander, and I were also taken below to similar accommodations, where we were assigned three bunks in a stack of four. We were demoralized—to say the least—as it was a far cry from the Atlantic crossings we'd made before the war and even the Pacific crossing to Japan, where our cabins had been comparatively deluxe, very private, and comfortable. It was somewhat distressing to think these would be our quarters for the next thirty-six days at sea.

Looking around, we watched as the enormous room started filling up with women and children, some of whom were crying. Others were just running around. Across two aisles, my mother suddenly spotted a young girl—a teenager by the name of Kiku (Japanese for "Chrysanthemum") Schneider, whom she knew—whose father and late mother had been friends. She looked totally forlorn, and when my mother asked her where her father was, she said he had been sent to where the men had been assigned. My mother tried to console Kiku by telling her she had nothing to worry about, that she would be safe and could see her father during the day, and they could eat all their meals together. That seemed to make her feel better, and she wiped her tears away.

A little while later, my father and Enno arrived and told us to take our belongings and come with them. As we climbed back up to a deck where there were cabins—which we had thought were just for officers—my father, who had been speaking with Colonel Schanze and who had seen the accommodations, told us he had arranged for my mother, Alexander, and me to have one of the cabins with a porthole on the basis that Alexander was carrying an American passport. We were relieved and overjoyed that we wouldn't have to sleep in a room with hundreds of others, who could very well have become seasick or had other problems. That's when we had begun to better understand the reason for the DDT.

Our new cabin had two lower and two upper bunks on each side of the wall, for a total of eight bunks, but we seemed to be the only ones occupying the cabin. There was a porthole at the end of the narrow room, in between the bunks. My mother and I chose the lower bunks opposite each other and Alexander chose the bunk above mine. While my father and Enno were still topside with us, we asked them to take us down to their deck and show us where their bunks were located. When we entered the large room, we realized it was the mirror image of the one to which we had originally been assigned, and when we came to their bunks we saw Mr. Schneider, Kiku's father, sitting on his bunk in the next row looking just as forlorn as his daughter. In his hand he was holding a box, keeping it close to his heart, not knowing what to do with it. When my mother asked him if she could help, he answered, saying these were the ashes of his wife and he wasn't sure how best to keep them safe. Because his was the lowest of the four bunks, they both decided the safest place would be right under his bunk, where no one could trip over the box or accidentally knock it over. He was grateful for the advice and smiled, saying he was happy to have seen my parents again. With that we had to leave to go topside again, as by now the bunk room was filling up, and we weren't supposed to be there anyway.

Back in our cabin—it was hardly a roomy stateroom but certainly a lot more comfortable than we'd been earlier—we began unpacking and putting our clothes in the drawers beneath the bunks. We knew it was time for lunch when we heard the ship's gong. Exceedingly hungry, we went immediately to the giant mess hall, where we were told to wait to be assigned seats and to find our men. My parents, Enno, Alexander, and I got in a chow line, where we happily received real food, albeit from cans. By then we couldn't have cared less where it came from, as long as we were given something fairly decent. Soon after lunch, the SS *Marine Jumper* made its way slowly out of the harbor, through the Straits of Uraga, and into the Pacific Ocean bound for our first stop—Shanghai.

My memory of those early days on board the *Marine Jumper* is hazy. I do remember, though, that on the first day at sea everyone was summoned on deck for the usual fire drill and an introduction to the emergency procedures. We were given detailed instructions on where we were to assemble and to which lifeboat stations we were assigned. Curious as to what route we would be taking to Germany, we asked the seaman who had issued us the instructions to give us a brief description. From what he told us, we were heading south and passing the island of Shikoku, east of Honshu, and then continuing southwestwardly toward the East China Sea. From there we were going to enter the Yangtze River and continue on until we came to the Huangpu River, which in turn would take us to Shanghai.

After several days, we dropped anchor between the Bund and Pudong (which at the time was just a vast stretch of farmland) in the middle of the Huangpu River, where we were scheduled to pick up additional passengers who were being sent back to Germany. Upon arrival we were met by hundreds of *junks*, all trying to sell us their wares. The way they showed them to us was ingenious, in that they would balance the item on top of a long bamboo pole that reached all the way up to the first open deck. There we'd have a chance to examine their merchandise and then either refuse the object or keep it and throw the money down to them. It was quite a scene as junk after junk would fight furiously to be the first to show their wares.

Having the cabin to ourselves had been too good to be true and was too good to last, because at Shanghai a woman with her teenage daughter joined us. Fortunately, they were both very pleasant and kept pretty much to themselves. After a day in Shanghai, where we were not permitted to disembark, we were on our way again, sailing back down the Huangpu River to the Yangtze River and passing the islands of Changxing Dao and the smaller Hengsha, as we were heading back toward the East China Sea.

Once seaborne again, I met a young girl about my age with whom my parents were not too enamored—why, I never did find out—but we had a good time palling around together anyway. Also, at times—although it was strictly forbidden to fraternize with any of the officers and seamen—I was approached by a Captain Gross, who engaged me in a conversation. At age thirteen, although shy, I was feeling very grown-up and was especially pleased that this American captain was so attentive and interested in what I had to say. Yet in the back of my mind, I wondered why he was asking me so many questions. Why, I mused, did he want to know all about my life so far? Having been told we were to keep to ourselves, it made me nervous and fearful to even be seen talking to him. He reassured me that as a captain, he was in charge of fraternization issues, and I had nothing to worry about. Once I stopped worrying, I decided I'd ask him a lot of questions, too, and started to look forward to my meeting him for walks around the decks. It was good exercise and the fresh sea air was invigorating, although as we sailed farther south and hit the equator south of Singapore, it became too hot, in spite of the ocean breezes.

It was on one of those walks that he asked me whether, while in Japan, we had heard about the Nazis' sending Jews to concentration camps during the war. I told him not to my knowledge but that I would ask my parents if they had heard anything. When I asked my father, he reminded me that we had no communication except for my little radio—he did not want me to divulge that we also had his shortwave radio, which at the time was contraband—and although he knew that concentration camps had been built starting in 1933, they

On deck, walking with Captain Gross.

were supposedly for those who had opposed the new regime. They were also for communists or other real or imagined offenders, including some Jews who had been sent there because they were opponents of the Nazi regime, not simply because they were Jewish. He was not aware of any mass incarceration and annihilation.

On my next walk, I told Captain Gross what my father had told me, so he proceeded to tell me that after Germany had declared war on America, all persons of Jewish origin had been systematically sent to concentration camps both in Germany and in Poland, either as slave laborers or for extermination in gas chambers. It was a state-sponsored program by the Nazi regime, under which more than six million Jews had perished. In addition, five to ten million people, including ethnic

Poles, Soviet civilians and prisoners of war, people with disabilities, homosexuals, Roma, and political and religious opponents, were murdered by the Nazis. This information was all too overwhelming and horrifying, and I'm not sure I even believed Captain Gross at the time.

That evening, my father went to look for Captain Gross, determined to hear directly from him the unbelievable story I had told him. He wanted to be sure I had heard the captain correctly and was not making it up. What he did not know—because we arrived in Japan before Hitler had started rounding up Jews living in Germany at the end of 1941—was that the rumors of his heinous agenda were not confirmed by the US State Department until November 1942, and not until December 1942 did the Allies expose and then denounce the atrocities. Captain Gross told him that the first large-scale deportation of Jews began in October 1941 and that the gassings had begun in December of that year. My father was rocked by what Captain Gross told him and confirmed that I'd heard correctly. It was hard for us to understand what we were only now hearing, and that it had taken so long for us to learn this unbelievably shocking news. The memory of all that the SS had done to the Jewish people on Kristallnacht way back in 1938 made my parents realize that what they had witnessed in Berlin had just been the beginning of the Jewish persecution, the atrocities, and the mass murders that followed.

Continuing on through the Straits of Singapore and Malacca, through the Andaman Sea and across the Bay of Bengal, we arrived in Colombo, Ceylon (now Sri Lanka), where we docked. It was a sunny, hot, and humid day with temperatures in the high 80s. What surprised us most of all was being greeted by guards and police officers dressed in what looked like black or navy blue wool suits. Apparently—or so we were told when we asked how they could stand wearing those hot wool suits—dark clothes actually radiated the heat better. We didn't know this then, and it made no sense, but if that was what they believed in Ceylon and it worked for them, we saw no reason to question it.

After we'd spent the day in Colombo, we set sail again, this time through the Arabian Sea to the Gulf of Aden. One morning, an announcement came over the loudspeaker that a fellow passenger had died the night before and there was to be a burial at sea, which everyone was invited to attend. Having never seen a burial at sea, my parents decided they would go and suggested we come along. While we were all assembled on the aft deck, the body, which had been wrapped in a white sheet, was rolled out on a gurney, and a priest proceeded to say a short Mass before several seamen lifted a board with the body on it off the gurney and walked it to the railing. There they tilted the plank toward the water and commended the remains of this poor soul to a watery grave in the sea.

We continued up through the Suez Canal to Port Said, where at times the banks of the canal were so close to our ship on both sides

Burial at sea on the SS *Marine Jumper*.

that we could almost touch the trees and houses lining them. Once out in the Mediterranean, the weather cooled down quite a bit as we cruised along near Greece, Malta, Tunis, and Algiers. When we entered the Strait of Gibraltar and passed the famous Rock of Gibraltar, it had been almost a month since our departure from Japan.

The weather was still pleasant as we entered the north Atlantic Ocean, but in the Bay of Biscay we encountered a storm that was the most frightening we had ever experienced. The seas were so rough and the wind so strong that we thought this was the end of the line for us all. At one point the ocean loomed like a tall wall of water to the side of us, and the next minute the water came crashing down on our ship with such force that no one would have survived had they been on deck. No sooner had the wall crashed into the ship than she was carried way up on the next wave and ended up as if on top of a mountain of water before the wave dropped her back down again into the valley of the ocean waters. The same cycle repeated itself over and over for what seemed like hours. My mother, Alexander, and I, after watching for a while, decided we'd had enough, particularly because we were beginning to feel seasick. We went to our cabin, where we threw ourselves on our beds, letting our bodies roll with the motion instead of fighting it. When it seemed the storm had subsided and it looked safe enough to go out again, my father came knocking on our door to suggest that we go for a walk with him on the outside deck. It was the last thing any of us wanted to do, but he was very persuasive and promised us we would feel a lot better if we got some fresh air and something to eat. After a lot of coaxing and discussion, we finally agreed, and sure enough we began feeling better. Such were the mundane realities of our lengthy trip at sea.

With just about a week to go, we started talking about the future and making plans for our time in Germany as well as for our eventual return to America. We talked about what each of us wanted for the future and about how we would go about achieving our goals. We had all survived the war—which mercifully had by now been over for nearly eighteen months—in relatively good shape, though marked by some of its privations and a sense of isolation. We agreed that after seeing all our family, our first order of business would be to do whatever was necessary for us to be able to return home to New York City as soon as possible. Fortunately, Enno and Alexander had received their Certificates of Citizenship when they were still in Japan and were therefore no longer listed on my mother's passport. Although both were still underage—Enno had turned sixteen a little more than three weeks before we left Japan, and Alexander was going to be eleven in four months—they were free to apply for their own passports.

Enno, just before disembarkation.

Several days before our scheduled arrival in Bremerhaven, we started packing, anxious to disembark soon after the ship docked. The temperature had begun dropping, and it was turning much colder as we proceeded northeastward into the English Channel, passing Guernsey on our starboard side and heading toward the North Sea. Suddenly, in the distance, on the port side, we were able to make out a long stretch of white terrain, which as we came closer was a dramatic and very beautiful sight. These were the famous White Cliffs of Dover and were so white because they are made of chalk. It was fun to see them, as I remembered them immortalized in the famous World War II pop classic of the same name. It also reminded me of the 209th MP station, where we had heard the song played over and over. I felt a touch of nostalgia come over me for those first days back in Yokohama after the war had ended and we had newfound friends in all the MPs.

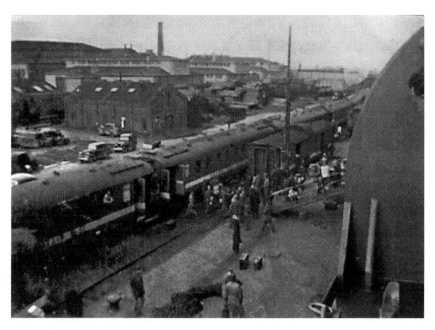

Arrival in Bremerhaven on the SS *Marine Jumper*—March 23, 1947.

Once in the North Sea, having passed Amsterdam and having come closer to Bremerhaven, our port of disembarkation, the ship was forced to slow down, as it had to cut its way through thick sheets of ice that had formed in the Weser River during what had been the coldest winter there on record. It matched the reception we were given and the feelings we had when we finally docked. It was March 23, 1947.

We had been at sea a full thirty-six days, and although it felt good being on land again, it was definitely not how we remembered it. It was a dramatic contrast with the receptions we had received on previous arrivals before World War II. Now, ten years after the last time we had docked in Germany, there were no banners, no streamers, no bands playing music, no family, nothing. All that awaited us was a third-class train that was to take us to an internment camp in Ludwigsburg. To make matters worse, it was a gray, cold, dismal day and the surrounding area was totally destroyed, just as it had been in Japan.

Part Three

HALLO, GERMANY

*W*e had prepared to be ready early, so when it came time to disembark, we were among the first to leave the ship. At the bottom of the gangplank, we were told to go directly to the first waiting train with our bags. By arriving at the train early, we were able to find five seats together in the same railroad car and were able to choose exactly where we wanted to sit. After we had placed our bags on the racks above, we settled down on the hard wooden benches and waited for the rest of the passengers to make their way down the gangplank to enter the train.

When everyone was aboard, the train took off, winding its way slowly out of the station from beside the dock. All we knew was that it was going to be an all-day train ride lasting well into the evening. By the time we pulled out of the station, we were wide-awake, anxious to see what the countryside looked like.

The last time we had visited Germany, my brothers and I were only six, four, and one—too young to have been able to remember much of anything. This, despite the fact that our parents had told us a great deal about our families during the years we had spent time together in Japan. Each described in great detail the various cities and the countryside in which they and their parents had lived, but we were not able to visualize much of what they told us. None of us was prepared for the many scenes of complete destruction and devastation we passed—just like in postwar Japan—and we were shocked at the amount of rubble, twisted steel, and shattered glass we saw strewn about along the way, especially in the Ruhr and the larger cities such as Frankfurt. It had become a wasteland. At most of the railroad stations we saw injured and disabled men, some without arms or legs, which they had lost during battle or bombings. We saw little children begging for food. It was a scene of horror. My parents, who had known Germany in its prewar days, were devastated to see all that their country had become since they had been there last.

As the train rolled into the Ludwigsburg station, an announcement was made that we were to get off and go to a camp close by. We were told first to stow our belongings in a locker at the train station, as there would not be enough room at the camp to store everyone's luggage.

The camp in the small town of Ludwigsburg was located just outside the southern city of Stuttgart. It had been a German prisoner-of-war camp during the war and simply changed hands when the war ended. It was now a *Stalag 17*–type prison camp run by the American occupation in the American Zone. We stowed our bags in a locker at the train station, and when we arrived at the camp we found that it was segregated. This meant that my mother, Alexander, and I were sent to a section for women and children and my father and Enno were sent to another section, for men and boys. The last time I saw my father before we were separated, which by then was evening, he was being handed sheets and sheets of paper—a very long, extensive questionnaire he had to fill out and sign.

Meanwhile, the three of us were shown our cots and given a few skimpy blankets that didn't look as if they could keep us warm. Luckily, our cots were right next to one another, so we could tuck in side by side. The winter of 1946–47 in Europe was the harshest on record, and the shortage of coal made it almost unbearable. Not for the first time, we wore everything we owned. Early in the evening, after a meager dinner consisting of a watered-down potato soup, we fell onto our cots exhausted from our long day, having been up most of the night before. I had a hard time falling asleep, however. The bleak and depressing countryside was still fresh and vivid in my mind.

The following morning, we ventured out to familiarize ourselves with the surroundings and to look for breakfast. Once again, this consisted of a watered-down potato soup. To our shock and amazement, we saw that the camp was surrounded by barbed wire, and at each of the four corners high above the ground were square towers in which MPs stood guard with rifles. They were a far cry from the friendly and generous MPs of the 209th MP station in Yokohama. But back there, we had been rescued by them; here, we were guarded by them. We could only sit around and wait.

After yet another cup of watered-down potato soup, my mother told us we had been released and were going to go immediately to Stuttgart. She wanted to get in touch with her and my father's families to let them know where they could find us. My father had not yet finished filling out the copious amounts of de-Nazification papers required of him, so he and Enno had to spend another night at the camp before he could be cleared and released.

That afternoon, we walked to the train station in Ludwigsburg. When we went to our lockers to pick up our bags, we found one of them had been pried open and the contents stolen. It was another blow, because much of what had been left of our personal belongings was now also gone. Needless to say, my mother was deeply upset. She immediately reported the theft to the stationmaster, who very politely apologized but said there was little else he could do about it.

Stuttgart, the sixth-largest city in Germany, was roughly nine miles (sixteen kilometers) south of Ludwigsburg. It took us just twenty minutes by train from Ludwigsburg. I never found out how my mother was able to pay for our tickets. Even before leaving Japan, we had been made to surrender all our remaining currency. It had all been confiscated, and we had not yet been reimbursed with any Reichsmarks. In effect, we were penniless. From the train station my mother took us directly to the famous Hotel Graf Zeppelin, from which she had planned to call her parents and siblings in Hamburg, as well as my father's family, who had fled the Russians and landed in Bavaria.

On our way to the hotel, we found ourselves horribly distraught as we walked along the rubble-strewn streets, seeing how badly the once-beautiful city had been destroyed. It was also heartbreaking to see how many war-wounded men were bravely going about their business. The utter devastation was so complete and surreal that we could never have imagined it without seeing it with our own eyes.

Suddenly, to our great surprise and joy, we ran into Captain Gross. He was just leaving the hotel as we were arriving and stopped to say hello. After exchanging a few pleasantries, he asked my mother how she was doing. She told him quite well, considering that we were flat-out broke because we had not yet been issued any local currency in exchange for the Japanese yen that had been taken from us in Yokohama. Visibly embarrassed that we had been left penniless, he proceeded to take out his wallet and hand my mother 300 reichsmarks, saying he was very sorry but hoped that would tide us over until we were reunited with my father and our Japanese yen were exchanged. We were deeply touched. Here was an American captain of Jewish origin whose country had been at war with Germany for the past four years, and yet he could still be kind to the three of us, who were of German origin. We thanked him profusely and thought how magnanimous it was of him to have been so generous and kind.

The concierge at the hotel told us we would be able to find refuge in a local Red Cross shelter. That meant that my mother was able to call the various family members and tell them where we would be staying for a night or two until my father and Enno could join us. She was also able to find a kind waiter at the hotel restaurant who, when he heard where we had just come from and what we had gone through, gave us something to eat, despite the fact that we did not have ration tickets. When my mother inquired where we could get the tickets, he told us we would have to be issued ID cards and would need to register at the place of our residence first. This presented a momentary problem, because we had not yet established where our residence would be and were not likely to know until we had been in touch with the rest of the family.

We devoured the food the waiter gave us, thrilled to have solid food to eat. The next stop we made was at the Red Cross. Once again, we were badly shaken at the sight of the many men we passed who had lost legs, arms, or both and had not yet been able to get prostheses. Turning the corner into the next street, we saw something we deemed highly unusual. There, in front of long planks of wood, sat a row of women, all with hammers in hand, chipping cement off perfectly good bricks and throwing the cleaned bricks on a pile. They proceeded to take another cement-caked brick off the pile of rubble, knock off its cement, and throw it on the cleaned pile. That procedure went on throughout the day in almost every city, and it was thanks to the many *Trümmerfrauen* ("rubble women"), as they were known, that the rebuilding of Germany had slowly begun.

On our way to the Red Cross, my body started to ache, and suddenly I felt hot and fatigued. When we arrived at the Red Cross building, we were shown the three beds that had been assigned to us halfway down a giant hall. The hall was filled with just two rows of beds, each row lined up against a long wall on either side of the entrance. At the other end of the room there was an exit door. When we saw those rows and rows of beds, we prayed we'd only have to stay one night.

By now I knew something was very wrong, as all my muscles were aching and I fell into my bed in a pool of perspiration. My mother took my temperature, which, much to her dismay, was 104 degrees.

She gave me an aspirin, and I must have fallen into a deep sleep immediately, because the next thing I remembered I was waking up to muffled voices. Squinting through half-closed eyes, trying to see what was going on, it looked like there was a tall man standing between my mother's and my bed. I thought I recognized the man as my mother's younger brother, Hans Waldemar, known as Hanni. I found out later he had come for us in the middle of the night. Not wanting to take me out in the cold night air because of my high temperature, my mother thought we should wait until daylight to leave. She asked my uncle to meet us the next morning, being certain that by then my father and Enno would have been released and be on their way to the Red Cross to join us.

By morning I was feeling a bit better. My temperature had come down considerably, so my mother bundled me up and we went outside to meet my uncle. A short while later my father and Enno appeared. My father had been fully de-Nazified, a process that had been put in place by the Allied occupation to ferret out any hidden Nazi criminals. He had been cleared and released. He told us of having met Crown Prince Wilhelm August of Germany, who was in the camp hospital. He was the eldest son of the late Kaiser Wilhelm II of Germany and a great-grandson of Queen Victoria.

Meanwhile, my uncle Hanni had come to pick us up in his car to drive us to my father's family, all of whom had fled the Russians in January 1945. They had left behind their intact, furnished estates in Silesia and had relocated to Murnau by the Staffelsee. This was a small Alpine village in Bavaria near Garmisch-Partenkirchen, the home of the 1936 Winter Olympics, where one of my father's sisters had moved to before the war.

We piled into the car and were off mid-morning on our three-hour drive south to Bavaria. My brothers and I sat in the back, and at our urging, our parents began giving us detailed descriptions of the relatives we could expect to meet and how they were related to us, as now we were curious to know more about our next stop. We were instructed to watch what we said and not to be too jolly, because there was no telling what these people had been through. Our father reminded us that his family had been through a great deal of trauma, that his brother and sister had been killed, so that we should be sensitive to a reunion.

With great anticipation, we arrived at a typical Bavarian house with its slanted roof, white stucco exterior, balconies, brown wooden shutters, and flower boxes that adorned many of the windows. It was located just outside Murnau, a charming village south of Munich at the foot of the Bavarian Alps, where Gabriele Münter and Wassily Kandinsky had gone to paint in the summers of 1909 to 1914. It was, and still is, a beautiful area and a great source of inspiration to innumerable artists.

A decade had gone by since we had last seen our relatives from Silesia, and now we were about to have a bittersweet reunion. Greeting us with open arms was our grandfather, the doctor and professor. Having heard stories of the approaching Russian troops' brutality two years earlier, at age seventy-three, he had fled his home in Breslau just before the Russians came to occupy the city. He'd had no other choice but to leave and move to his home in Hirschberg. This meant leaving behind his large practice and all that he had worked for and built up during his life there. Staying was just not an option.

He had been driven by his youngest daughter, Irmgard, to Wolfshau, near Hirschberg, his summer home. Irmgard was known in the family as Irmchen. At age twenty-six, she had taken over the running of my grandfather's household after he had lost his wife, our grandmother, twelve years earlier. Irmchen also took to driving him after his White Russian chauffeur, Rufin, was drafted into the army. One day, she had to go to Dresden on personal business and tragically did not make it

My grandfather Professor Dr. Wilhelm Ercklentz.

back. The officer who was driving the bus in which she was a passenger failed to notice a red light at dusk, which had signaled him to stop at a German roadblock. When he didn't stop, his car was shot at and a bullet hit Irmchen, who was the only passenger standing, killing her instantly.

My grandfather, upon receiving this shattering news, had no alternative but to drive to Dresden to pick up his deceased daughter and bring her home. Having heard this, a close friend of the family asked one of the men working on her estate to accompany my grandfather so he would not have to make the very sad and long trip alone. Upon their return home, Irmchen was given a funeral and buried a few days later. This was another devastating blow and was a difficult time for the entire family.

Shortly thereafter, my grandfather drove his little Fiat roughly 385 miles (620 kilometers) to Murnau in Bavaria—despite bombers overhead and American, French, and English troops approaching—to stay in the home he had bought for his daughter Gabriele, who was living

My father's youngest sister,
Irmgard Ercklentz.

there with her husband Paul Meyer-Spee. Paul was an artist from the
Black Forest before the war, and met Gabriele while he was in Breslau
restoring the Dom there. They had married and moved to Murnau
during the war, where my grandfather had built a house for them and
where they had spent the war years with their young son, Michael. In
Murnau, my grandfather established a new practice. He was still going
relatively strong for his age, despite having suffered catastrophic losses.
He was an indomitable man. Not only had he recently lost his beloved
youngest daughter, but a year earlier he had also lost his youngest son,
Hima, who was killed in a bombing raid while racing down the hall
leading to the stairs to the basement of his office building in Frankfurt.
The devastating explosion catapulted him through a shattered corner
window and onto the street below.

Then we met Wilma, my father's second-oldest sister, and her
husband and six children, who lived on an estate just southwest of
Breslau called Schmolzhof. In January 1945, the children had said a

My father's youngest brother, Hima.

tearful good-bye to their mother, who was pregnant and had to leave for a nearby hospital to give birth. Several days later, though—because Russian troops were rapidly approaching—the hospital was evacuated and everyone was moved to a Red Cross train. At Görlitz, Wilma left the train, which had no heat or food. She was a long distance west of Breslau, so local friends and relatives managed to find her a room in the basement of a hospital there. Shortly thereafter, her youngest daughter, Christina, was born.

On January 26, 1945, the five other children—after having closed up and locked their estate and taken only the most necessary items, such as their duvets and warm clothing—left all their possessions, thinking they would be back in a fortnight. They fled from the invading Russians in their horse and carriage. The only adult with them was Wilma's sister-in-law, Adele, who had left her villa nearby with her nephew and foster son to be with Wilma's children. Their idea was to trek west.

Traveling slowly through ice and snow, in brutally cold temperatures, they were forced to change plans. Because the four older girls

were walking alongside the carriage on foot, the large group was unable to go very far each day. The decision, therefore, was not to try
to go all the way to Bavaria, but to stop at our grandfather's house
near Hirschberg first—in the town that was known as Wolfshau—
believing they could get a good meal there and sleep in warm beds.
Their father was unable to be with their mother or his many children,
because he had been drafted into the army. Luckily, he was not fighting on the Russian front. In fact, he was stationed in the vicinity as a
supply officer. He had been informed of his wife's trek and her where-
abouts by his brother, who had connections and access to a working
telephone. To his children's great surprise, he appeared on February 1,
bringing with him some of the food supplies he was helping transport
to the west, but sadly he had to leave them four days later to return to
his post.

It took Adele and the children fifteen long days to reach Hirschberg from Breslau. The icy roads, snow, hail, and freezing temperatures made it difficult for the children and the horses to move quickly.
Normally, the journey would have taken roughly two and a half hours
by car, at the most, but since they were on foot they needed to make a
number of stops to try to warm themselves and find something to eat.
They also needed to sleep wherever they could find shelter. It had been
one of the cruelest winters on record.

Once at Wolfshau, the children remained with Adele for the next
two months, during which time their mother, my aunt Wilma, arrived
with their newest sibling. They were overjoyed at having another sister but were even happier when they learned that our grandfather
had found room for them all on a railroad car that was hitched to a
Red Cross train going west. He wanted to be sure they would arrive
safely in Murnau with his new granddaughter. The thought of no longer having to walk great distances was an immense relief to them all.
Nevertheless, a trip that would normally have taken eight hours by

car ended up taking them six very cold, challenging, and exhausting days.

It was also a frightening trip, as it turned out the train was not as safe as everyone had hoped, and almost from the beginning they were under attack by low-flying Russian fighter planes. This, despite the fact that the train cars were clearly marked with a Red Cross symbol on their roofs, which was the international sign they were not to be strafed or bombed. Once past the Ore Mountains, closer to Nuremberg, out of nowhere came more low-flying fighter planes—British, this time—and once again they started strafing the train, forcing it to stop. The seven older children, the baby, and the two women had to crawl underneath their beds and lie there until the planes flew off again. It was so cold that they were shivering, terrified they might not survive the attack and praying no one would be killed.

We were also reunited with my aunt Gabriele. And, of course, there was the indispensable Adele, along with her nephew and foster son, whom we'd never met before. At this already full and crowded house, the five of us arrived—fortunately for them, with very little luggage—to spend a few weeks together and to catch up on the past decade.

We spent most of the days talking, walking, and getting to know the seven cousins whom we'd never met before, as well as the two sets of aunts and uncles we didn't really remember. We took turns telling each other what we'd been doing in the past decade, but most important were the elaborate tales we told one another of our more recent war experiences, of which there were many. Hanging over all of these exchanges was the knowledge that we, and especially my grandfather, had suffered the painful loss of two young family members: Hima and Irmchen.

It was a very strange feeling: in the US and Japan, we had friends but no family to speak of; now we were surrounded by family but had

My parents with my father's sister Gabriele and husband, Paul Meyer-
Speer, and my cousin Angela von Wallenberg in Bavaria, 1947.

no friends in the area. As typical teenagers, we spent a lot of time with
our newfound cousins, roaming around the area looking for things to
do and ways to entertain ourselves as best we could. We went for walks,
picked flowers, and found many different types of wild mushrooms in
the woods, which we brought home to our families. Fortunately, we
had been taught to distinguish between the edible and the poisonous
kinds. We also picked dandelions. Then one of the designated chefs of
the day would puree them, much like a puree of spinach, which actually was quite good and nutritious. Other times we would play games.
We learned to amuse ourselves with very little. Our parents, aunts, and
uncles, providing for a family of twenty-one, struggled to find enough
food and ration tickets necessary to purchase meat, breads, eggs, and
butter.

On one occasion, between chores, my mother took some time to
give herself a manicure and pedicure. This caused quite a stir, because

none of our relatives had ever seen anyone paint their toenails red before. It only reinforced how different we had become from our German families since living in New York, never mind the long years in Japan.

One of Wilma's five daughters, my cousin Angela, was nine months older than I, so we spent more time together than we did with the others. At age fourteen, she and I loved spending hours in front of a mirror primping, for lack of anything else to do. Having seen Rita Hayworth in the movie *Gilda* in Tokyo, I would sometimes put on a show for Angela. I'd start by throwing my head forward, letting my hair fall over the right side of my face just as Gilda had done. I thought it was a most seductive move, and then I started singing "Put the Blame on Mame," taking off imaginary gloves and throwing them her way, just like in the film. She was a great audience and frequently egged me on to perform some more. Other times, we went swimming in the Staffelsee—a pretty, serene lake in Murnau. It was one of the warmest lakes in Bavaria, and sometimes a friend of our cousins, Gerhard von Selzam, dropped by in his rowboat to pick us up. His grandparents owned Wörth Island in the middle of the lake, so we had permission to go swimming on the banks of their property.

Because Murnau was in the American sector of Germany, Angela's oldest sister, Adi, took a job as a secretary at the American Murnauer Barracks. Often, she brought home food from the canteen that otherwise would have been tossed out. She also brought home cartons of cigarettes, which were akin to owning gold, as one could purchase just about anything with them. It was by far the best currency—better even than reichsmarks. Alexander, then eleven years old, was a great kid and very creative. Just as he had done in Japan, he loved to spend time with the soldiers at their barracks, and he, too, brought home food they gave him. Wilma and her husband, Gotthard—who had safely returned from the war zone in the east by then—had in the meantime acquired a cow and horse. The cow was useful, as it provided us with milk. My cousins used the horse to ride into town—without the benefit of a saddle—to go shopping. The horse could also pull a cart and take our grandfather to town or to his office there.

Having lived in the house with three generations for a little more than three weeks, my parents knew it was time for us to move on and start our trek north to Hamburg to be reunited with our maternal grandparents. A final reunion was arranged with the remaining members of the family. A date was picked, and everyone was asked to bring something to the party. In addition to the twenty members who were living in the house in Murnau, our father's oldest brother, Bernhard, was also invited. He, like his father, was a professor of internal medicine and had likewise been forced to leave his practice in Breslau. He had set up his new office in Mittenwald, a town approximately twenty-five miles from Murnau, south of Garmisch-Partenkirchen. Although divorced from his wife, he lived there with his companion and on occasion with his two daughters.

My father's oldest sister, Hildegard, along with her husband, son, and daughter, were expected as well. They came from Pürgen, a town where they had settled after the Russians drove them out of their home in Silesia. It was approximately thirty-one miles north of Murnau, so not too far a distance to go by train. That brought the total number of family members to twenty-eight. It was a bittersweet reunion. After having survived the worst, most destructive, costly, and terrible war in the history of mankind, there was much joy that day, as we celebrated our family's being reunited once again. But we did not forget those who did not survive. For them we had a moment of silence and prayer.

After many tearful good-byes with promises to keep in close touch, the five of us departed on foot down to the station in Murnau and boarded a train bound for Munich. The hour-and-a-half ride was a

The 1947 family reunion in Murnau.

My mother, Heinz and Hildegard Staroste, my father,
Michaela Staroste, and Enno.

lot more scenic than our train ride to Stuttgart had been the previous month. It was good to see the countryside awakening from that harshest of winters. Once we arrived at the station in Munich, my father went to buy our tickets to Hamburg, as we had to change to a train that would take us there directly. The trip was going to take the better part of the day, only this time it was not under the auspices of the Allies. That meant we had to stop at the border between the American Zone and the British Zone and get off the train with our bags to have them searched. Only then were we permitted to board again. This procedure had to be followed on every train traveling between all four zones—the American, the British, the French, and the Russian—into which Germany had been divided. Fortunately, our route only required one such stop.

Upon our arrival at the *Hauptbahnhof* in Hamburg, we were met by the same Uncle Hanni who had met us late that night at the Red Cross in Stuttgart the previous month. He took us to a small hotel around the corner from my grandparents' house on the Oderfelder Strasse. They were not currently living there because their house had been taken over by the British and made into an officers' club. Instead, they had both gone to live at their hunting lodge in the country, to which we were headed the next morning. Naturally, we were curious and asked our parents if we could take a walk around the neighborhood. Because it was already dusk, they suggested we wait until the morning. They did not want us to run the risk of being kidnapped, raped, or murdered by the criminals who were said to be lurking inside the many ruins, waiting to pounce on unsuspecting women and children.

In the evening, Hanni took us to dinner and shared his ration tickets with us so we could have a piece of meat. He told us he had already applied for ration tickets for all of us in Wentorf, the village in which we were going to live with our maternal grandparents until we could return to America.

My maternal grandparents' townhouse, on the Oderfelder
Strasse in Hamburg, which miraculously survived the
bombing.

The following morning everyone was up early. We ate a meager
breakfast, after which my mother took my brothers and me for a
stroll around the neighborhood. She made a point of passing by our
grandparents' townhouse, where my mother had grown up after her
family returned from Kiel. From pictures we'd seen, it didn't really
look as if it had changed much. The ivy still covered the front of the
house like a thick, green, fluffy blanket. It was quite obvious from
the unkempt state of the garden that the British officers who were

housed there were less interested in tending roses than my grand-mother had been.

When we returned to the hotel, my father was already waiting for us to start on the last leg of our trip, to our temporary home away from home with our grandparents. We boarded an elevated train at the Klosterstern station around the corner from our hotel. This took us out to Grosshansdorf, at the end of the line. The one taxi from Wentorf—operated by a man named Rayze—had broken down and was therefore not available to meet us. That left us no other choice but to walk the last ten miles. It was the longest distance any of us had ever walked, but fortunately, almost four hours later, as we were coming up to the home stretch, we saw Rayze coming toward us in the distance, driving the repaired taxi. It was just in the nick of time, because by then we were all so exhausted, we were ready to collapse. By the time we rolled into the driveway of the hunting lodge, we had regained our

My maternal grandparents' hunting lodge, the *Jagdhaus*, in Wentorf.

composure and were in much better shape to greet our grandparents, whom we children barely remembered after our ten-year absence.

It was an emotional, joyful, and exciting reunion, particularly for our mother, who had not seen her parents in almost nine years. The last time they had all been together had been in Hamburg, when my parents had stopped by after they had been to Berlin and were on their way home to New York. It was on that trip to Berlin—on the night of November 9, 1938—that they had witnessed firsthand the horrors of the SS and their actions against the Jews during what is widely remembered as Kristallnacht, the night of broken glass. They had heard that all across Germany synagogues went up in flames, shops were looted, businesses were ransacked, and Jews were incarcerated. In the streets of Berlin, my mother watched the windows of a jewelry store being smashed. She confronted the thugs, telling them to stop being such vandals, only to be shouted at that if she didn't like it she should leave Germany. She told us she and our father had gone back to the hotel after the extremely upsetting incident for "a double Cognac." The episode they had witnessed in the streets was an early warning of what would eventually turn into one of the worst horrors of the twentieth century, the extent of which we had first learned about from Captain Gross on the *Marine Jumper*. It was also the last time our parents had been to Germany until now.

My grandmother had arranged a hearty welcome-home luncheon with delicious venison that my grandfather had shot in the fall and that she in turn had preserved in glass jars in order to have meat for the winter months. With it she served a very tasty red cabbage and mashed potatoes, topping the meal off with a delicious red berry pudding served with vanilla sauce, known as *Rote Grütze*, which is a popular north German dessert. It was the best home-cooked meal we'd had in more than five years, and we felt spoiled and happily satisfied.

It had already been quite a day, and during lunch we covered so much territory that the meal had gone late into the afternoon. When we got up to go upstairs and unpack the little we had brought, our grandmother stopped us in our tracks, saying, "Children, never go out empty-handed," whereupon we each picked up some of the used dishes and glasses and brought them into the kitchen.

My grandparents' hunting lodge consisted of a living room, dining room, veranda, sitting room, three guest bedrooms, a bathroom, plus a powder room on the ground floor and three bedrooms and a bathroom on the second floor. By the time we arrived, the part of the hunting lodge that was left to my grandparents was the downstairs living room, dining room, and veranda, plus the master bedroom and one guest room on the second floor, which they were permitted to keep for their youngest son—my mother's younger brother, Hanni. The kitchen, however, had to be shared. The rest of the rooms were occupied by four families, all refugees from the northeastern part of Germany, who had fled the Russians in 1945.

It was required by law that each house owner give lodging to refugees, if there were spare rooms in the house. By today's standards, it would be hard to imagine how this arrangement would work, but work it did, albeit with everyone pulling together and being considerate of one another. Before we arrived, the house had been divided up and my grandparents were left with the allotted five of their ten rooms. An elderly couple was moved into the third bedroom upstairs, their daughter with her son was assigned one of the guest rooms on the ground floor, a woman with her daughter moved into the sitting room off the front hall, and a woman with two children occupied the second of the three guest rooms. Half of the third guest room had been turned into a bathroom and the other half into a kitchen for the two families who were assigned the sitting room and guest room downstairs. As it ended up, two families shared the facilities in one part of the house and now, with us in residence, four families shared our kitchen and bathrooms.

Initially, my parents took over Hanni's room, as he was living in Hamburg and traveling a lot; Enno slept on a wicker chaise on the veranda; Alexander and I slept on the floor in the square upstairs hall leading to the three bedrooms and bathroom. This meant that each evening the two of us had to make up our beds, and each morning the elderly couple had to pass by us on the way downstairs to the kitchen. Since they were early risers, they had asked whether they could be the first to use the kitchen.

There was very little to unpack—a far cry from the forty bags with which we had started out in 1941—so my mother suggested we all go for a nice long walk. She wanted to show us the little village where we could do our shopping. There was also time for her to show us the woods where our grandfather went to stalk deer as early as 4:30 or 5:00 in the morning. When we returned, it was still light enough for us to go into the garden to see where my grandparents grew much of the food they lived on, such as potatoes, turnips, tomatoes, lettuce, cucumbers, and squash. They also had mature apple, pear, and cherry trees and had planted raspberries, strawberries, red currants, and gooseberries, most of which my grandmother made into fruit compotes and jellies or jams. She had learned to can them in glass jars and then hermetically seal them with a rubber ring. My grandparents' great pride and joy, though, was their flower garden, where they grew the most beautiful roses, lilies, peonies, zinnias, foxgloves, and tulips. They had arranged the planting in such a way that almost all spring, summer, and fall one or another flower or shrub would be blooming.

When we returned to the house, my grandmother had already set the table in the dining corner of the living room. On a little cart she had all sorts of cold cuts, an assortment of wonderful black breads, and margarine made from a plant, called *die Feine Sanella*, a bland, ersatz butter. She also had leftover pudding from lunch. When she saw that we had come in, she called to us to wash our hands and come to dinner.

If we didn't always come right away, she was in the habit of calling out "*Ich sitzte*"—"I'm sitting"—which meant we were expected to appear immediately.

By now it was almost the end of April. Springtime was known to be erratic in that part of Germany, but we were lucky because a few days after we arrived, the weather turned sunny and quite a bit warmer. Aside from being able to look out their veranda windows and see the woods in the distance—forests my grandfather had leased for ninety-nine years from the district of Lauenburg for his hunts—we could also see vast acres of farmland. There were farms and farmers all around us. My grandparents had befriended a good number of them and could therefore buy homemade sausages and other foods from them.

Once we had settled in and become more familiar with our new surroundings, my grandmother began to take us shopping either on foot or on the bicycles we had found in the potting shed. We even found a tandem, with which we ended up having hours of fun. As my grandmother introduced me to the local tradespeople, I also met some of their children and befriended those who were closer to my age or to the ages of Enno and Alexander. They began to include us in their activities after they were reassured that we Amis (slang for Americans) could be trusted.

May turned out to be a beautiful month, with the trees and plants throwing out buds once again, turning the entire landscape into a sea of luscious hues of green. It was a welcome, rather mild month, after the cold and wet days of winter, and there was little rain. The freshness of spring was conducive to our spending more time outdoors. As the days grew longer, we had more time to take our bicycles or the tandem out to explore the surrounding area and the neighboring villages.

The two tradespeople who had become most important and very much in demand in our lives were the local tailor and one of the refugee ladies occupying a guest room who was a seamstress. Enno, Alexander, and I were rapidly growing out of our clothes, forcing us to become creative with hand-me-downs. Some of Enno's clothes were too big for Alexander and me and had to be taken in, and some of ours had become too small for us and had to be let out. If none of that worked, we became creative and made one dress or suit from two of the outgrown ones. This was mainly because there was still very little in the way of clothes or fabric to be had on the market. Showing great foresight, the tailor had bought up quite a variety of quality materials before the war, fearing there might be a shortage one day. Now he was able to sell us some of that fabric—of which he had a nice supply from which we could choose—and would cut and sew the material into a needed garment. Fortunately, my parents both still had their German bank accounts, into which they'd been making deposits before the war in order to have local currency for our annual summer vacations. These were now a source of cash with which we could pay the tradespeople.

I often sat and watched the seamstress, Frau Wichman, who came over to our part of the house at least once a week to alter or sew a new dress, skirt, or slacks for my brothers and me. She was a woman in her early sixties who had lost her husband in the war and had fled with her parents and her one son from eastern Germany, landing at my grandparents' doorstep. As a young girl, she'd had an accident that had left her with a permanent limp—one of the reasons she had chosen a sedentary profession. It was more comfortable for her to sit and sew. She wore glasses when she needed to sew close up, and when she wanted to see if I was following what she had taught me. When she saw that I had mastered the simplest of stitches she had me sew a seam or hem a dress. After a while, I became her helper and would work with her for hours. My mother sometimes gave her a dress she no longer wore, and Frau Wichman would redesign it and make it into something more suitable for a teenager. It was lots of fun, seeing something I had worked on come together into a pretty new dress, and it inspired me to take a sewing class in the neighboring village.

The tailor had a daughter, Lisa, with whom I had become friendly, but because she worked as a farmhand nearby, I really was only able to see her on weekends. On Saturday nights, the local pub occasionally held a dance. My brothers and I and some of Lisa's friends from the village would go to the pub and dance to what is best described as northern German country. Everywhere we went, we went by foot or on our bicycles, which was wonderful in the spring, summer, and fall. It was less pleasant in winter.

Having been a city girl almost all my life, I was not at all familiar with farming. Because of this, I asked Lisa what her duties as a farmhand were. She told me her first job started at 5:00 in the morning, when she had to take the farmer's horse and carriage loaded with empty milk cans out to the fields where the cows were grazing. There she took out a small three-legged stool and a pail and started manually milking all the farmer's cows, of which there were quite a few. I asked why they were still milking the cows by hand, and she told me that was because so far the machines had not been perfected, and frequently blood would be found in the milk.

She told me she would gladly pick me up one morning, because she passed our house every day. Milking a cow seemed like a rather novel idea, so I said I'd give it a try. She said she would come by at 5:00 the next morning but would not knock on the door. Instead, she would just call out "Yoo-hoo" to signal that she was waiting outside our house on her wagon.

Sure enough, at 5:00 the next morning I heard the "Yoo-hoo" and immediately ran downstairs, opening the front door and quietly shutting it behind me so as not to wake anyone. The wagon she rode on was quite high, so it took a moment to climb up, but then Lisa gave her horse a swift snap of the whip and we were off in the early dawn, trotting over to the fields in which the cows were waiting anxiously to be relieved of their milk.

I watched as Lisa went about her job, and since it looked relatively easy, I asked her if she would let me have a turn milking one of the cows. She agreed but said I should realize the cows were sensitive to someone else's touch, especially the touch of a novice like me. She told me to take two of four udders, and hold one in each hand, then start alternately pulling down on one udder and then the other in a rhythmic motion. At the first pull, I was amazed at how difficult it was to get a stream of milk out of just one udder, let alone two. After several tries, I realized I didn't stand a chance of getting enough milk out of either and gave the stool and pail back to Lisa. She thought the whole thing terribly funny and laughed out loud, watching me struggle. That was the end of my milking career.

Another early morning activity was stalking deer. My grandfather would wake me up around 4:00 in the morning, when it was still dark. I'd jump out of bed, get dressed, and meet him downstairs. With his walking stick in hand, we would start out into the woods. It was one of my favorite activities, especially going with my grandfather. He was such a delightful, thoughtful, and interesting elderly gentleman, having traveled the world.

Entering the woods and walking deeper into the forest, I was amazed at how still it was. Except for an occasional call of a male cuckoo in the distance or the crow of a rooster from a nearby farm, everything was totally still. My grandfather would take me to one or the other of his favorite stands and we would climb up and sit there in total silence while waiting for a deer and her family to appear. From time to time, we would also see a stag or hear the rustle of leaves when a pheasant flew through the trees overhead. Although he had also shot wild boar in his day, I never got a chance to see one, nor did I see any wild rabbits or hare.

After a long while and several deer sightings, he would motion to

My grandmother with my grandfather upon his
return from a shoot.

me to follow him, and down we'd climb from our perch, walking back
home in silence, arriving just in time for breakfast, both quite hungry and looking forward to a hearty meal. It was fun sitting down for
breakfast on the veranda where my grandmother had already set the
table the night before. She would put out a basket of assorted breads
and some soft-boiled eggs, covered with little quilted hats to keep them
warm. It was always a thoroughly enjoyable time, as my grandfather
had so many fascinating stories to tell about his many far-flung travels.

Having spent most weekends in their hunting lodge since long
before the war, my grandparents were known to everyone in the village.

It was one of the reasons we had milk and eggs and even occasionally some butter. The farmers frequently brought food over to them, especially when they had baked muffins or rolls. If they had extra eggs or milk left over after having sent the mandatory amount to the market, we were sure to be the beneficiaries.

When my grandmother wasn't shopping or organizing her now-enlarged household, she was in her garden tending to her flowers, vegetables, and fruit trees, all of which she had planted with my grandfather. The only time I ever found her relaxing and sitting down was after dinner when the dishes had been done and she was finally finished with all her household chores. Many times I found her playing solitaire in the evening, and since she'd taught me how to play canasta, a popular game in those days, I sometimes challenged her to a game. She was quite the competitor, and when I mentioned this to her, she said I should have seen her on the tennis court in her youth, when she would slam the ball into her opponent's side of the court so hard the ball would seldom

The planted garden.

come back. With that she'd demonstrate with her still-powerful right arm, an imaginary racquet in her hand.

During this comparatively idyllic time, my father had begun to show overt signs of frustration. "Enough is enough," he said, more than once. He took his family responsibilities seriously. He had done everything he could for all these years, to be met at every turn with setbacks and enforced idleness and isolation. Six long years he had been in professional limbo. Though he had managed to provide perfectly well for us under the circumstances, he could no longer tolerate living like the refugees with whom we shared the hunting lodge. He wanted to get a move on, and soon.

At the end of the summer of 1947, my father started the process of applying for reentry permits for himself, my mother, and me, wanting to return to America as soon as possible. He had never been happy living in Germany, and he couldn't wait to get back to rebuilding his life in New York City, which he loved more than anything in the world. In doing so, he discovered it would be far better if he were to live in the American Zone, nearer the authorities who could help him with the US Department of Immigration. Since we were living in the British Zone, and the trip to Frankfurt in the American Zone would take at least four hours each way, he decided that a commute was out of the question. It would have been too time-consuming and costly. Instead, he decided to move to Frankfurt with Enno to establish a residence there and try to find a job with an American company. Enno, at age sixteen and holding an American passport, was not only able to get a job as an American civilian, but it also gave him access to the army PX. This was a godsend, because it allowed him to buy coffee and cigarettes—which were like gold on the black market—as well as sugar and all sorts of canned goods and candy. Meanwhile, my father found a job with the Coca-Cola Company in Frankfurt. Between the two of them, they were making a tidy income.

✦ ✦ ✦

In Frankfurt, my father soon found a room with connecting bathroom in a building in the middle of the city. His landlady—noticing that my father and Enno did not yet have ration tickets—told them where to register to become eligible. Seeing that Enno was wearing a US Army civilian uniform, she also told him that if Enno was able to buy cigarettes and coffee at the PX, he should do so, because, as she bluntly put it to him, "*Wer nicht schiebt wird geschoben*" (He who doesn't push will be pushed). What she meant by that was that if he didn't start bartering on the black market, he and Enno would surely starve, because the ration tickets were certainly not going to sustain him and his growing young son. Having access to the PX was what saved all of us from further hunger, as Enno could buy a whole carton of cigarettes for a dollar and then barter a single pack for almost anything we needed or wanted.

My mother, Alexander, and I meanwhile helped our grandparents prepare the garden for winter, harvested the fruit that was still left on the trees, and took in the vegetables that by now were ready to be picked. While Alexander helped my grandfather prune the trees and gather wood, some of which he had to chop, I helped my grandmother clean and cook the fruits and vegetables and prepare them to be preserved in sealed glass. From time to time my grandfather also took Alexander shooting. I once saw them bring home a deer, which the hunt master would then cut up for my grandmother to preserve.

The very gray days were beginning to get shorter, and even during the midday hours it was difficult to distinguish between land and sky. In that part of northern Germany the days were uniformly gray, cool, and frequently misty and foggy. It was a time of year I did not like at all, remembering the freezing weather in Karuizawa. It was, however, a time to enjoy sitting around the old-fashioned tile oven in the living room. In those days there was no central heating. Instead, each room had a *Kachelofen* (a tile oven) in which one built a fire in the early morning that kept on heating the room throughout the day with the addition, from time to time, of more wood or coal. It was during those days that I came to cherish our *gemütlich* (cozy) home away from home. It was a bucolic setting, conducive to reading and writing letters to my friends in New York, as well as to the wonderful nuns at Sacred Heart.

What a surprise it was, soon after, to receive "care packages" and letters from them, filled with all sorts of clothing for my brothers and me. Tucked among the clothes we found candy bars we hadn't seen in more than six years, and we were ecstatic about this. I was happy that my friends had not forgotten me after so much time had passed. Things were looking up, and life was beginning to improve.

When my father and Enno came home for the long weekend at Christmas, they brought with them two suitcases full of coffee, tea, cigarettes, sugar, chocolate, and canned goods, as well as soaps, all of which Enno had bought at the PX. They took the train from Frankfurt to Hamburg on December 24 and once again had to get off the train with their suitcases at the border town of Celle between the American and British Zones to show the British inspectors what they were bringing in with them. As usual, Enno was able to prove his US citizenship, and the inspectors were satisfied.

They arrived in Hamburg five hours later and found a taxi to take them to Wentorf, arriving just in time for our Christmas Eve dinner. After dinner, when all the dishes were done, I decided to surprise everyone with a cake and a few pies to present to them on Christmas morning. It was fun to finally have the ingredients necessary to bake. I finished a sponge cake I'd topped with a chocolate buttercream icing, and from the pantry I took out a glass jar of plums and one of cherries, which I'd helped my grandmother preserve, and proceeded to bake two delicious fruit pies—a plum and a cherry—and when all was done, I hid them in the pantry and went to bed. On Christmas morning, I had planned to present my cake and pies to my grandparents, who I thought would be delighted with my presents, but I thought better of it when I heard we'd have many family members coming for dinner.

On Christmas Day, we were invited for lunch by a cousin of my mother's, who lived in another village nearby, and in the evening Uncle Hanni arrived with more family from Hamburg. It was a happy and festive occasion—despite the still war-torn conditions in Germany—because we were so grateful to have survived the war and were able to celebrate Christmas together. There were still no presents that teen-agers might have enjoyed receiving, but our parents found a beautiful Irish setter for the three of us. We named her Diana—after the goddess of the hunt, for she was indeed a hunting dog. She was also associated with wild animals and woodlands, which my parents agreed was a most appropriate name for her in our hunting country. My grandmother gave

Diana, our beloved Irish setter.

us mementos from her and my grandfather's earlier trips to Asia and South America. My grandfather gave us watercolors he had painted on his many trips around the world. We loved receiving them, as they were beautiful works of art, and we have all cherished them to this day. In turn, I was pleased and proud to be able to present the cake and pies.

My grandmother had set the table beautifully, with a green table-cloth and a number of silver candlesticks she'd brought with her from the house in Hamburg. For the centerpiece she had nestled a pair of silver pheasants in branches of evergreens. Christmas music was playing in the background as we sat down to a superb dinner prepared by one of the women in town who was a chef extraordinaire. She had prepared an acorn squash soup for starters, which was followed by a roast of venison with red currant sauce, red cabbage, and mashed potatoes. For dessert we had my pies with *Schlagsahne* ("whipped cream") my mother had whipped up from cream bought from one of our neighboring farmers.

Friday, we celebrated the second day of Christmas—a holiday in most of Europe and known in England as Boxing Day—by visiting the local farmers, bringing them some of the coffee, sugar, and cigarettes that my father and Enno had brought from Frankfurt as Christmas presents. It was our way of saying thank you for their having shared their produce with us over the past year. They in turn were so thrilled and grateful that they promptly asked us back for *Kaffee und Kuchen* ("coffee and cake") on Sunday afternoon because, having received sugar from us, they would be able to bake some of their cakes and pies and serve them to us with a freshly brewed cup of coffee and the ever-present *Schlag*. My father and Enno had to take the train back to Frankfurt, but we were happy at the thought that they would be back the following Wednesday for the long New Year's weekend, laden with more delicious goodies from the PX.

The *Jagdhaus* after a snowfall.

The 1947–48 entry in my grandparents' guestbook,
underneath a watercolor by my grandfather depicting our
travels, at our first Christmas together again, after the war.

The winter was rather mild, but on occasion we awoke to a beautiful, crisp, white landscape.

It was during that long winter that I became restless. At almost fifteen, I missed my pals, and although I did write them a lot, it just wasn't the same. Sitting with the understanding seamstress did help, because I could tell her all my teenage troubles and she in turn would give me advice. She distracted me with her stories, and soon we'd either have finished or altered one of the dresses. I felt I had at least accomplished something. I often found myself being moody, particularly if my mother asked me to do something I didn't like doing. Without getting angry, she would say to me, "Hildegarde, this has to be done, so you might as well make it fun. Now you can either do it with a pleasant attitude"—because as a typical teenager I was not always pleasant—"or you can do it with an unpleasant attitude. It is your choice and your choice alone. I can assure you, though, you will feel a lot better about yourself if you do it with a pleasant attitude." I would know that she was serious, because Hildegarde was a name I was only called when I was in trouble.

In the spring of 1948, my father thought we would enjoy a change and invited us to visit him in Frankfurt for a few days. The afternoon we arrived, my father wanted to show us the city. The medieval center of the city had been totally destroyed, and between five and six thousand residents had been killed in the air-raid attacks, including our Uncle Hima. Even the historic Paulskirche had been razed. My father led us through the rubble to his office, and Enno showed us his, but he did not take us to the PX. In 1949, the city of Frankfurt-am-Main became a part of the State of Hesse. Later, the headquarters of the US high commissioner for Germany were moved there and stayed until 1952.

The sights were depressing beyond belief, and once again we

Alexander sitting on a Jeep with my mother and me by his side, amidst the rubble that was all over Frankfurt.

Enno in his civilian
US Army uniform.

thanked the Lord that we had been spared the direct bombings in both Japan and Germany.

That evening after dinner, my father told us that Rita Hayworth was expected at a US Army baseball game sponsored by the Coca-Cola Company, to which he had been able to get tickets for all of us. Having seen the movie *Gilda* in Japan and having loved it, I had become a great fan of Rita Hayworth and was excited to soon be seeing her in person. There was a great deal of commotion around her at the baseball game, but at one point I got up my courage and walked over to where she was sitting and asked her for her autograph. Without hesitation, she took out her pen and signed my autograph book. I was over the moon.

My mother, Alexander, and I were scheduled to return to Wentorf, but when my father informed us that he heard there was to be a currency reform in the next few weeks, he suggested we stay until he was certain it would take place. On Friday, June 18, 1948, after the banks had closed for the weekend, there came the announcement that the date for the currency reform was set to take place on Sunday, June 20. On that date, the reichsmark was to be legally replaced by the deutsche mark, which was to become the basic unit of the new currency. This meant that each person was going to initially be able to exchange RM 60 for DM 40, with the remaining RM 20 to be exchanged for DM 20, within the next sixty days. Smaller notes and coins remained in use, but at one-tenth of their value. However, this did not include the Russian Zone. Meanwhile, my father, as head of the family, had to report all monies he had in his possession, as they were to be converted later that year. Tax reforms were going to be initiated as soon as possible after the currency reform.

June 20, 1948, marked the turning point in the redevelopment of western Germany in the postwar period. Replacing the old reichsmark with the new stable deutsche mark had a major economic impact and was the cornerstone of the economic miracle that followed. Overnight, new goods appeared in shops, the widespread black market came to a halt, and once again there was an incentive to go out and earn money. The political and economic recovery of western Germany was on its way.

It was a new beginning, and everyone was looking to the future with renewed hope. People had confidence that the time had finally come to be able to think about rebuilding lives in a peaceful, economically stable, and encouraging atmosphere. My father was certainly encouraged by all that had transpired, and he began planning for our future with renewed vigor.

Once my father had found a source of income and was settled with Enno in Frankfurt, he turned his attention to Alexander and me. Neither of us had been to school since arriving in Germany a little more than a year earlier, a fact that caused him great concern. My mother didn't seem too disturbed that we'd missed a year of schooling. She felt we had already been to the equivalent of a trade and finishing school, because I had learned to sew, garden, bake, and help take care of a household. Alexander had also learned gardening as well as chopping wood, hunting, and being a general handyman. One day, while chopping wood for the fireplace, he accidentally chopped off his thumb, so my parents had to rush him to the hospital. My father almost fainted seeing his son's thumb hanging by just a thin sliver of skin, and the rest of us were horrified and felt sick at the sight. My mother, as usual, took charge and bandaged his hand and thumb to stop the bleeding. Fortunately for Alexander, the thumb could be re-attached, and after about forty-five minutes he was sewn up, bandaged, and ready to go home again.

Meanwhile, my father enrolled us in the not-inexpensive Schule Schloss Salem, near the *Bodensee*, known as Lake Constance, in Baden. This was the sister school of Gordonstoun, in Scotland. Both were founded by the distinguished and renowned pedagogue Dr. Kurt

Hahn. Neither Alexander nor I felt very enthusiastic about being sent away to a boarding school in a country in which we'd never lived and whose language we had not as yet mastered, but we had no choice. The schools in Wentorf would not have given us the education my father wanted us to have, and there was no space to come and live with him in the one-room flat in Frankfurt. He felt we would be much better off in the beautiful countryside of southern Germany. He also felt it would do us good to meet some German children, with whom we could spend time to improve our German. We still hated the idea, but we agreed to go after our parents promised to come and pick us up if two weeks into the semester we were still unhappy and hadn't adjusted.

On the day of our departure, after having said good-bye to our grandparents, my mother took Alexander and me, with suitcases in hand, to the Hamburg Hauptbahnhof, and off we three went.

On the train leaving for Schule Schloss Salem.

Alexander waiting for the train in Hamburg, 1948.

The train made a stop in Frankfurt, where our father joined us for the last leg of the trip. We easily found a taxi at the station to take us to our boarding school half an hour away. The driver, in a heavy southern German accent, asked whether we would like him to take the direct route to Salem, or the scenic one along Lake Constance via the famous rococo church, Birnau. We opted for the scenic route, stopping briefly in Birnau to see the interior of the beautiful pilgrimage church situated on a hill overlooking the lake. It had originally been built as a monastery for the Cistercian monks of Salem in the eighteenth century.

As we neared Salem, which is set in the most gorgeous hilly countryside, I had butterflies at the mere thought of being deposited in this strange but magnificent-looking *Schloss*. The taxi driver stopped a few hundred yards in front of the gatehouse and told us that from there we would have to continue by foot. On the way to the large baroque gatehouse, we stopped for a bite to eat at the Gasthof zum Schwanen—an inn on the Salem Castle grounds.

My father filled us in on more of the Salem School's history. He told us that Dr. Hahn, who was Jewish, publicly protested the rise of Hitler and the Nazi regime. Consequently, he was arrested and exiled to England in 1933, where he lived most of the rest of his life. In 1934, Dr. Hahn founded the renowned British Salem School, Gordonstoun, in an abandoned castle in Scotland and based it on his evolving educational principles. He later founded Outward Bound in 1941.

My father concluded his history lesson by saying that Kurt Hahn's credo was, "There is more in you than you think." He also believed that each student had more courage, strength, and compassion in him or her than he or she could possibly imagine, and he felt strongly that his students should learn this truth about themselves early on. It was Dr. Hahn's belief that each child is born with innate spiritual powers and the ability to make correct judgments about moral issues, which he believed a child lost because of the influence of what he called our "diseased society" and the impulses of adolescence. That philosophy was one of the many reasons my father had picked this school.

When we had finished lunch, my mother said it was getting late and we were expected at school shortly. Entering through the lower gatehouse, we came to the administration offices, where my father was asked to register us. He first filled out my papers and was told that I would be greeted momentarily by my roommate-to-be, who would show me to our room. Next, he took care of Alexander's papers. It was only then that he learned Alexander would be entering Schloss Kirchberg, an offshoot of Salem, where the lower school took their classes and had their dorms. It was just a few miles south of Salem, closer to the shore of Lake Constance. Alexander was to be taken to his room there by one of the seniors on duty. I quickly said good-bye to my parents and Alexander, and just then my roommate, Erika, came to greet me. As I turned around to wave good-bye one more time, I could see Alexander going off with one of the older boys and our parents waving good-bye as they hailed a taxi. My apprehension about the future was soon lightened when Erika assured me that I would find the school to be like no other and that the students were a welcoming and helpful lot.

I quickly learned that Erika, like me, had been born in Hamburg. She immediately made me feel at ease. We walked up a path past a long wing of the castle to the abbey and the entrance to the school wing beyond. Walking down the long corridor toward the main part of the school, Erika pointed out the various classrooms on the right and the courtyard, used for recess, on the left. At the end of the hall, we turned left and walked down another long hall, passing the music room and more administration offices on the right. Just beyond them there was a very wide staircase leading up to the boys' dormitories on the second floor and the girls' dormitories on the third floor. Erika motioned to me to follow her up the stairs to the second landing. The stairs, which were made of wood, were uneven and worn, showing signs of centuries of use. Turning left at the top of the second landing, we walked through large double doors that had glass windows on the upper half. They were the entrance to our long hall of dorms, all of which were situated on the left side. On the right side, there were windows that overlooked the courtyard and the abbey beyond. On the steeple's face, there was a large clock, which Erika said would help to keep me on time. Punctuality was taken seriously at the school, she said. Just then I heard the tolling of two church bells and, looking up, saw it was already 4:30 in the afternoon.

Our dorm was the first on the left. The heavy wooden door led into a long, narrow room with a large window straight ahead at the end. Erika pointed out my desk to the right of the window. Lined up along the wall and closer to the door were a chest of drawers and a towel stand. Erika pulled open a pair of curtains to reveal a bed with two legs folded up onto the springs. She pulled the wooden frame down, flipping out the legs, and when the contraption was horizontal it became a bed with a mattress on the wooden frame. She told me I would find sheets, blankets, and pillowcases in the chest of drawers, and although we had to fold the bed up in the morning, we could leave all the bedding on the mattress, which had to be secured with two wide canvas straps. The wall to the left of the window was Erika's side and was the mirror image of mine. That was the extent of our dorm. There was a large bathroom and a locker room with multiple sinks, showers, and toilets at the other end of the hall.

Because I had arrived on a Saturday, I was free on Sunday afternoon to tour more of the school and familiarize myself with my surroundings. Erika was very helpful, despite the fact that she was two classes ahead of me. We got along famously from the start, mainly because we were not in competition with one another. She told me that everyone at school was bound by the honor system, meaning we had to keep track of two salient issues, namely punctuality and order. She explained that if I were to be late for class or meals, I'd have to give myself a "PU-MI"—a punctuality minus—and if I didn't keep order in my room or desk, I'd have to give myself an "OR-MI"—an orderly minus. If one had more than three in a week, one would be restricted from going into town to take a special trip to Überlingen or anywhere near the lake. She told me that was a punishment to be taken seriously, because among many of the fun things to do there was to go to the local ice cream parlor and order an *Eis im Schatten* (ice cream in the shade), which got its name from a little Japanese paper umbrella that was placed on top of the ice cream scoops.

She also felt I should know some more of the basic beliefs and philosophies of the school. Dr. Hahn had prescribed several palliatives for modern life. One was physical education, the pursuit of physical fitness and challenges on land and sea, as well as long endurance tasks. It was to help students strengthen their natural physical aptitudes and overcome their weaknesses. Manual skills and crafts were stressed, as well as rescue operations such as lifesaving, firefighting, and first aid, all of which were part of the curriculum at Salem.

Before turning off the lights, Erika also told me that on Monday morning at 6:20 a.m. a fellow student would open our dorm door and call out, "*Guten Morgen! Aufstehen! Dauerlauf!*" ("Good morning! Get up! Endurance runs!") and then close the door and leave as quickly as she'd come in. Whereupon we'd have to jump out of bed, get dressed in our running clothes, and be at the double doors outside our room just before 6:30 a.m. At the sound of two dongs from the abbey bell tower, we had to be ready to run down to the first floor, out the back

The Schloss Salem with the abbey and school wing in the distance on the left.

The northern gatehouse to Schule Schloss Salem.

door behind the staircase, and go for a half hour run around the castle grounds, the gardens, or the immediate area surrounding the castle. She said the most important thing I had to do when we returned was to immediately rush to the bathroom and take my shower, because if I got delayed, the boys on the lower floor would be back from their run and take all the hot water.

After breakfast, it was off to Mass in silence, and when it was over, we were told to go to orientation, where we were given general guidelines of what was expected of us. My father had told me that Salem had high academic and extracurricular expectations of its students and was interested in imparting a sense of respect for the individual, responsibility to the community, and an awareness of the importance of the democratic process in sustaining both—one of the many reasons he had chosen this school for us. When orientation was over, we headed to assembly, at which our headmaster, Prince Georg Wilhelm of Hannover, whom I had met earlier at breakfast, spoke to the entire school.

Our choir rehearsing in Schloss Salem's *Kaisersaal* (Emperor's Hall).

Nothing was scheduled for the afternoon, so Erika took me on a walk into the tiny village of Salem. It was such a clear and beautiful sunny day that we could see the Swiss Alps in the distance. On the way, we passed an apple orchard and found delicious-looking ripe apples lying on the ground near the road. Since nobody seemed to have claimed them, we picked up a few and snacked on them during our walk.

That evening after dinner, we had Vespers, and then it was time to get ready for bed. Because I had some time left before lights had to be out, I decided to write my parents a letter, telling them that so far I'd had a very nice time and that if things continued along the same lines, I would probably want to stay at least until our school vacation.

Among the students I gravitated to most were several girls who also happened to be from Hamburg. It was probably because Hamburg was a relatively cosmopolitan city that we related to one another and had many interests in common. My best friend there—Ruthi von Cramm—who to this day has remained close, lived in a castle that had been built early in the twelfth century but had been in the von Cramm family since the fourteenth century. It was in a village about a two-hour drive south of Hamburg called Oelber am weissen Wege. Ruthi was the niece of Baron Gottfried von Cramm, one of seven brothers, who was the famous German tennis player of the 1930s and who in 1935 was the undisputed No. 2 tennis player in the world, after Fred Perry. In 1936, however, he refused to give up playing tennis with his Jewish friends, as Hitler and the Nazi party wanted him to do—at six feet tall with blond hair, blue eyes and nearly unrivalled athletic prowess, he was an Aryan poster child—which placed him on shaky ground with the increasingly totalitarian regime. A three-time Wimbledon finalist, he was never able to beat his opponents—Fred Perry in 1935 and 1936 and Don Budge in 1937—despite the fact that minutes before von Cramm's match against Don Budge was to begin, Hitler personally called him on the phone and ordered him to win his match so that the German tennis image would not be tainted and disgraced. Not too long after losing the final at Wimbledon, he was imprisoned because he was accused of being a homosexual, which was strictly forbidden under paragraph #175—a provision of the German Criminal Code that made sexual acts between males a crime. After six months, however, he was released after pressure from several influential friends and members of his family who had contacted Hermann Goering, then the *Reichsmarschall* (Marshall of the Empire)—a title he had been given by Hitler.

Ruthi and I frequently visited each other, and during school vacations we spent hours talking about our past and present lives, among other things. In the course of our conversations, and quite by accident, we discovered one day that our mothers had been friends since childhood in Hamburg and had gone to school together. Another time, she told me about her maternal grandfather, Eduard Pulvermann, a Hamburg businessman, who in 1920 founded the now-world-famous annual Spring Derby in Hamburg. He was half Jewish and was under constant surveillance since November 1941 because the Gestapo, having broken into his office in Oslo, Norway, during the German occupation, found in his vast correspondence copies of letters he had written to friends abroad. In several of these, he had commented on how much the food in Germany had deteriorated and had signed them "With best wishes" or the like, rather than with the mandatory "Heil Hitler." In addition to being considered unpatriotic for having made such derogatory remarks against Germany, it was also against the law. For this the Gestapo sentenced him in January 1942 to two years in "protective custody," a euphemism for the power to imprison people without judicial proceedings. Two years later, instead of being freed, he was taken directly to the concentration camp Neuengamme, near Hamburg, where he was murdered on Easter Sunday, 1944.

A number of boys in my class had also suffered badly under the Nazis, as well as others in classes above me. One classmate, Count Berthold von Stauffenberg, whom we called Stauffus, was the oldest of the five children of Count Claus Schenk von Stauffenberg, the officer who masterminded Operation Valkyrie, the failed assassination attempt on Hitler's life on July 20, 1944. Also in a grade or two above me was another good friend, Jan von Haeften, whose uncle Werner von Haeften was one of several officers who, with von Stauffenberg, was involved in Operation Valkyrie. Both men were arrested on the day of the assassination attempt. Without trial, they were shot by a ten-man firing squad in the courtyard of the War Ministry in Berlin. When von Stauffenberg was about to be shot, von Haeften, in a last dramatic gesture of defiance, threw himself into the path of the hail of bullets. On July 23, three days later, Jan's father was arrested, tried in the people's court on August 15, and sentenced to death. That same afternoon, he was executed in a shed at Ploetzensee, also in Berlin.

I was not aware of all this history at the time I was going to school, because the war was hardly ever discussed. It was still a time for healing. So many millions had suffered and died at the hands of the Nazis—six millions Jews exterminated, along with millions of non-Jews deemed to be enemies of the Nazi regime. The latter groups perished by execution or died in concentration camps throughout Europe.

Among them were a large number of fathers, uncles, and other relatives of many of my schoolmates, who over the years had been involved in trying, unsuccessfully, to eliminate Hitler and rid their country of the Nazi scourge. We were so preoccupied—with our studies, our extracurricular activities, our church, and our trips to town—that the subject of wartime difficulties hardly ever came up. Everyone was happy the war was over, happy to be alive, and tried to forget the painful recent past. No one was the least bit interested in rehashing their experiences or dwelling on traumatic memories. Little things like going to the town of Überlingen, sitting in a café having an ice cream, meant everything. As teenagers, the focus was on the future, which looked a lot brighter than the past had been. Life was beginning to improve, ration tickets were being phased out, and food was starting to come to the markets more abundantly. I considered myself lucky, because although we had shared war experiences, unlike many of my schoolmates, I had not lost a father, did not have a mother who was imprisoned at a young age, and had not been separated from my siblings.

During the middle of the term, I discovered, much to my surprise, that Erika had a boyfriend named Ferdinand von Bismark—the great-grandson of the Iron Chancellor Otto von Bismark, unifier of modern Germany in 1871. Everyone called Ferdinand "Bissy." At the time, Bissy was a count, but he became the Earl of Bismarck upon his father's death in 1975. His family estate in the north—Friederichsruh in Aumuehle—was just a half hour's drive from Hamburg. He, like

Erika, was two classes ahead of me. After so many years of convent school, it was great fun going to school with the opposite sex. Just in the choir alone, having male voices made a big difference, and when in my first term we started making preparations for a performance of Mozart's *The Magic Flute*, we had a delightful Papageno, a Tamino, a Monostatos, and a Sarastro among a number of other boys. I was chosen to sing the role of the mezzo-soprano genie by Paul Stern, the head of the music department, and Ilse, who gave me singing lessons. After watching the Queen of the Night sing her very dramatic coloratura aria from high up on a hill, having suddenly appeared from behind a curtain, I decided right then that despite the fact that I was a mezzo-soprano, I would become a coloratura soprano. But it was just a dream. Many singing lessons later, I was still a mezzo.

My first term, the winter of 1949, went by very quickly because I had many activities with which to occupy myself. I was having such a good time that I completely forgot about my initial apprehensions. It was also not as cold as I thought it would be, though I was deathly afraid the morning endurance run would be so cold it would bring back my chilblains and I tried to stay inside as much as possible, .

It turned out to be an uneventful term because we were all studying very hard. Two events, however, do stand out.

The first was sometime early in February, when a prankster pinned a piece of cheese on the door of one of the boys' dorms. That was cause for a serious school assembly, at which Prince George Wilhelm announced the cheese incident, and asked the perpetrator to come forward. With food as scarce as it was, he told us it was not appropriate, no matter how small the piece of cheese, to use it even if only as a joke. The whole school had been preparing for a big carnival celebration, but when no one came forward to confess to this distasteful infraction, the prince announced that the carnival celebration would have to be canceled. With that, we were dismissed. Furious that no one had come forward, we all vowed to get to the bottom of this incident so that we might be permitted to resume our plans for the carnival festivities. Before we had a chance to investigate, the prince came into the dining room during dinner that evening, asked for silence, and announced that, happily, the student who had pinned the cheese on the door had come to him in private to let him know it was he who had played the joke. He also announced that he was delighted to be able to tell us that we could now continue our plans for the carnival celebrations. Fortunately for us, Dr. Hahn's honor system was alive and well and working in Salem.

The second memorable event was when all the girls decided to gang up on the boys by playing a trick on them for always teasing us. Because all their armoires were outside their dorms in the wide hall, we had easy access to their clothes. One day we decided to take out all their ties, knot them together end to end, and string them up in the dining room from one corner to another at ceiling height. The next morning, they all appeared without their mandatory ties, and when they saw what had happened to their ties, they vowed to get even.

That night, we had just fallen asleep in our hide-a-beds when, unbeknownst to us, the boys snuck into our room, dumped stinging nettle between Erika's and my beds, proceeded to lift up our beds with us in them, and let them come crashing down without straightening out the legs. With that, we rolled right down onto the floor and into the stinging nettle. They repeated this in every one of the girls' rooms and had a good chuckle while we were all trying to wash off the sting from the nettles.

The last three days of February and the first of March were filled with fun extracurricular activities, and everyone was very creative making their costumes out of the little materials available. On the evening of March 1 a dance was held in an empty room in the basement. It had been decorated all in red, and above the entrance door there was a sign saying "Welcome to Hades." We danced until 10:00 p.m. and drank only water or juice throughout the evening, but we had the time of our lives, laughing and telling jokes and stories. When it was all over, everyone went straight to their respective dorms and fell into bed having had such a happy and carefree time.

That evening, several boys had asked me to dance, but there was one in particular who I felt was very special. When, at the end of the evening, he asked if I would go for a walk with him that weekend, I was pleased at the thought that he might have taken a liking to me too. He re-introduced himself by saying his name was Adalbert and that he would meet me outside my dorm on Saturday afternoon right after lunch at 2:00 p.m. and would bring his camera. That was Tuesday evening, and it seemed like forever until Saturday came along. But when it finally did and lunch was over, I rushed to my room, combed my hair, and put on what I thought was my prettiest outfit—a white blouse with a gray skirt, a brown sweater, and brown suede sling-back shoes. It was still cool outside, so I took along an old poncho my grandmother had bought in Peru at least fifteen years earlier and had passed on to me. Promptly at 2:00 p.m. there was a knock on my door, and there he was, smiling and looking very handsome. We walked and talked for at least three hours, occasionally sitting on my poncho on a bench in one of the villages. Spring was in the air and I felt very comfortable in his company, so much so that I wondered whether I was falling in love.

At that point, school took on another even more exciting dimension. Thinking what I was feeling was what is called being in love, my spirits soared. I was full of energy, and everything I did was with great enthusiasm. Everything seemed so effortless, and when I'd run into trouble with a difficult subject, I knew where I could find help. Since Adalbert was two classes ahead of me, I did not see him as much as I would have liked, but when he too was cast in *The Magic Flute* (as a priest), it enabled us to be together at rehearsals. Because we were coming to the end of the winter term and going home for Easter, the number of rehearsals increased. At the end of the dining room, behind a heavy curtain, there was a stage where we had begun building sets. Every afternoon between the end of our sports period and dinner, we had an hour to practice. On weekends we had to give up a lot of our free time to ensure the production would be ready on time. It didn't bother me—I was happy, having a wonderful time, and I couldn't think of anything I would rather have been doing.

At the end of the term, Alexander and I met up once again and together took the train back to Hamburg, where our mother picked us up. It was good to see my parents and grandparents again, but when the time came for us to go back for the spring term, we actually looked forward to returning to school. In many ways it was a time of liberation. We were liberated from our parents, liberated from the war, and I was liberated from the confines of a convent. Having successfully made the trip home from school after the last term, my parents felt we were old enough to take the train back to Salem by ourselves. When the Easter holidays were over, we were sent off to make the eight-hour trip, with a few of the goodies Enno had bought at the PX packed in our bags.

In the spring term, Erika was no longer my roommate, but instead I was assigned a much larger corner room, which I shared with Ruthi and two other girls. Happily, the room was much sunnier than the previous one and was just around the corner from the bathrooms. In the meantime, the opera rehearsals were going full force again, as we were still a long way away from being ready for the dress rehearsal. We had just two months left before our performances were to take place.

In May 1949, there was good news. The *Luftbrücke*, also known as the Berlin Airlift, which had begun in June 1948 in response to the Soviet blockade of Berlin—the United States, Britain, and France had been flying in supplies to the western sector of Berlin after the

Russians had cut off all routes by land and sea—was winding down when the Soviet barricades were lifted. At the end of September, Luft-brücke finally ended its operation after more than a quarter million flights. It had been considered the first battle of the cold war—which was won by the Western Allies without a shot having been fired—and the Allies had supplied millions of tons of food, as well as fuel and hope, to two million stranded West Berliners for more than a year.

Now July was upon us, and with that came the long-awaited performance of Mozart's *The Magic Flute*. My costume and that of the two other genii were simply long, white flowing robes sewn out of white sheets. They were the easy costumes. However, Papageno and Papagena were a different story. It had taken weeks to make their costumes because every feather had to be sewn on to an undergarment separately and by hand. Dress rehearsal had been scheduled for the day before the first performance and none of us thought we were anywhere near ready. The dress rehearsal had so many flaws in it that even the Sterns were worried that the opening night would be a flop. On opening night, however, to our utter amazement, everything came together perfectly, as it is wont to do, and we received a standing ovation. The comments were very gratifying, and I had my first experience with the "smell of the greasepaint and the roar of the crowd."

At the end of July, Alexander and I once again took the train home together for our summer vacation, which lasted just six weeks, meaning we had to be back before the middle of September. My friend Ruthi was about to turn eighteen, and she invited me to a house-party weekend at her family home, Schloss Oelber, to celebrate her coming of age. I had only just turned sixteen. She invited many of her friends from Hamburg, Hannover, and even from the Frankfurt area.

It was 1949, and Dior was all the rage. The famous designer had just shown his new three-quarter-length dresses and skirts, and I was dying to have this latest fashion. When I came home from school, my mother called in the seamstress with whom I had been sewing and asked her to bring some pretty summery prints so we could make a party dress. I picked what I thought was a stunning blue-and-green flowery cotton print on a white background and went straight to work. Frau Wichman had brought some of the latest patterns along, and among them we found a perfect two-piece Dior model. The top had a sweetheart neckline and a cinched waist with a peplum attached, and the full skirt had a stiff tulle petticoat, equally as full, underneath it. Because time was running short, Frau Wichman did the cutting and I did the basting. When all was put together, I had a fitting and then the sewing machine came out. In those days I had an eighteen-inch waist, which was accentuated by the fullness of the three-quarter-length skirt, which in turn happily hid the fullness of the hips I'd acquired by eating so much bread and the many potatoes they'd served at school. It turned out to be just what I had envisioned, and I couldn't wait to wear it to Ruthi's party.

By now, much of the rubble of the cities had been cleared and my fear of traveling alone had subsided to the point where I felt comfortable taking the train from Hamburg to Oelber by myself. There, I hailed a taxi to go to the Schloss. When I arrived, I was greeted by Ruthi and her mother. They showed me to my room and told me to meet them for tea in the salon as soon as I had unpacked and freshened up. Coming downstairs, I saw they both were already in the salon, so I quickly joined them. We sat and talked for a while, and of course I had to tell Ruthi's mother all about my mother and what she had been doing throughout the past two decades after marrying my father and moving to New York City.

After a while, Ruthi suggested we go on a tour of the Schloss and its many rooms, then walk around the large park to the stables and the vegetable gardens. On our walk, she told me that ever since it had been in her family, Oelber had been a working farm, the reason Ruthi and her siblings always had enough food during the war—albeit just the basic staples like potatoes and root vegetables.

Ruthi then told me in a quiet voice why I hadn't met her father. During the war, he had been conscripted into the army and sent to the Russian front. Fortunately, he was not wounded before being transferred to France as adjutant to a general there. Having joined up with his battalion, he was on a surveillance drive of the area with three fellow soldiers when a low-flying plane strafed his vehicle, killing his three companions and badly shattering his legs. He was found by his wife, who worked for the Red Cross, in a church where he had been left with other wounded soldiers. Along with her stable boy, they drove to the nearby village to bring him home. That was in the summer of 1944. The doctors suggested his leg be amputated, but he refused to give up and lose his leg. After multiple operations and continual use of morphine to ease the pain, spanning over an entire year, he never regained the use of his legs and was just not up to joining in and enjoying the evening's festivities.

Meanwhile Ruthi's mother had gone to prepare for the party that evening, and it was time to get back to the Schloss to help her. She needed us to organize the seating arrangements and other finishing touches. That done, we all went to change and Ruthi said I should come down around 7:30 p.m. when the guests would be arriving. By the time I was ready, it was 7:45 p.m. and a number of guests had already arrived. As I walked down the few steps into the salon, I couldn't believe my eyes: There was Adalbert, who had come all the way from his Schloss near Heidelberg. I was ecstatic but had to rein in my emotions, as there were a number of older guests and I had to be on my best behavior. We spent most of the rest of the evening together, as Ruthi had seated us next to each other at dinner and we danced the night away.

The next morning, I called my parents and asked them if I could invite Adalbert to Wentorf for a few days, because he had already come this far and it would be fun for me to return with him on the train. They agreed. That afternoon, we left for Wentorf together. It was the first time my parents and grandparents had a chance to meet Adalbert. Although my mother and father liked him a great deal, my father was afraid I would want to stay in Germany because of him, so he convinced me to come to America, when we were granted entry, with the promise that if I still felt as strongly about him, we could visit each other the following year.

In the course of our conversations that evening, he revealed that his father had been murdered by the Nazis. They had come to arrest him at his Schloss in Leutershausen before dawn one morning in the summer of 1944, taken him to prison, and executed him that same day. It was a horrific, painful memory for Adalbert, his sisters, his mother, and his grandmother, all of whom were at the Schloss that morning and all of whom were helpless to do anything about it. Had they tried, it would only have made matters worse and endangered their own lives as well.

It was wonderful having Adalbert at home with my family, and when we went on long walks through the woods, I showed him the places my grandfather had taken me stalking for roebuck and deer. We also cycled on the tandem into the neighboring villages if there was shopping to be done. Then, close to the end of his stay, he came down with a high fever. He was shivering and had to stay in bed. My mother was a wonderful nurse to him, covering him with plenty of blankets and giving him aspirin and occasional alcohol rubs. When the doctor came, he diagnosed Adalbert with bronchitis and told him to stay in bed until the fever subsided so he wouldn't get pneumonia. A week later, Adalbert was up and feeling well again but had to leave almost immediately, as he was needed at home for the upcoming harvest season. His family's Schloss was surrounded by many acres of farmland.

Just after his departure in August, while listening to the news on the radio, we heard that the US court at Nüremberg—where the war crimes trials had been held since October 1945—had finally come to a conclusion, with the conviction of nineteen additional war criminals. Because several of them had been responsible for Adalbert's father's death, he, like the rest of us, was thankful that justice had finally been done.

At the start of our second year in Salem—by now our familiar and much-loved boarding school—Alexander and I left in a happier frame of mind than the year before. Once again, we arrived on a Saturday in order to get settled and find our room assignments. I was placed in an even larger room, this time with six girls, most of whom were my classmates. Once we had the school calendar and our class schedules worked out, it was time to visit the Sterns to see which opera they were planning for the coming year and when I could schedule my singing lessons.

I popped into the music room and found they had already decided that with the voices they had available at school, they were going to go into rehearsal with a three-act, rather than four-act, version of *The Marriage of Figaro*. I had never heard the opera before, so when Mrs. Stern told me that she and Mr. Stern had picked me to sing Cherubino, the Count's page, I didn't know what to expect. They told me not to worry— it was another mezzo-soprano role in which I'd be playing a young boy, and it was the most enthusiastic, fun, and playful role in the opera.

Shortly after school started we were told that the Federal Republic of Germany (more commonly known as West Germany) had officially come into existence with a new constitution and that Bonn had been chosen to become its new capital. West Berlin, too, was granted a constitution. Konrad Adenauer, referred to as *der Alte* ("the old one"; he was seventy-three), was elected Chancellor of the Federal Republic with the support of the Christian Democratic Union (CDU) he had founded and the liberal Free Democratic Party (FDP). He would remain in office for the next fourteen years, until his retirement, at eighty-seven, in 1963.

By the middle of December—just before the Christmas holidays were to begin—more good news arrived. West Germany had received the first allotment of funds from the Economic Cooperation Administration, thereby becoming a full participant in the Marshall Plan. The seeds of the German economic miracle were sown.

Christmas in Wentorf was once again the festive and *gemütlich* family gathering, with everyone contributing their share to making it a wonderful holiday season. Although Christmas shopping still left a lot to be desired, new merchandise was beginning to trickle into stores. My grandmother loved chocolate, as did my mother and I. My grandfather enjoyed cigarillos but allowed himself to smoke only two a day—one after lunch and one after dinner. My mother loved clothes, and a new scarf or gloves were in my budget, although she used to say, "I don't want anything. My best present will always be if you all do well in school and behave like ladies and gentlemen, because remember, the way you behave will ultimately reflect on your father and me." That was my parents' constant reminder. My father smoked cigarettes, so I asked Enno to bring home a carton of Chesterfields, his favorite brand, for which I promised I would reimburse him. Enno, Alexander, and I decided we would forgo presents for each other, because there wasn't much we could buy anyway with the small allowances we were given.

When we were a lot younger, we were told that while we were taking our baths and getting dressed for dinner, we had to be very well behaved, because Santa Claus would be coming down the chimney and leaving presents for us. When Santa had made his delivery and left, if we were all dressed and ready, we were allowed to enter the "Christmas room," where the bare tree had been transformed with real candles, multicolored balls, treasured ornaments, silver tinsel made of tin, and topped off with a golden star. In the background, Christmas music was played, and our presents had been placed around the tree in such a way that each one of us had our own little area, to avoid any fights. Underneath the tree there was always a crèche—a ceramic baby Jesus in the manger, with Mary and Joseph flanking him. They were surrounded by ceramic sheep, a shepherd, donkeys, cows, and the three wise men with their camels lined up outside, bearing their gifts of gold, frankincense, and myrrh. As impressionable young children, it was a solemn occasion when we entered the Christmas room, but it would soon turn to mayhem as we excitedly unwrapped our presents.

Now it wasn't much different. My father—who had always been most particular about the type, shape, and decor of the tree—was in charge of finding the tree and getting it ready in its stand and mounting the gold star on the uppermost point, usually with help from my brothers. Then it was my mother's and my turn to hand him the balls, and if there were other ornaments, they would be next, followed by the most important ritual—the hanging of the tinsel—which he insisted had to be hung one strand at a time. The end effect would be very regal. Last, but not least, the candle clips, with real candles in them, had to be placed in such a way that the candles were far enough away from anything flammable, especially other branches.

While all this was going on, my grandmother was busy in the kitchen starting to prepare our Christmas Eve dinner, with the help of the same local farmer's wife who had cooked for us before and was a great cook. I joined her when we'd finished the tree and started baking my fruit pies again. My grandfather, being the eldest, was excused from having to do anything. He kept to himself to read, which was his

My parents coming home after having picked a bag full of cep mushrooms.

usual daily pastime. Alexander brought in wood for the stove and the fireplace, and Enno read a book while waiting for someone to engage him in a project that needed to be done.

Our celebrations began on the early side, as it would soon be dark. After helping to set the table, I went upstairs to dress so as not to be late. By the time we were all gathered in the living room, my father had lit the candles on the tree, on the fireplace mantel, and the four candles of the Advent wreath lying on the coffee table. From time to time, he'd have to change the record on the Victrola, as music was of utmost importance to us all and added so much to our holiday. Alexander had lit the fire in the kachelofen earlier in the morning. He then lit the wood in the fireplace, which made the room warm and toasty. At that point, my grandfather made his contribution to the evening by popping open a special bottle of Sekt—a German sparkling wine—and offering us each a glass. He regaled us with tales about his many travels around the world, what China was like at the turn of the century, and how he never needed a passport to travel the world in those days.

Then it was time for dinner. The menu consisted of a hot *Steinpilz* (cep mushroom) soup, made with mushrooms our parents had picked in the late fall on one of their walks through the woods.

This was followed by roast loin of venison from a deer my grandfather had shot. It was served with a fresh-from-the-garden red current sauce and the usual red cabbage and mashed potatoes or *spaetzle*, a southern dish not unlike noodles or pasta. For dessert, my grandmother had once again made the family favorite, Rote Grütze, which she served with a light vanilla sauce. With that we ate homemade Christmas cookies given to us by our neighbors. My grandfather, who claimed he could identify most of the white wines from the Rhine, the Rhineland-Palatinate, and Mosel—his favorite regions—could also distinguish between an *Auslese, Beerenlese, Spätauslese*, or a *Trocken-beerenauslese*. Doubting he could really tell the difference between all those wines, we tested him a few times by not showing him the bottle. He almost always got it right.

There were two more terms to go before the summer holidays, during which I spent most of my free time preparing for the upcoming performance of *The Marriage of Figaro*, practicing and taking singing lessons almost daily to learn my arias, which I had to sing in Italian. Once the other performers and I had our parts more or less memorized, we started rehearsing the scenes where we interacted with one another. There was quite a bit of recitative involved, and timing was critical. Sadly, in this production there was no role for Adalbert, so our time together was once again diminished and limited to occasional walks.

During the spring term, Ruthi was hospitalized with acute appendicitis. While she recuperated at a friend's house, I went to visit her one weekend and to bring her back to school with me. She had found some cigarettes in her friend's living room and offered me one, while taking one out for herself. I refused, knowing our school rule, but she said one puff wouldn't hurt me—after all, it wasn't as if I were really smoking. I took one drag and started coughing so uncontrollably that I almost choked. That was the end of my smoking days—or so I thought at the time.

We ended the school year with our performance of *The Marriage of Figaro*, and once again, we received a standing ovation on opening night. Unbeknownst to us, there was someone in the audience from the Amerikahaus in Munich. He was so impressed by our performance that he invited us to present the opera at the Amerikahaus for three consecutive nights at the end of the spring term.

At right: Cherubino, as played by me in *The Marriage of Figaro*
at the Amerikahaus, Munich.

The whole family after having watched my performance in Munich.

Having been established by the American Military Authority in 1945 as the American Reading Room on the Beethovenplatz, it was renamed the Amerikahaus in October 1947. It contained a library, a reading room, a children's library, a record and film department, a concert hall, lecture classrooms, and large exhibition spaces. There was much excitement over our trip to Munich, and I was particularly pleased because I'd never been there before. My parents promised they would come with Enno to watch our last performance, then take us back to Salem to pick up what few belongings Alexander and I had and from there take us home to Hamburg.

With that, the happiest year and a half of my teenage years had just come to an abrupt end.

That same summer—the summer of 1950—my father left his job at the Coca-Cola Company. He had heard from the American consulate in Hamburg, which had opened up again in 1946, that the United States Immigration and Naturalization Service (INS) had restored their quotas—shut since the war—and that his, my mother's, and my entry papers had come through. This meant we would finally be able to return to America. He was overcome with joy, as were the rest of us. He had worked so hard for so long to have this day come to pass. We immediately wrote to all our friends back in New York to tell them the good news. Later, we learned that we were among the first wave of postwar immigrants to come—in our case, to *return*—to America.

At the end of July, right after the whole family returned from Munich, my father and Enno left on a freighter, the *American Merchant*, sailing from the Port of Hamburg. It was by no stretch of the imagination a luxury liner—unlike the ships we had sailed on before the war—but the price was right. The freighter had accommodations for just twelve on board, and—as my father later reported—they were perfectly comfortable. Everyone had their own room and bath, and when it came to meals, they ate in the officers' mess. The ship made one three-day stop in London, during which my father took Enno along to visit with two friends from his banking days twenty-five years earlier at J. Henry Schroder Banking Corporation. Almost in disbelief at having been able to return to their adopted home after all this time, they arrived in New York Harbor a week later, docking at a Hudson River pier.

The plan was for my mother, Alexander, and I to follow once my father could find an apartment and get us re-established in his beloved New York. In anticipation of our departure at the end of September, Adalbert had invited me for a long weekend to his home near Heidelberg, to meet his mother and sisters, shortly after my father and Enno left. Because he had agreed to take our Irish setter, Diana, I was to bring her along and leave her with him in her new home. My father knew of my plans, and before leaving for America he took me aside and told me in no uncertain terms that nothing was to happen that could lead to my becoming pregnant—and that if it did happen, I should forget about ever coming home again. I was not to disgrace the family. In those days, a young girl was supposed to wait until her wedding night before going to bed with anyone. The Catholic Church forbade it as well. Because my father had put the fear of God in me, there was no way I was going to allow myself to act on my desires and do what would normally have come naturally. Nevertheless, I spent five wonderful days with Adalbert at his home, although during that time, we received some very sad news from Ruthi. She told us that one of our mutual friends in Salem had hanged himself. None of us could understand what could have possibly brought on such a drastic action. Our friend had successfully made his *Abitur*, had been rewarded for this achievement by his parents' gift of a new car, and had been planning a pleasant trip with his classmate Bissy Bismarck. His suicide was completely inexplicable.

Several days later, when the time had come to return home, it was emotionally wrenching for me. Not only had we lost a dear friend, but I was also leaving Diana and the boy with whom I had fallen in love. My first night back in Wentorf, I went to bed crying uncontrollably, whereupon my darling grandmother came into my room and sat at the edge of my bed trying hard to console me. The next day, I couldn't and wouldn't even try to get out of bed. That went on for three days, during which no one—not my grandmother, my mother, Alexander, nor anyone else—could give me solace. However, when, on the fourth day I received a letter from Adalbert, in which he wrote saying he might be coming to America to visit me during the Christmas holidays, my unhappiness lifted. Now I had something to look forward to, with renewed hope and joy. I wrote back, and that began a new phase in our relationship. From then on, we wrote each other every day and continued our romance long-distance. My trip to the post office and waiting there for the arrival of the mail was now the highlight of each day. Even when Adalbert went back to school and I was helping my mother pack us up to leave for America, we kept writing to each other. Then, in late September, the day came when my mother, Alexander, and I boarded the United States Lines freighter at the Port of Hamburg for the trip back to New York.

My mother had a hard time leaving her parents, who by now were in their sixties. Although they were in good health, she nevertheless worried about whether she would ever see them again, not knowing how soon she could afford to take a ship back to Hamburg. Alexander and I were all packed and ready when the faithful Rayze came in his (brand-new) taxi to take us to the port. There we were to board the same freighter, the *American Merchant*, that my father and Enno had taken two months earlier. My grandparents were at the door to see us off, and as we hugged and kissed, we were all reduced to tears. The three and a half years that we had spent in Wentorf with them—although under difficult postwar circumstances—had nevertheless been happy ones family-wise. Everyone had pulled together to overcome the challenges that had been thrown our way, and we had learned many valuable lessons. This, after all, had been the second time our parents and grandparents had lived through a world war. It was said that the First World War was the "war to end all wars," but as it turned out, World War II ended up having been the costliest, most destructive, and brutal war in the history of mankind. It was a conflict that we as a family had experienced not only in Japan but also in the aftermath of a Germany in recovery.

We arrived at the Port of Hamburg, bid farewell to Rayze, and boarded the ship. At the top of the gangplank we were immediately assigned our cabin, which we found was quite comfortable and spacious. It actually slept four but was only being occupied by the three of us. My mother took the lower bunk by the porthole, and Alexander and I were left the double bunks across the room from hers. Alexander, being a boy and the youngest, slept on the upper bunk that folded down at night. Once on board, we dropped off our bags in the cabin and immediately went topside to watch the ship pull out of the harbor. My mother was quite emotional, and I could see the tears streaming down her cheeks. I tried to console her, but all she could do was give me half of a thankful smile.

The freighter was actually quite cozy. There was no having to navigate multiple levels of cabins or eating in large, crowded dining rooms. We took our meals in the officers' mess, which was just like sitting down to a large family meal. Among the younger passengers on board was a student at Swarthmore College in Pennsylvania named Dabney Althofer, who offered to teach me how to play Scrabble to while the time away. It was great fun. Like both my father and Enno, we too made a stop in London. We arrived in the city, which had been badly bombed by the Germans during and beyond the Blitz, but fortunately some of the main attractions had been spared. We proceeded to take them in and visited with friends of my parents who had invited us for lunch at their home in the country. Three days later, we were back on board, sailing for New York.

The voyage home on the Atlantic was relatively smooth and uneventful. Unlike the larger steamships on which we had traveled in earlier years, there was not much to do on board except read the books from the ship's limited library or take a walk around the deck, especially when the seas were rough. My father had taught us long ago that fresh air and exercise were the perfect antidotes to seasickness in rough sea weather; he said that unless we allowed ourselves to roll with the motion, or went outside, we could become terribly seasick. In those days, stabilizers were unknown.

Fortunately, everyone on board was perfectly agreeable, which made for a harmonious crossing. I continued to play Scrabble with Dabney almost daily, but as we got closer to our arrival date, I was so excited and distracted that I was no longer able to concentrate. Thinking about what lay ahead began to occupy my mind. I wondered whether my friends from a decade ago would still remember me and whether we would even recognize each other. We were all just little seven-year-olds in 1941, and now we had become teenagers, some of us almost old enough to vote.

Part Four

HELLO, USA

*I*t was in the early morning of Monday, October 2, 1950, that we were scheduled to arrive in New York. Not wanting to miss watching our entrance into New York Harbor and seeing the Statue of Liberty as we approached her, I spent most of the morning on deck. Suddenly, in the distance, through the lifting haze, I spotted the looming statue's majestic shape. My mother and Alexander had joined me by now, and all of a sudden I had a great urge to hug and squeeze them both as tightly as I could. I must have startled them with my enthusiasm, but in a split second they hugged me back, and this time tears of joy started rolling down our cheeks. The emotion I felt when the Manhattan skyline appeared was overwhelming. It was hard to believe that we were actually back in New York City. The scene unfolded like a dream. Tugboats came to greet us and guided our ship to dock on the west side of Manhattan. It was an amazing panorama—all those tall gray buildings, regimented ranks along perfectly straight streets, north and south, east and west, representing all the dynamism, energy, and potential of a great new era. A sea of yellow cabs poured down the avenue that banked the river and across the streets, and some were already waiting at the entrance to the pier.

We were all packed and ready to go the moment we were permitted to disembark. My mother, with Alexander's US passport and our entry permits in hand, suggested we walk down the gangplank ahead of her so she could keep an eye on us. We proceeded through passport control and on to customs. We had nothing to declare but our happiness and joy.

Waiting for us on the pier were my father and Enno. I couldn't help but burst into tears again. Added to all the excitement of returning to New York were deep, pent-up emotions—mainly those of fear of the unknown, apprehension about what lay ahead and not having the slightest idea what I was going to do once we were settled in our new home. We had been away almost a decade. Much of that time had been spent not feeling free, being trapped by events, trying to survive, and basically being in limbo. Now, suddenly, the time had come for us to act.

After much hugging and kissing, my father hailed a yellow cab. This time we didn't have the forty pieces of luggage with which we had departed so long ago—which was symbol enough of our vastly diminished circumstances. He asked the driver to take us to the Hotel Wales at 1295 Madison Avenue between 92nd and 93rd streets, explaining to us that the apartment he had found was still in the process of being painted and wouldn't be ready until the end of the week. When we arrived at the hotel, we found it to be a far cry from the hotels we had stayed in before the war, but it was a vast improvement over all those in Japan and Germany. We settled in quickly and started making plans for the future.

Enno had already enrolled and started his last year of high school at the Collegiate School, which he had left in 1941 and where they now had kindly offered him a scholarship. They were unable to offer a second one to Alexander but promised that when Enno graduated the following year, they would grant him one for his entire high school years from ninth through twelfth grades. Wasting no time, our father enrolled Alexander in St. Ignatius Loyola, the parochial school on Park Avenue and 84th Street, where he was able to start immediately and complete his last year of grade school.

I had finished high school in Germany at seventeen, so technically I would have been ready to enter college, but at that point I was sick

With Alexander, our parents, and Enno in a reunion photo soon
after our return to New York.

of school. It had been such a struggle having to learn, in German, all
the subjects I had originally been taught in English. Also, with no one
earning any money, I was ready to go out into the real world and see
what it was like. That meant I had to get working papers, which was
my first order of business. At some point, my parents had reconnected
with Marieli, their Eurasian friend from Japan, who had been released
from prison and had come to America after the end of the war and
gone to work as an interpreter. She suggested to my parents and me
that I apply for a job at Time Inc. because they had an international
department where she felt I could probably fit in.

Shortly thereafter, I took the Fifth Avenue bus down to 49th
Street and walked the half block west to 9 West 49th Street, the original home of Time & Life. At the large reception desk downstairs, I was
told to go to the personnel department. Once there, I nervously asked
the receptionist where I might find someone who could help me get a

job in the organization. She gave me a slip of paper to fill out and told me to hand it back to her when I was finished, and then to sit and wait.

Not too long afterward, a very nice older woman came out and asked me to come into her office, where she proceeded to interview me. She gave me more papers to fill out and showed me to a small cubicle where I would have some privacy. A while later, she stuck her head into the cubicle and asked me how I was doing. I told her I was just finishing up, so she motioned to me to come back into her office. The first thing she told me was that she had noticed on my application that I was only seventeen years old and she could not offer me a job unless I had working papers, that it was against the law to hire minors without them. I told her that I had already been downtown to apply for them and that I was waiting for them to be mailed to me. Hearing that, she told me that when she had them in hand, she could offer me a job as an office girl, delivering mail, for twenty-five dollars a week. I thanked her very much and left her office. Once I was out on the street, I looked for a telephone booth to call my parents. I found them at the hotel and was excited to give them the news of my swift employment. I had a job, was going to be paid, and I would be able to contribute to the family finances.

A few days later, I received a call from the Department of Labor telling me my working papers were ready. I told them I would pick them up straightaway and made plans to take them directly to Time & Life on my way home. I called the lady in personnel, and she told me to come by and drop off the documents in order for her to arrange the necessary paperwork for my employment. A week later, I was formally hired.

I started work at Time Inc. on the twenty-third floor, where the Time International offices were located. There, right off the elevators, was the office girls' desk, where two of us were stationed at all times. We were known as OGs and did everything from making coffee first thing in the morning to sorting and delivering mail, sharpening pencils, and running errands. At the end of the day, we made the rounds of the offices and picked up any mail left in the outgoing boxes on the writers' desks and worked with the mailroom when there were larger packages or boxes to go out. Most of the week things went pretty smoothly, except at the end of every week just before *Time* magazine was put to bed and press time approached. Then things would get pretty tense, as everyone was pressured and under the gun to meet the deadline. During one of those weeks when pipe, cigar, and cigarette smoke was once again floating over just about every writer's desk, I bummed a cigarette from my colleague at the OG desk and decided to try smoking once more. This time I didn't cough and choke at all, but actually felt a relaxing sensation throughout my entire body. "This is not bad," I thought to myself, as I took another puff, feeling very grown-up and sophisticated. I took up smoking, and my preferred brand was filtered Parliaments, which came in a cardboard box.

While my mother, Alexander, and I were still in Germany and my father was looking for a place for us to live, he also went to visit his many friends at the various banks he had dealt with in the 1930s, hoping they would be able to offer him a job. At that point he was forty-seven years old, had been out of the workforce for almost ten years, and soon found that the banks were loath to hire someone from the outside when they had so many young trainees to promote ahead of him. It certainly didn't help that he was German. There was also a question of whether, at his age, he could get health insurance. It was a difficult market, but my father was a proud and persistent sort and kept on looking, refusing to collect unemployment insurance or go on welfare.

My mother, in the meantime, saw to it that we were clothed and fed. There was a kitchen in our hotel apartment, and she shopped at the local market and washed our clothes at a laundromat. She was tremendously supportive and encouraging to all four of us. Not too long afterward, when our parents returned from having looked in on the progress that was being made at the apartment, they told us it was ready for us to move in. Now all that was left to do was to pack up what little clothes we had in the hotel and call the storage company that was holding the shipment the Tillitses and Carlie had sent to us after we left Hamburg.

The thought of finally being able to make the move and get settled in our own apartment was an extremely happy one. After the movers had delivered everything, the three of us pitched in and went to work unpacking and placing everything just where our parents asked us. The apartment was at 142 East 80th Street, on the top floor of a four-story walk-up between Park and Lexington Avenues. It was an old-fashioned building, but what my father liked about it was that it was on the Upper East Side, not far from our old neighborhood—and, crucially, it was just about affordable. It also had the right amount of rooms and was open and sunny with exposures to the east, south, west, and north.

There was a living room and next to it a library, or third bedroom, which was assigned to me. Down the hall were two bedrooms connected by a sink area. My parents moved into the first one down the hall from my room, and Enno and Alexander shared the other one. Farther down was a bathroom, and past it there was a dining room, a pantry, a kitchen, and a maid's room with bath. My parents had beautiful taste, and the apartment ended up not only being very comfortable but also looked quite wonderful with all the furniture they had collected while in Japan. Carlie, too, had moved to New York from Vienna and gave us some of the upholstered furniture she had shipped from Vienna and didn't need in her apartment. Because it didn't fit into our color scheme, my mother and I went about making slipcovers for the pieces. We also sewed curtains on a secondhand Singer sewing machine for the four windows in the living room as well as one for my room. Another good friend of my parents, Karl von Clemm, had recently lost his wife—one of my mother's best friends—and was moving out of their large country house into a much smaller apartment in the city. He offered to lend my parents additional furniture to tide them over until they could afford to buy what they still needed.

By Christmas of that year, we were all settled in and had so much to be happy about and lots to celebrate. We were alive and well and back in the city that had been our father's lifeblood. He had worked very hard to have us all return to the country he had loved ever since he was a young boy in Silesia. Staying in Germany had never been an option for him.

After the New Year, when our father had still not found a suitable job, he realized that he had simply run out of money, and one day discovered he had just enough money left to buy a Sunday *New York Times*. The Warburg family had been good friends of my mother's family in Hamburg, so she decided to visit Freddie Warburg, a partner at Kuhn, Loeb & Co., to ask whether he might be able to help out with a loan until my father was able to find a job. Without a moment's hesitation, Freddie wrote out a check for the sum of $10,000—a huge amount of money in those days—and told her to tell my father there was no rush for him to repay the loan, that he was happy to be able to help. Several years later, after my father had landed on his feet and found a job as a financial vice president at a chemical company in New Jersey, he and my mother went to Freddie Warburg's office on Wall Street to thank him for having extended them a loan and to repay him. Freddie thanked my parents but told them it was not necessary, he had been happy to help. With that, he tore up the check right in front of them. It was an incredibly generous act, greatly appreciated by our entire family.

I continued taking the Lexington or Fifth Avenue bus down to

Time & Life, and once I had learned the ropes and felt grounded in my job, I started calling the friends I'd left behind in 1941. My best friend had been Celeste Cusachs—we called her C.C.—whom I had met when we summered in Southampton in the late '30s. Although we did not go to school together, we nevertheless saw each other on weekends during the school year. I had no idea whether, after all those years, she would remember me but thought I would give it a try. When she answered the phone and I identified myself, she not only remembered me but said she was overjoyed to hear from me. She wanted to know right away when we had arrived back in the city, where we were living, and what I was doing. She was also curious to know where we'd been all through the war years, because we'd last seen each other ten years earlier. I told her I was working at Time & Life, and before I could finish, she asked me when we could see each other. She too was working in publishing, in an entry-level job similar to mine. We made a date to meet on the following weekend.

When we saw each other again, it was as if we'd never been apart. We picked up right where we had left off, of course bringing each other up to date and filling in the past decade. Ten years older, she still had the same beautiful, shiny dark brown hair, an aquiline nose, porcelain skin, and brown eyes—she was just taller. When I told her all about our adventures, she was stunned, because in her case, other than attending school, summering in Southampton, seeing her friends, and graduating from high school, not much had changed in her life. She listened in disbelief to some of my stories and was amazed to hear how much I had loved my high school, Salem, because she certainly hadn't felt that way about her own high school.

Late in the spring of 1951, C.C. invited me to drive to Southampton with her to spend the weekend at her mother's house, a cottage on First Neck Lane, across from the Meadow Club. There was no Long Island Expressway yet, so we had to take the Jericho Turnpike all the way to the Veterans Memorial Highway in order to bypass Smithtown and connect with Route 27 East. I will never forget driving down Hill Street that first day, returning to where we had spent two very happy summers in 1937 and 1938. It all came back to me: the beautiful, tall, tightly clipped privet hedges lining the street, behind which you could faintly see white clapboard houses, the Catholic church that we passed on our way to turn into First Neck Lane. A wonderful feeling of serenity came over me, and I felt as if I'd finally come home again.

That weekend, I saw C.C.'s mother and her two much older half-sisters, Dysie and Helen. Both had married and were living elsewhere but just happened to be out visiting their mother. In those days, cars were not really used much in the village. We either walked or rode bikes to where we wanted to go. On my first day in Southampton, we walked across the street to the Meadow Club, where I remembered having taken tennis lessons a dozen years or so earlier and where the US Open used to be played on all-grass courts. We watched some friends playing tennis for a while then had a soft drink by the bar, and there I met friends I had known before the war. Everyone always wanted to know where I'd been those many years, and once again I'd have to take my disbelieving friends through our adventures.

After that first weekend and many more like them the same summer, my social life started to pick up as C.C., old friends from the past, and some new friends started inviting me to their parties. There, I would meet boys, who in turn would ask me out on dates. Later in the fall, they would invite me to go on college football weekends, mostly to Yale and Columbia, because the campuses were relatively close by. I was a newcomer to those weekends, and it was fun to sit in the stands with a group of enthusiastic friends. What I did not enjoy were the after-parties in the various clubs or fraternities, where there was so much drinking going on that frequently you'd see boys and girls that were drunk, sloppy, and probably unaware of what they were doing in public. My father had always warned me that if I or my date had too much to drink, I should call a taxi instead of getting into a car with anyone not sober enough to drive. So aside from worrying about myself, I also had to worry about my date. I was fortunate that I hardly ever had a problem, because the boys I dated were seldom ever so drunk that they couldn't drive. To be on the safe side, I always carried enough money to be sure I was able to find my way home in a taxi by myself.

One day in the early spring of 1951, I was on my lunch break from work with a friend at a famous restaurant on Fifth Avenue between 45th and 46th Street called Schrafft's, when a man approached our table. He asked me whether I would be interested in doing a toothpaste commercial for television. He told me he'd noticed what a nice row of white teeth I had behind my smile and wanted to cast me. My guard immediately went up, thinking this could be just another pickup line, but I said "Why not?" to him, whereupon he asked me for my telephone number. By now I'd become a bit more suspicious, so I asked him for his business card and told him I'd call him after consulting with my parents. With that, he pulled out his card and handed it to me, saying he hoped I would call him soon. Printed on the card, I saw that he was an account executive with the advertising agency Kenyon & Eckhardt, and it looked as though he might very well be legitimate after all.

The next day, I called and told him I had talked it over with my parents and that they saw no harm in my filming a commercial. I said I would be happy to accept his offer. (My father was quietly delighted, because years earlier he had paid dearly to have my teeth straightened.) Straight white teeth behind a smile was, in my father's opinion, a most important attribute for a woman to have, and now it looked as if I was at least getting some benefit from having had to wear braces as a child.

After giving me the details of what I was to wear, what I needed to do, and where I was to go, I was booked for a day to shoot the commercial at a studio in Astoria, Queens. I was told that my per diem would be $125. I almost fainted, because that was five weeks' pay at my current job. Of course I had to ask my boss for a day off for personal business and was thrilled when she gave me permission.

On the appointed day, I headed out and arrived at the studio promptly at 7:30 a.m. I was completely new to this business and learned a lot in a hurry. I was amazed by how many people it took to film a toothpaste ad. There was a producer and his assistant, a cameraman and his assistant, a lighting man and his assistant, and a script girl and her assistant. There were also makeup artists, hairdressers, and gofers. *All this talent just to shoot a film of my pearly whites*, I thought. I wore a typical shirtwaist dress, looked at the camera, and smiled like crazy.

At the end of the day of the shoot, when I was given my check, I was told that if I wanted to continue doing commercials, I would have to join the Screen Actors Guild and the American Federation of Television and Radio Artists. *Wow*, I thought, *join a union so I could work in films and live television?* It had never occurred to me to work in either, but I was intrigued, particularly by the staggering pay. That started me on what I thought of as a new part-time career. I immediately joined SAG and AFTRA and went about finding an agent to represent me.

The year 1951 had been so unbelievably eventful and had gone by so quickly that when our entire family was invited to celebrate Thanksgiving with our parents' dear friends the Gillespies and their six children, we had much to talk about and even more to be thankful for.

Meanwhile, our parents had reconnected with a lawyer friend of theirs, Teddy Thiesing, who, like my father, had emigrated from Germany to America as a young man. He was also my godfather, so this was a most happy reunion. He was a warm and welcoming host, as was his much younger wife, Connie, whom he had married while we were abroad. With the Christmas season approaching, he invited us for dinner at his duplex apartment in New York. Long before the Depression, he had bought the apartment on East 57th Street. It had a two-story living room in which he traditionally placed a fifteen-foot fully decorated fir tree, although he did not use real candles. However, entering his living room was a very dramatic and beautiful sight. The tinsel sparkled, mirroring the lights of the tiny bulbs, and the multi-colored balls had been hung by size, with the largest on the bottom, becoming smaller on the way up to the smallest on the top. It was a dazzling display. When dinner was over, we lingered for a while longer, and then it was time to go to midnight Mass at St. Patrick's Cathedral.

As teenagers, we always celebrated New Year's Eve at home with our parents, as it was an evening—as they liked to describe it—of "forced merriment." They felt we were safer at home. Occasionally, they invited a few of their good friends, as well as some of ours, to join us after dinner and offered us all—teenagers included—a glass of bubbly to ring in the New Year.

The New Year had dawned, and with it came many changes. In the last year I had been transferred from the twenty-third floor all the way up to the thirty-third floor, where Henry Luce—who with Briton Hadden had founded Time Inc. in 1923—had his offices. Henry Luce's right-hand man, Roy E. Larsen—originally the circulation manager and then general manager of *Time* and for many years president of Time Inc.—had his office on the same floor, as did the managing editor, Roy Alexander. They were a delightful group of brilliant gentlemen, which of course made it a pleasure to be working on the same floor as the executive offices.

I continued to be transferred from one floor to another and was learning all about the many different magazines and meeting many of the writers, researchers, and photographers along the way. By the following spring, I had been on virtually every floor except for the twenty-first floor, where the *Fortune* magazine offices were located and where I eventually ended up. Ralph Delahaye "Del" Paine was publisher and managing editor and was married to Nancy White, who at the time was working in the fashion department of *Good Housekeeping* magazine. She ended up as fashion editor and later as editor of *Harper's Bazaar*. When I told my parents where I had landed, I discovered, much to my surprise, that the Paines were friends of my parents and the Gillespies.

I met most of the writers at *Fortune*. One, by the name of Hedley Donovan, would later become managing editor after Del Paine retired, and editor-in-chief of Time Inc. after Henry Luce retired in 1964. Another writer who had made quite a name for himself with his 1956 bestseller titled *The Organization Man* was William Hollingsworth "Holly" Whyte, who later became an urbanist and people-watcher, publishing a half dozen more books. And then there was Charles J. V. Murphy, who was a friend of the Duke and Duchess of Windsor and who much later wrote a definitive biography on the duke and duchess and their lonely years of exile. To me, the workplace was a beehive of intellectualism, a far cry from the years of relative cultural isolation my family had known for so many years.

The days at Time Inc. were extremely happy ones. I felt fortunate to be working in such a classy organization, having the opportunity to get to know so many of the editors, writers, researchers, and executives who were an interesting and integral part of the organization. Although our OG desk was no longer right off the elevators, but rather behind a large reception desk near a kitchenette, many of them would frequently stop by to get a cup of coffee or to chat on their way to or from the elevators, or they'd just stop by if they needed something. It was exciting to be exposed to so many brilliant minds and to be able to learn from them. At *Fortune*, there was a receptionist, Lorraine McPhal, whom I had come to know quite well. From time to time she would ask me to relieve her if she had a lunch date or had errands to do outside the building. I was glad to oblige, because it would give me a chance to see what was happening in the front office and to see the various people who came to visit.

One day, around noon, a short, slight, elderly gentleman walked in, and I immediately recognized him as the Duke of Windsor. He had come to see Charles J. V. Murphy. Knowing who he was, but not quite sure by what name I should announce him, I politely asked, "Who may I say is here to see him?" He must have thought I was a dunce, mistakenly thinking I didn't know who he was—the whole world knew who he was, after his having abdicated the British throne "for the woman I love." He answered, almost in a whisper, "the Duke of Windsor." I picked up the phone, dialed Charlie Murphy's number, and announced the duke just as he'd told me to.

My life had started to settle into a manageable routine. I worked by day, and at night and on weekends I went out on dates with friends or with one or another young man I'd met either in the city or on Long Island. We went to dinner or a movie, took in a Broadway show, or attended parties together. The first musical I was invited to was the unforgettable Pulitzer Prize–winning *South Pacific*, by Rodgers & Hammerstein. It starred Mary Martin as Ensign Nellie Forbush and Ezio Pinza as the French plantation owner Emile de Becque. I had never seen such a romantic and beautiful production. Another fun thing to do, particularly on a rainy afternoon or evening, was to take in what was then known as a double feature. Until the arrival of television, the movie houses showed newsreels of important events around the world—one in particular that comes to mind was the trial of Ethel and Julius Rosenberg for their part in World War II espionage and their subsequent execution in the electric chair in 1953—before showing two movies for the price of one admission ticket.

At the time there were also two very popular nightclubs we enjoyed going to for dinner and dancing or for a nightcap after a show. They were Sherman Billingsley's Stork Club and Gogi's Larue. The former was aptly named because although not a private club, it was much like one, in that on any given evening one would see a number of friends as well as celebrities who were out on the town. When television started to make its debut, it was great fun, because Sherman Billingsley would send out telegrams to a young crowd—usually a group of friends who knew each other well—inviting them for a complimentary dinner with dancing. All he asked of us in return was that we sign a release allowing a TV camera crew to broadcast us live while we were enjoying an evening at the Stork Club. Needless to say, being on television was quite the novelty and the invitation was a coveted one.

By that time my romance with Adalbert had long since evaporated. It had been too much to expect that we could maintain our relationship a continent apart as teenagers both living exciting, youthful lives. There was now no one special in my life who I was crazy about, but I was happy and content. Free as I was, though, and being a romantic, I still thought it would be fulfilling to have someone in my life with whom I could perhaps fall in love and eventually marry. I enjoyed visiting friends—going to their weddings and bridal showers or out to dinner—but I would have much preferred to have gone with someone special, rather than just on another random date.

As the weather improved and warmed, C.C. and I started going out to Southampton again on weekends. By now the countryside was beginning to turn many different shades of green as buds and leaves appeared and trees and flowers bloomed. The fresh country air was in stark contrast to the polluted city air, and we always loved breathing it in, knowing how good it was for our lungs and our well-being. More and more people began driving out to the Hamptons, and the moment the school year came to an end, mothers could be seen driving out in their station wagons filled with children, suitcases, toys, and bicycles.

They were going out early to tend to their gardens and to open up their houses for the season, which happened anywhere between Memorial Day and the Fourth of July, depending on the weather. It was then that the traffic would start building up, usually right after lunch on Fridays, so that at times the normal two-hour drive to Southampton could take up to four hours or more.

On the Saturday of the Fourth of July weekend, the Meadow Club usually held its annual Independence Day dinner dance, officially opening the season. There would be at least three more such dances in the course of the summer, and they were always a great deal of fun. Lester Lanin—a famous bandleader of the era—and his orchestra knew just how to play the crowd. At the end of the evening, he would give out different-colored hats with his name stitched on them, which he used as a novel and smart advertising gimmick. He was one of the early ones to put his name on some form of clothing.

I loved to dance, so these parties were always the highlight of the summer. I made sure I had a date—preferably a good dancer. One time, when most of my male friends either weren't out for the weekend or already had a date, C.C. arranged a blind date for me. He was a nice enough young man, but for whatever reason, we just didn't click. I could see that this was not going to be one of my better evenings, so the moment we'd finished dinner and I had a couple twirls around the dance floor with him, I took "French leave" and walked back to the "Barn," the name of C.C.'s mother's cottage. It had not been one of the best nights, but mercifully it was over fairly early for me and I fell into bed, happy to be home.

Back in the city the following Tuesday, I was once again manning the reception desk, having relieved Lorraine during her lunch hour. A well-dressed man wearing a gray suit, white shirt, blue-striped tie, and a taupe fedora with a black hatband walked into the reception area, looking at the series of *Fortune* covers that were hanging on the wall

opposite my desk. I asked him, "May I help you?" in my best receptionist manner, whereupon he turned around and then did a double take,
visibly amazed at seeing me sitting there. I was a bit taken aback until
he introduced himself as Arthur Merrill and asked whether I'd been
at the Meadow Club in Southampton that past Saturday. I thought it
an odd question but replied that yes, I had indeed been in Southampton and that I'd also been to a dance at the Meadow Club. By now I
was curious to know why he was asking, but before I could pose the
question, he explained that he'd seen me dancing there, but when, after
dinner, he went looking for me to ask me to dance, he wasn't able to
find me. Not knowing who I was or how to get in touch with me, he
was naturally stunned but very pleased to see me at *Fortune* magazine
just three days later. He said he couldn't get over the unbelievable and
amazing coincidence of having found me. With that he asked me for
some tear sheets and after I told him where he could find them, he
departed.

That afternoon at around 4:00, Lorraine buzzed me and said there
was a man calling for me on her phone line and that I should pick up.
It was the same man who had stopped in for the tear sheets, calling me
to thank me for my help. He also wanted to ask whether after work
I would meet him for a drink at the Café Pierre in the hotel on the
corner of 61st and Fifth. He was quite distinguished-looking and had
told me he was a banker—just as my father had been—so I saw no
reason not to accept. It seemed safe enough. The Café Pierre was a rep-
utable spot in one of Manhattan's better East Side neighborhoods—
and anyway, I'd found him to be very attractive.

We met not too long after 5:00 p.m., and after ordering me a
bourbon old-fashioned and a martini for himself, we started the usual
introductory conversation. He told me he was a banker at the Mor-
gan Guaranty Trust Company downtown, and I told him bits and
pieces of my earlier life. In the course of the conversation, I mentioned

I had lived in Japan during the war, whereupon he told me he had been a supply officer on the USS *Tuscaloosa*, a United States Navy New Orleans–class heavy cruiser, and he had been in both the Iwo Jima and Okinawa operations. On the *Tuscaloosa*, he'd been through the maelstrom of kamikazes, who had come at his ship out of the sky from all directions. After a while, he asked whether I would join him for dinner, but I had made plans to have dinner with my parents, so I asked him to give me a rain check. The next day, he called to ask me out again, and from then on we saw each other pretty regularly.

What followed was a whirlwind courtship in New York, on the North Shore of Long Island, and in the Hamptons. There was no doubt that I had fallen deeply in love, and it seemed so had he. I couldn't wait to introduce him to my parents, and he in turn invited me out to Long Island to meet his parents.

We continued seeing each other almost every day or evening that fall, enjoying our time together and meeting each other's friends, going to movies, galleries, concerts, and playing tennis on weekends in the country. I had forewarned my father of my beau's intentions, and when he hesitated because of my age, I reminded him that he had married my mother three months after she had turned twenty. I promised him we would wait until the following year, because we had just met that August. In the end, he said he would give us his blessing, so the way was paved for my beau when he went to ask my father for my hand in marriage.

It was soon afterward that we decided to become engaged. We chose a date in mid-December, before the many Christmas holiday parties would begin crowding the calendar. My godfather kindly offered to give us our engagement party at his apartment on East 57th Street, the one with the double-height living room in which he always erected the giant Christmas tree. My mother and I started making preparations for the party, which was set for December 18, 1952.

Life in the early 1950s, with World War II over, was frequently referred to as the "golden era," as times were finally improving. It was also a very creative period. Hundreds of products were invented that we now take for granted in our everyday lives. After the memory of the Depression and World War II, we as a nation relished those relatively peaceful years. New York during the fabulous '50s was an exciting place to be living. The two years since our arrival back on American soil had been filled with so much to do, things to learn, and friends to meet, that there was hardly time to keep up with all that was going on in the world, despite the fact that I was working at a large news organization.

I did follow the Korean War, and General MacArthur's career, having been so impressed with him during World War II and seen him in the flesh. After he left Japan in 1950, he was put in charge of the United Nations Command in the Korean War, which had broken out about the same time as we returned to New York. It was a position he held until April 1951, when President Truman relieved him of his duties, for insubordination. The general had made public statements that were contrary to the administration's policies. He was such a popular war hero that his removal was controversial, to say the least. As people who had seen General MacArthur in all his glory in Japan, it surprised and disappointed us to see our hero brought down.

Arthur and I were married two months before my twentieth birthday, on April 25, 1953, and settled into an apartment on the fifteenth floor of a building in the East 60s that overlooked all of downtown Manhattan. It was so open that one could see all the way down to the Empire State and Chrysler Buildings. After a honeymoon in Bermuda, I returned to work at Time Inc., and my husband to the First National City Bank, which he had joined shortly before our wedding.

It was just about the time when black-and-white TV sets came on the market, although we did not own one until my in-laws gave us one for Christmas the following year. There was, however, a large TV screen in the reception area of the Time & Life Building on which we could watch the latest news. We watched the report that the American communists Ethel and Julius Rosenberg, who had been accused, tried, and convicted of conspiracy to commit espionage—having passed information about the atomic bomb to the Soviets during the war—had been executed in June. A month later, there was much joy when the news was broadcast that President Eisenhower had ended the war in Korea.

That summer, I discovered I was pregnant and joyfully started preparing myself for motherhood. I wanted everything to be perfect for the little stranger who would enter the world in the following February and change our lives forever. In those days there was no way of knowing the child's sex before it was born. I can't remember where my mother found it, but miraculously the bassinet in which both my brothers and I had slept as newborns appeared. All I had to do was have the stand and legs painted, launder the dotted Swiss fabric that draped it, and send the mattress to the cleaners. It would be just like new again. Aya, the nanny who had taken care of the three of us when we were born, said she would come out of retirement to help me with the baby.

My parents were over the moon about the news that they were having their first grandchild and my mother would frequently go baby shopping with me. My father, having found a job as a financial VP at a chemical company, was busy at work during the week, but since we lived nearby, we would often have dinner together on weekends. Alexander, by now, was going to the Collegiate School and Enno was at Columbia University. Both were still living at home, which also gave me a chance to see them when we went to visit my parents.

In the spring of 1955, my agent, seeing that I had my figure back after the birth of my son, sent me to audition for the Miss Rheingold contest, which carried with it a $50,000 prize. This was a mind-boggling sum—almost $1,000 a week if averaged out over a year, when I was earning twenty-five dollars a week at my day job. I had heard of the contest but never dreamed I would be chosen as a contestant. Nevertheless, I entered on a lark.

I was told to go to the Jade and Basildon Rooms of the Waldorf Astoria Hotel, where the judges would be screening applicants. When I arrived there, I found the rooms teeming with hundreds of registered models, all waiting in line to show their photographs and be interviewed. I joined the queue, and soon it was my turn. The first judge I met was the president of the company, a Mr. Philip Liebmann, who was followed by executives from the advertising agency Foote, Cone & Belding; the photographer Paul Hesse; and actors Irene Dunne, Bob Cummings, Rosalind Russell, and several others. They all sat behind a long table, engaging us in conversation, studying us, and thumbing through our portfolios. At the end of the line, if one passed muster, one would be given a blue slip, which meant "Come back tomorrow." If you were not the type they were looking for, you were given a pink slip, which meant "No need to come back."

I was excited when I received a blue slip and ventured out the next day to repeat the same exercise. The only difference was that some of the judges had changed. At the end of the second day, I again received a blue slip and was asked to return once more. To my surprise, there were only thirty-six of us remaining, and at that point we were asked whether we would be available to serve as an ambassador for the brewery for an entire year if we were to win the election. If we answered in the affirmative, we were given a contract to sign and asked to come back the following week. That evening when my husband came home from the office, I told him what had happened. We proceeded to weigh the pros and cons of having to be available to the company for a whole year and decided it was definitely worth it, especially because I had

Aya to care for our baby if I had to be away for any length of time.

A week later, when we returned, there were only six finalists left. We figured they had vetted us all in that past week and assumed they had chosen the six with the cleanest records and the least amount of baggage to partake in the first leg of the campaign. We were assigned a chaperon by the name of Eleanor Nolan, who was going to be with us throughout the six-week campaign, organizing and coordinating all of our schedules. The campaign was scheduled to begin on Monday August 1, and to run for six weeks, ending on Sunday, September 11.

We were booked for photograph sessions and wardrobe fittings almost immediately, but not before being formally introduced to one another. We were: Myrna Fahey (the actress and Elizabeth Taylor look-alike); Gretchen Foster (Loretta Young's niece); Cheryl Johnson; Maggie Pierce; Carol Toby; and me. I went by the assumed professional name of Hillie Merritt, which I had used previously when modeling. The deadline for both our pictures and our "uniforms" was mid-July, as the photos of all six of us had to be strung up wherever Rheingold beer was sold, and we needed to be packed and ready to begin campaigning on August 1, 1955. Our wardrobe consisted of identical pale blue Anne Klein shirtwaist dresses with matching lightweight wool jersey coats, pale blue shoes, multicolored handbags, and many pairs of white gloves for each of us.

During the six weeks we campaigned along the eastern seaboard and on the West Coast. Most days started out early in the morning, when we were picked up in chauffeur-driven limousines. We campaigned all day, attending local fairs or riding in parades on a special Rheingold float. We were driven down Main Street in personalized convertible Cadillacs, waving to the crowds. We made personal appearances at various store openings where Rheingold beer was sold. Once, we were even driven around town in our own two-seater bubble-top Messerschmitt KR200.

Chauffeured in my very own bubble-top Messerschmitt KR200.

All six Miss Rheingold contestants, on the campaign trail.

Most of the time our day ended around 6:00 p.m., but on occasion if there was a convention of brewers or a meeting of advertisers, we would have to stay for an early reception, after which we were driven home again. The campaign in the east took us all the way from Upstate New York through Connecticut, New York City and all its boroughs, and down to Atlantic City in New Jersey. Traveling with us was John R. "Bunky" Hearst Jr., a grandson of William Randolph Hearst, who was a photographer with the Hearst-owned *Mirror* newspaper. He had been hired to photograph all of us throughout the campaign and to record our many and varied activities. Everywhere we went crowds gathered, asking us to let them photograph us with them and their friends or family members. I was amazed by how many people—old and young alike—asked us for our autographs. Of course, we were flattered beyond belief. It gave us a real insight into what it must be like to be a celebrity.

After also traveling all along the West Coast, we were brought back to New York City, where a farewell dinner was held for us at 21, and our wonderful six weeks of campaigning had come to an end. Not sure when we'd see one another again, we tore a one-dollar bill into six pieces, giving each of us a sixth of a dollar, with the vow that we would put the dollar back together again in 1957, when the reign of the winner of our contest would be completed, and we could plan a reunion. Like so many vows made at emotional moments, we did not keep the promise, and though I reunited with Gretchen Foster and Maggie Pierce, I never saw the other three again. We parted that evening each wishing the others good luck, for the voting was over. The next step in the roughly three months ahead was for the ballot boxes to be emptied and the votes counted, in what had become the second-largest election in the country, next to the one for president of the United States. In the Miss Rheingold election, one did not have to register to vote, and one could vote as often as one's heart desired. The time had come to sit it out and wait patiently until the winner was announced.

There were so many millions of votes pouring in that they were counted by simply weighing them. As the bags of ballots arrived at Rheingold HQ, it began to look very favorable for me, as apparently—I was told much later—I was running considerably ahead of the others right from the start. It was just as Maggie Pierce had predicted one day in Twentynine Palms after watching the reactions of the crowds. Therefore, unbeknownst to me, I was being scrutinized closer than ever. Much to the chagrin of the Liebmann executives and the advertising agency, they discovered I was not a US citizen. But I had come to America exactly five years earlier, which was one of the requirements needed for citizenship. The other was that one had to have been married for at least three years. Fortunately for me, I qualified on both counts and therefore had no trouble getting my citizenship quite quickly, with the help of the legal department at the brewery. Although Rheingold Beer had come from Germany—the originators of Rheingold beer were a German-Jewish family who had come from the town of Ludwigsburg, north of Stuttgart (the same town we had ended up in after the war)—they had not been keen on having a non-citizen representing their company, despite their German background, and my brand-new US citizenship solved the problem.

Samuel Liebmann, a member of a prominent Jewish family, had emigrated to America in 1850, settled in Brooklyn with his wife and three sons, and opened a brewery there. The company, which was flourishing at the time of Samuel's death in 1872, continued under the management of his three sons. In 1903, when the three brothers retired, their six sons took over. Beer production grew continuously so that by 1914 their annual output was 700,000 barrels. The company survived Prohibition by producing lemonade and a drink they called Near Beer.

At the end of Prohibition in 1933, the company once again started beer production; and in the late 1930s, Dr. Herman Schuelein, who had fled Hitler's Germany, where he'd been general manager of the famous Löewenbräu Brewery, became one of the senior managers of the company. It was in large part due to his experience and leadership that after World War II the company experienced unheard-of growth. Together with Philip Liebmann, Dr. Schuelein developed a dry lager beer they decided to market under the brand name of Rheingold, naming it after the Wagner opera, due to its golden color. In 1939, Dr. Schuelein came up with a clever marketing idea when the company chose Jinx Falkenburg as the first Miss Rheingold in 1940. From then on, for the next twenty-five years, the brewery held an annual Miss Rheingold contest, letting the beer-drinking public decide who would be the next Miss Rheingold to represent the company as their goodwill ambassador. During the height of the campaign in the 1940s, '50s, and '60s, the Liebmann Brewery had a 30 percent share of the New York beer market.

After our tour, the wait went on. I was pleased to be back home and eager to devote more of my time to my little son, who up until then had been lovingly cared for by Aya, his father, and his four adoring grandparents. I also continued modeling and filming television commercials.

About a week before Thanksgiving, I was at home with my twenty-one-month-old son, when the doorbell rang. I looked through the peephole and saw a man standing outside whom I did not recognize. Without opening the door, I called out, "Who is it?" to which the man replied, "Western Union." In those days a telegram was not always good news, so when the man handed me the envelope with the telegram inside, I tore it open with a slight bit of apprehension, but then I saw it was from Philip Liebmann. I eagerly read the message:

"Congratulations on having won the 18th Miss Rheingold contest." It was signed Philip Liebmann. All I remember is being overcome with such joy at the thought of having won the title that I picked my son up out of his playpen and hugged him, rocking him back and forth and up and down in my arms, telling him, "I won, I won!" He looked so perplexed, not knowing what I was doing and what I meant that I put him back into his playpen and ran to the telephone to call my husband, my parents, and my closest friends.

Later that day, Eleanor, our chaperone, called to congratulate me and to tell me that she'd have to make appointments for my fittings— not only for my winner's dress but also for my entire wardrobe for the next twelve months of ads. I jotted down where I had to be and at what time and asked whether I needed to bring anything, to which she replied, "Just yourself." Looking at my calendar, I realized the week ahead would be a very full one. So much had to be accomplished before the end of the year, which was just six weeks before my first scheduled appearance and roughly two months before the major photo shoot, which would take place in California.

There would be plenty of press coverage of my win, including by the legendary syndicated columnist, radio host, and gossip monger Walter Winchell. Much to the consternation of the Rheingold execs

New York Novelet: A young German girl married a Wall Streeter several years ago . . . Blessed with a baby and all the thrills newlyweds know . One of the bride's gal-pals (a model) suggested: "Why don't you take up modeling so your afternons won't be dull?" . . . So she did . Seh just won the Miss Rheingold Contest . . Using the name Hillie Merritt . . . Her real name is Hildegarde Merrill . . . Wife of Arthur Merril, whose kin founded the Wall St. firm of Merrill, Lynch, Pearce, Fenner & Bean.

and the staff in general, he leaked the news, in conspiratorial tones, that I was not really a "Miss" but a "Mrs."

Once the excitement had settled down, my first stop was to be at Fira Benenson's atelier. She was the designer who'd been chosen to make my winner's dress—a beautiful long gold satin evening dress appliquéd with sequins—as well as a short white taffeta cocktail dress studded with rhinestones for a Christmas dinner ad. Both dresses had to be ready for a press conference that was being called for mid-December.

The day of my press conference, Thursday, December 15, finally dawned. The time had come to return to the Waldorf Astoria Hotel, this time to the Carpenter Suite, to meet the gathered reporters. A room had been reserved for me to change into my Fira Benenson winner's evening dress, which Eleanor had brought to the hotel. (It was to become the Rheingold centerpiece of the New York Historical Society's *Beer Here* exhibit fifty-seven years later.) Soon a makeup artist and hairdresser arrived. Amid much excitement, they began their work. The makeup artist started doing his magic, and when he'd finished, the hairdresser fixed my hair. Then it came time to slip into my beautiful gold satin dress, to go and meet the waiting journalists and photographers that had assembled. The hairdresser had placed a crown on my head and secured it tightly. As I was leaving the room, Eleanor thrust a scepter into my hand, and out I floated. For a moment I was startled by the flashbulbs popping all around me. But then I caught myself and started smiling and posing for the cameras, just like I'd seen celebrities do. It was, after all, a very happy day, and I wanted the photos to reflect that. In fact, the past few weeks— since I'd learned of my win—had been a heady and intoxicating period. As I was being interviewed by the journalists who had been sent by most of the local and many of the out-of-town newspapers, I had to pinch myself once again to see whether this wasn't all just a wondrous dream.

Right after having celebrated a few extremely happy Christmas days with my family, I started readying myself for the early morning trip to Lake Placid on December 30. The car ride took close to five hours, and upon arrival we were greeted by the Winter Sports Committee members and then shown to our rooms. I was asked to appear for a press conference and photo session later that afternoon and was told that the Major League baseball player Johnny Podres, who had been chosen as king of winter sports, and I would each be given long, velvet, ermine-trimmed capes to wear over our warmest clothes, as we were going to be photographed outside in the snow. From there we were told we'd go to dinner, after which the thirtieth annual coronation procession would commence and we would be escorted to our "thrones." These were situated on the third and top tier of richly decorated platforms at the end of the huge Olympic Arena in front of an enormous

Meeting the press at the Waldorf Astoria
Hotel, December 1955.

Johnny Podres and I at the coronation ceremonies in the Olympic Arena.

painted backdrop of snowy hills and mountains. We were told it was there that we'd be crowned king and queen of winter sports as part of the grand pageantry that always preceded the spectacular ice show.

Once downstairs, I was handed the cape, which I threw around my shoulders. The time had come to proceed regally outside. It was then that I first met Johnny Podres, who was a delightful young man, and with whom I hit it off right from the start. He too had been given his ermine-trimmed cape. We were asked to step outside for the photo shoot, and once again the flashbulbs started popping from all directions. We were asked to pose every which way, and then Johnny was asked to kiss the queen, which he said he was more than happy to do. We had a lot of laughs, and being with a pro made the press conference less intimidating. That evening after dinner we were off to our coronation—my first duty as Miss Rheingold of 1956. The next day, it was all over and we motored back to the city, arriving just in time for me to give my son his evening bath.

With Johnny Podres in Lake Placid.

The overnight stay in Lake Placid was my first official duty, and from then on it would be a series of personal appearances at all types of civic, charitable, and social functions. I was also to be photographed for ads in newspapers, magazines, and billboards, as well as to appear in television commercials for *Rheingold Theatre*, a television series, hosted by the renowned actor Douglas Fairbanks Jr.

Next on the agenda was the trip to Los Angeles, where I was put up at the Beverly Hills Hotel. This time, I was not with five other contestants, but rather with my son and Aya. Although my husband had been invited, he had to work and opted out of flying with us. He did say he would take a long weekend in February and visit us then.

We left New York in rainy weather, looking forward to the California sunshine. Just as I'd expected, we landed at the Los Angeles airport on a beautiful, sunny afternoon. It was a pleasant change from the raw weather we'd left behind. My clothes and all their accessories were already hanging in the closet in my room when I arrived, all pressed and ready to step into. This simplified matters considerably, as all I had to do was unpack what I'd brought to wear when I was not working.

There was also a sheet of paper with my schedule on it, including changes of venue in the event of inclement weather. Upon studying the schedule, I saw that instead of thirteen ads, I was actually going to be photographed for twenty-six ads. Two different ads were needed for each month—a color photo of me involved in an outdoor activity for the billboards, newspapers, the backs of magazines, and for color posters and displays; then I would change my costume to be photographed in a black-and-white indoor photo that was related to the outdoor activity. Those would be placed inside magazines.

In the January toboggan shot, for instance, the coordinating black-and-white photo had me with three models in it who played the roles of three of my friends. In all party shots, everyone was always either serving and/or drinking Rheingold, except for Miss Rheingold. She was never shown drinking Rheingold, although she was permitted to pour it for others.

The day after our arrival, it alternately rained and drizzled, so our photo shoot was moved to an inside location. In this case it was to a warm, cozy, wood-paneled après-ski setting in a den with a wood-burning fireplace, in front of which I was asked to sit. Then the three models joined me for what looked like an après-toboggan cocktail buffet at which, of course, Rheingold beer was being served. By then I had changed into a white wool flannel shirt with a foulard and a full, black wool skirt. This was the photo that was going to be coordinated with the January color shot in which I was tobogganing.

Paul Hesse, the brilliant photographer, had been hired years earlier as the official photographer for all the Rheingold shoots. Because I'd already met him at the Waldorf in New York when I was trying out for the Miss Rheingold contest, he was not a total stranger. He gave me a warm welcome, and I immediately felt at ease. There was the usual kibitzing with all those who had assembled, before I was ushered into the makeup room to get ready. I was offered a cup of coffee and water and was asked to go and change into my après-ski outfit. The makeup artist then proceeded to once again perform his magic and was followed by the talented hairdresser, who within fifteen minutes had combed me out beautifully. Now I was ready to start working, and I returned to the den.

The four of us took our assigned seats and then the lighting crew went to work. They would focus different kinds of floodlights and diffusers on each of us. Paul had an assistant who would from time to time come up—almost to my nose—with a light meter and test whether the light was sufficient or whether more was needed. In the meantime, the person responsible for props brought in a number of bottles of Rheingold from the cooler and placed them strategically on the table he had brought in earlier that day, and placed some others in the hands of the two male models.

By the time everyone was dressed and ready, the props were in place and the lighting was perfect, and a test shot was made. While the film was being developed, we were told we could break for lunch. Sandwiches were ordered in for us, and we perched ourselves on barstools in the kitchen. A half hour later, Paul's assistant called to say we should take our places. The afternoon session was about to begin. It was a pretty simple session in that the stage had been set and all preparations had been made earlier in the day. All we had to do was pose according to Paul's instructions. When Paul felt he had plenty of good shots, he told us we could change back into our street clothes and go home. He would let us know if he needed us to come back the next day for any reason. It was something most photographers did for insurance, in the event something had come out wrong. The afternoon had gone by very quickly, and it was nice to have finished relatively early. I reached the hotel in time to have a chance to play with my baby at the pool. The temperature by then had risen into the 70s, and I was able to give my son his dinner out on the terrace.

Thursday the temperature was warm enough, but it had turned quite windy. Once again, we couldn't shoot outdoors, although the snow machines were already being shipped in for the next day's shoot. I was told to relax but to stay in the hotel so I could be reached in the event the wind calmed down. The forecast for the next two days was going to be picture-perfect. This meant that we'd be able to shoot the outdoor scene, with me tobogganing on totally manufactured snow.

Friday and Saturday turned out to be two glorious days with the temperatures in the mid-60s to low 70s. The weather for the shoot was perfect—not so warm that the snow would melt and not cold enough for it to turn to ice. The routine was pretty much the same every day we had a shoot. After breakfast, the makeup artist would come to my sitting room and get me ready, then I'd slip into the clothes I was meant to wear that day. The hairdresser, who had already been waiting, would comb me out; I'd kiss my son good-bye, and I'd be picked up and driven to the designated location.

The snow scene turned out to be hilarious. All around us there was either grass or a regular road, with flowers blooming, but there on the hill the snow machine had manufactured enough snow to make it look as if it had snowed all night. I was placed halfway down the hill on my sled, which had been anchored on the other side of the hill, so the sled wouldn't start sliding down while the picture was being taken. Needless to say, there was a certain amount of urgency to getting the shot, so there was a lot of pressure. Having nothing to do, I just sat on my sled watching all the activity going on around me. When Paul and his crew were ready, he would call out to me to smile or to tilt my head to the right or left. Mainly he shouted out, "Look like you're having fun!" Which, of course, I did. I was having the time of my life.

On Sunday, I woke up to foggy weather. The phone rang relatively early, and it was one of the Liebmann executives who had traveled out with us, telling me we would not be working that day. That allowed me to give Aya the day off and take my son on a nice long walk around the hotel and to the pool, where it was still too chilly to take a swim. On the way back, I spotted a soda fountain on the lower level of the hotel, where I decided it would be fun to have lunch. In the afternoon, after

Tobogganing with a canine actor for the
January ad.

my son's nap, we ventured out to West Sunset Boulevard and across to Will Rogers Memorial Park.

Monday it rained, so the shoot was held indoors again, but by Tuesday it had cleared, although it was still a bit windy. And so it went. Fortunately, it cleared over the following weekend and it was a pleasure to be able to go outside again. All that rain did wonders for the flowers, so when it came to photographing the gardening shot for the May ad, there were many more from which to choose. After following the usual morning routine, I was picked up and driven to a garden that had been rented by Paul, as it had a profusion of a large variety of flowers that were in full bloom. I was asked to stand in front of some of those flowers and to hold on to my wide-brimmed pink hat with my left hand. On my right arm, they hung a big basket filled with cut blooms, but apparently Philip felt there were not enough surrounding me. Before I knew it, I saw flowers being dug up and planted closer to where I was standing. I hated to think how the owners would feel when they returned to see their garden in disarray, but there was little I could do about it. The rest of the month was sunny most every day, making it possible to keep on schedule. For the June ad, we went to an amusement park, and for the July shot Paul had once again rented someone's backyard, this time in the woods, where it was made to look as if I was hosting a Fourth of July barbeque. For the August ad, Paul had rented a motorboat and we went out to sea, where I was shown how to steer it, so I could look authentic in the photo. The September shot took place in a barn, where a hoedown was taking place, and for October we shot one with a stuffed elephant and donkey in front of a plain white brick wall, with multicolored streamers hanging down all around me. For the November ad, I had been fitted with a very handsome shooting costume. There in the woods, I was perched on a fence with a cocked shotgun in my left hand, patting a hunting dog with my right. Finally, for the December shot, once again the snow machines were brought out to manufacture snow in front of a house, where on the mailbox were the numbers 1956. The beautiful white sheared beaver coat I wore was, sadly, the one piece in my entire wardrobe I did not get to keep, as it had been loaned out for just the day. There was one other shot—the Western one—in which I was dressed in a cowboy outfit with a ten-gallon hat and a pair of brown cowboy boots. I was sitting on a surrey with a fringe on top with a Lassie look-alike right beside me, on my way to deliver a case of Rheingold. All in all, it was a wonderful month and I was sad to be going back to cold New York.

Back in the city, I was on call every day to appear at a charity function or other event. One in particular was the White Elephant Ball, where my escort had to actually wear the head of a white elephant made of papier-mâché on his head. Another time, I rode in a horse

With my Lassie look-alike.

and buggy in the Steuben Parade, dressed up in a Bavarian dirndl. In another parade, I rode on the Rheingold float, which resembled foam, wearing a long pink "Southern belle" evening dress with a large straw hat and long pink streamers. Other times, I attended ribbon cuttings at store openings, attended several tennis matches, and rode on top of the backseat of a Cadillac in the Columbus Day Parade.

Enno and Alexander were more amused than anything else by my new role in the world. They both remarked that they had to laugh out loud when, driving back to New York from New Haven or Cambridge, they were greeted by giant billboards of their sister lining the highways.

In the spring there was great excitement in the air, when it was announced that the Oscar-winning actress Grace Kelly was engaged to Prince Rainier of Monaco and would sail on the SS *Constitution* for her April wedding in Monte Carlo. She was to become Her Serene Highness, the Princess of Monaco, and would give up her movie career. It was just about then that I was told I would be leaving shortly to begin filming the Rheingold commercials with Douglas Fairbanks Jr. That was thrilling news. This time my husband was invited to join the group.

We first flew to London on a Pan American Clipper, where we each had an actual berth, much like the one on our train to San Francisco fifteen years earlier. It was a terrific treat, because it afforded us a great night's sleep and none of us had jet lag the next day. In London, where the first commercial was shot, it showed Douglas and me touring London, stopping across from landmarks—such as the Houses of Parliament and Big Ben—and feeding pigeons in Piccadilly Circus.

A few days later, it was on to Germany, where we shot four more commercials. One was in a typical German *bier stube* (beer hall), another at the Nymphenburg Palace, where we toured the ateliers of the Nymphenburg artisans who were creating the china. Before departing we were led to the adjacent store in which some of the china was sold.

With Douglas Fairbanks Jr. in London.

Fortunately, the weather held out for us, so the third commercial was filmed by the Alpsee, a lake in the area, where we were shown having a picnic—with Rheingold beer, of course. There we were treated to a performance of a traditional folk dance popular in the Alpine region known as the *Schuhplattler*. It consisted of a group of men dressed in lederhosen and kneesocks clapping their hands and slapping their legs as they danced.

The last commercial we filmed was at Neuschwanstein Castle. We had to climb up the many stairs to the main part of the "fairy tale" castle, which had been built by King Ludwig II of Bavaria—often referred to as "the crazy king of Bavaria"—as his refuge. There we were filmed touring the numerous elaborate rooms, many with a swan motif. Outside on one of the umpteen terraces, we were able to see all the way down to the Alpsee, where we'd filmed the picnic commercial earlier. While standing on the terrace, my mind wandered and I couldn't help but think what a long, uphill road it had been since we'd left Germany six years earlier, and how lucky I had been to have experienced such a tremendous comeback after the difficult years during and after World War II. It was the first time I was able to return to Europe since we left in 1950, and it was heartening to see that both England and Germany were recovering well from the war. In Bavaria, my cousin Angie—who was still living in Murnau—was invited to be an extra in two of the commercials. I was so happy because I was able to hear from her how conditions in Germany were improving and how everyone on my father's side of the family was doing. The fortnight we spent in Europe was filled with exhilarating days, and the memories are precious.

We returned to America, and reality, toward the end of May. By that time I had formed a warm friendship with my "costar" Douglas Fairbanks Jr., my producer Rob Weenolsen, and his wife, Hebe, all of whom were a pleasure to work with. My "reign" continued uninterrupted and I resumed my ambassadorial duties as the events became more numerous during the summer. Another perk of being Miss Rheingold was that every week throughout the year, a case of Rheingold would arrive—a much-appreciated item in our refrigerator, particularly in the hot summer months in the country.

At the beginning of August, the 1957 contestants for Miss Rheingold were announced and their banners and photos started appearing all over town as their campaign went into full swing. Margie McNally, the eventual winner of the 1957 contest, competed against Diane Baker (who went on to stardom as an actress), Tami Conner, Kathleen Wallace, Beverly Christensen, and Suzi Rule.

The busiest days of the summer were Thursday, Friday, Saturday, and Sunday, when most towns put on all sorts of events and celebrations. That gave me time during the week to be with my son, who by now had entered the "terrible twos" and needed my attention. After a busy Labor Day weekend in which I attended a number of celebrations, we went back to the city, where I was given my fall schedule. One in particular was the Columbus Day Parade on October 8, in Binghamton, New York; it was memorable, to say the least. I was wearing the same dress and jacket with the mink collar I had worn for the October ad and was perched on the top of the backseat of a white convertible chauffeur-driven Cadillac. I waved to the crowds while Eleanor Nolan sat in the front seat next to the driver. After a while, my arms were getting tired so I switched back and forth, waving first with the left and then with the right, turning my head from side to side. For

Waving to the Columbus Day crowds, 1956.

the first time, I understood what Queen Elizabeth goes through when riding in her royal carriage.

There were only two more months left of my reign. The second-largest election in the country—the 1957 Miss Rheingold campaign—had come to an end, and everyone was anxiously awaiting the announcement and betting on who would win.

In the meantime, the campaign for the largest election in the country had come to an end on November 6. President Eisenhower triumphed over former governor of Illinois Adlai Stevenson and was reelected to serve for a second term. Ike had been a popular and charismatic president, who had ended the Korean War and in July had signed legislation that authorized "In God We Trust" to become our National motto. All was well in the country. Of particular interest to my family and me was the fact that, eleven years after the end of World War II, Japan became a member of the United Nations.

As the year 1956 came to an end and my duties were winding down, my family and I once again came together at Christmas. I couldn't help but reflect with them on the experiences we'd had and the distances we had traveled over the course of the past fifteen years. While exchanging presents, we chuckled as we reminisced about the Christmases in Japan, in particular the one in 1945 when there were no presents because there was nothing to buy and we had to sit on orange crates in our bombed-out house in Yokohama. What a comparison! It was thanks to my father who had persevered in his quest to return to his beloved America that we were able to celebrate the holidays in New York City with lots of wonderful presents. As we looked back on the many different lifestyles we had lived through on three of the world's six continents—North America, Asia, and Europe—during the most difficult of times, we gave thanks to God for having brought us safely back to this great country of ours.

EPILOGUE

As I reflect upon our family's experience during World War II of isolation, uncertainty, and quasi-detention in Japan, I am struck in hindsight by our tremendous luck—one might say divine intervention—particularly when I think of the millions of lives changed, of tragedies endured, of suffering and displacement. Had we stayed in America, we might very well have been interned, owing to my father's nationality and his association with a German bank. In any case, my father would never have found employment. Had we made it onto the Trans-Siberian Railway through Russia even a week earlier, we might have been caught up in the war between Germany and the Soviet Union, and God only knows what our fate would have been then. Had we made it all the way to Germany, we would have been caught in wartime, caught in the bombings, and most likely experienced the dislocations and violence suffered by my parents' families.

World events and timing meant we lived through the entire war in a state of uncertainty, frustration, and a good measure of distress when food was short and we were literally starving. Nevertheless, the experience brought us closer together—thanks mainly to my parents' resolve never to give in to feelings of hopelessness. They were our guides and our role models—stoical, loving, humorous, and dutiful. They saw us through schools and holidays, long journeys and dreadful winters, ruined cities and endless oceans, all the while coping admirably with what must have been a constant, nagging anxiety.

My father lost a younger brother and a younger sister—two civilians caught by chance in the violence. He also suffered a personal loss on a separate, material level, in that he spent so many of the prime years of his life unable to work, unable to advance his career, unable to support his family in the way he had always done in the past. It is a measure of his character that he stuck to his principles of hard work and resolve, so that when it became apparent that it would be impossible for him to resume working as a banker in New York, he found solid, meaningful employment as chief financial officer of a chemical company in New Jersey and continued working until his retirement in 1968 at age sixty-five. He had lived through the First World War, the resulting implosion of the German economy in the early 1920s, the Crash of '29, the subsequent Depression, World War II sequestered in Japan, and the doldrums and deprivations of postwar Germany, before finally being able to return to New York and rebuild a stable professional life. All the while he encouraged and advised us and watched with pleasure as we all strived and prospered.

After retiring, my father spent his remaining years researching and investing in the stock market, successfully growing the money he and my mother had saved for their old age. The income from those investments and Social Security—along with his share of the proceeds resulting from the sale of the chemical company where he had worked, and a small pension from the Commerz Bank—allowed my parents to live a relatively comfortable life.

In the summer of 1986, sixty years after my father had first come to America, my parents moved back to Germany, retiring to the same hunting lodge in Wentorf where we had spent three and a half years after the war. That same fall, they returned to America for the holidays to visit family—taking delight in their seven grandchildren—and to see their many friends. In February, after having spent a month in

Florida with my husband and me, my father quite suddenly had the urgent wish to return to New York. On Friday, February 13, 1987, several days after having arrived back in the city, he suffered a heart attack. He died at the age of eighty-four, with my mother at his side, in the city that had been, in his own words, his "life's blood."

♦ ♦ ♦

After returning to America in 1950 and with all of her children grown up and independent, my mother at last had time for herself but soon was restless for a busier daily life. She found satisfaction in part-time work with an organization called Students Abroad, and continued to travel to Europe to escape the heat of New York and to visit her parents, while my father stayed behind in New York. She kept to this routine even after my father retired, because her strong attachment to Germany and family ties never waned. My father had been the one striking out for a new life, the one who had made living in New York City his mission. My mother continued traveling between the two continents, spending the fall and winter months with us in Connecticut and Florida and the spring and summer months in her beloved Wentorf.

She passed away on March 23, 1995, a month shy of her eighty-seventh birthday.

♦ ♦ ♦

Enno was always the more serious among us—he was notably conscientious and applied himself to his studies with unflagging focus. Having finished his senior year at the Collegiate School in New York, he entered Columbia University in the fall of 1951. While in line to register at Columbia, he was greatly surprised to see Isaac Shapiro, his old friend from St. Joseph College in Yokohama, who was also in line registering, for the Law School. Enno was a few years behind Ike, because before finishing his secondary education he had gone to work to help support our family. Ike had had a most adventurous experience at the end of the war working as a guide and translator for the US forces in Japan when he was still a young teenager, as had Enno. He was then informally adopted by an American military family and taken to Hawaii with them to finish high school. It was miraculous that Enno and Ike were to become reacquainted in America, as they had always been close friends. He enjoyed his friendship with his bright, energetic childhood pal for the rest of his life.

Enno worked his way through Columbia by taking a job as a page at the NBC Studios at 30 Rockefeller Center. He graduated from Columbia in 1954 and went on to Harvard Law School. The following summer, he interned in the offices of the district attorney for New York County. Upon graduation in 1957, Enno joined the law firm of Curtis, Mallet-Prevost, Colt & Mosle in New York City. After a number of years there, he moved on to become general counsel to a financial holding company, eventually establishing his own private practice in New York City. Along the way, he wrote an acclaimed two-volume book titled *Modern German Corporate Law*. In 1969, he married, had two daughters, and eventually became the proud grandfather of three little girls.

We lost Enno in January 2014, after a short illness, three days before his eighty-third birthday, surrounded by his large and loving family. He died knowing that his fourth grandchild was going to be a boy.

♦ ♦ ♦

My brother Alexander, having spent the eighth Grade at St. Ignatius Loyola School, matriculated at the Collegiate School on a full scholarship in the fall of 1951 and upon graduation was accepted at Yale on a partial scholarship. While in New Haven, he played on the varsity soccer team, was an editor of the *Yale Daily News*, was active in the Yale Political Union, and became a member of the Fence Club and a senior society. He also worked at various bursary jobs to help pay for a portion of the remaining tuition. Upon graduation, he took a job at the private banking firm of Brown Brothers Harriman & Co., where he became a general partner in 1978. He married in 1964 and had three children. He now has seven grandchildren, five by his children from his first wife and two from his stepson, the son of his second wife, whom he married in 2006. Semiretired, Alexander lives in Connecticut, New York, and London and travels extensively—partially on business but mostly for pleasure.

✦ ✦ ✦

In early 1958, I gave birth to my second child—also a boy. The ten years that followed were mostly happy and rewarding, during which I continued modeling and working in television. At home, though, difficulties began to mount. Soon my husband and I realized that our marriage was coming to an end. We separated and eventually divorced.

During the initial years of our separation, when my husband lived on Long Island and I remained in the city with our boys, a friend of mine introduced me to David Mahoney, someone she told me was the one and only man in New York for me. How right she was. He would become the love of my life, my soul mate, and my second husband. He was a brilliant, ruggedly handsome, self-made businessman, with charm, grace, intelligence, street smarts, and charisma to burn. He had an unfettered love of life, business, science, and—happily—me. He was extremely generous with his time and his wealth, which he had accumulated over his long and successful business career. Having divorced his first wife a few years earlier and having received custody of their two children—a son and a daughter—he brought them into our marriage and we slowly started building new lives for ourselves and our four children. Over the years we were blessed with nine grandchildren—two girls and seven boys.

David Mahoney was an unstoppable force of nature. His spectacular career in advertising and marketing culminated in his being appointed chairman and CEO of Norton Simon Inc., but as is so often the case with successful, energetic people, he made his greatest mark in philanthropy, which he considered the most rewarding work of his life. His passion was the advancement of neuroscience and the need for that emerging field to capture the public's awareness. Even before his retirement, David founded the Institute of Neurological Sciences (now the Mahoney Institute for Neurosciences) at his alma mater, the University of Pennsylvania, and was appointed chairman of the Charles A. Dana Foundation in 1977. In 1990, after President George H. W. Bush declared the '90s to be the Decade of the Brain, David and I—with then-dean of the Harvard Medical School, Daniel Tosteson—established the Harvard Mahoney Neuroscience Institute, of which I am now chairman. In 1999, Columbia University honored David's many contributions to medical research with the creation of the David Mahoney Center for Brain and Behavior Research. All of these organizations operate and flourish to this day.

After almost three decades together, I lost this precious man five months into the new millennium. It was a time of unbearable sadness and grief, made tolerable only by the love and support of loyal family and friends.

My own journey continues. "Life is for the living," David used to say, so I have tried to live it wholeheartedly. I have dedicated this book to my brave, stalwart, and caring parents, for they embodied the grace, even-temperedness, resourcefulness, and faith that helped us all carry on. Today, I look back on touchstones of a long life that have to do with family, mutual support, love, caring, and persistence. I feel blessed and am grateful for the good fortune of my having had such remarkable, inspiring, and loving parents. I could not have asked for better role models. The long journey, often interrupted by unexpected events, meant having to adapt to the hazards of fate, being loyal and true to one another.

January 2016

ACKNOWLEDGMENTS

My parents, Hildegard & Enno Ercklentz;

My older brother, Enno W. Ercklentz Jr., who sadly passed away in January 2014;

My younger brother, Alexander T. Ercklentz who supplied many of the photographs;

My assistants, Debra Fallon and Virginia Somerville, who transcribed and typed much of the material;

My friend Parvaneh Foroughi, who helped me scan the photos;

My friend Anne Sutherland Fuchs;

My cousin Angela von Wallenberg-Pachaly Frisbie;

My friend Robert E. Frye, the documentary filmmaker and driving force behind this book;

My friend John Herman, MD;

My friend Jerome LeWine, who encouraged me to keep writing;

My late husband, David Mahoney, the former chairman and CEO of Norton Simon Inc.;

My cousin Adele von Wallenberg-Pachaly Mallman;

My younger son, Bob Merrill, who absorbed various parts of this story over his lifetime and spurred my memory;

My friend Jane Nevins, editor-in-chief emerita of the Dana Press, who worked on this project with me in its early stages;

My friend Paul Micou, the gifted novelist, who was invaluable in the completion of this book;

My friend Shirley Lord Rosenthal, editor and writer and A. M. Rosenthal's widow, who suggested a number of edits;

My friend and attorney, Edward F. Rover, esq.;

My cousin Irene Ruperti, who gave me encouragement and moral support;

My friend and colleague George Stamas;

My school friend Ruth von Cramm, who helped me reminisce about our postwar school years;

My "techie," Bruno Baumgartner, who Photoshopped many of the photos, most of which had faded; as well as Trinidad Ramirez and Gloria Medina, who cared for my well-being while I was busy writing;

My many friends and acquaintances who over the years strongly encouraged me to write about these not-well-known and unique fifteen years in my family's and my life and kept after me to do so for more than half a century.

Made in United States
Orlando, FL
26 August 2022

21601796R00183